Teacher Research in Language Teaching

THE CAMBRIDGE APPLIED LINGUISTICS SERIES

The authority on cutting-edge Applied Linguistics research

Series Editors   2007–present: Carol A. Chapelle and Susan Hunston
                              1988–2007: Michael H. Long and Jack C. Richards

For a complete list of titles please visit: www.cambridge.org/elt/cal

Recent titles in this series:

Teacher Research in Language Teaching

A critical analysis

Simon Borg

University of Leeds

 CAMBRIDGE
UNIVERSITY PRESS

CAMBRIDGE UNIVERSITY PRESS
Cambridge, New York, Melbourne, Madrid, Cape Town,
Singapore, São Paulo, Delhi, Mexico City

Cambridge University Press
The Edinburgh Building, Cambridge CB2 8RU, UK

www.cambridge.org
Information on this title: www.cambridge.org/9780521152631

First published 2013

Printed and bound in the United Kingdom by the MPG Books Group

A catalogue record for this publication is available from the British Library

Library of Congress Cataloguing in Publication data
Borg, Simon, 1965-
Teacher Research in Language Teaching : a critical analysis / Simon Borg.
    p. cm. – (Cambridge Applied Linguistics Series)
    Includes bibliographical references and index.
    ISBN 978-0-521-15263-1 (pbk.) -
    ISBN 978-0-521-76563-3 (hardback)
    1. English teachers–Training of–Research–Methodology.   2. English
    language–Study and teaching (Higher)–Research–Methodology.   3. English
    language–Study and teaching–Foreign speakers–Research.   4. English
    language–Study and teaching–Foreign speakers–Methods.   5. English
    teachers–Training of–Research–Methodology.   I. Title.

PE1066.B67 2013
428.0072–dc23   2012042709

ISBN 978-0-521-15263-1 Paperback
ISBN 978-0-521-76563-3 Hardback

For Helena, Nina, and Luca

Contents

Series editors' preface

Many applied linguists see classroom research as critical to the improvement of second language teaching and learning. Accordingly, the role of the teacher in such research is an ongoing topic of interest and discussion. Some argue that classroom research is a critical part of teacher education and that teacher involvement in research is a necessary aspect of their professional activity. Others take a position which they claim is more realistic – that language teachers have neither the time nor motivation to participate in research. This important debate within the field has continued without the benefit of clear definitions about the nature and scope of language teacher research or empirical evidence about existing practices of language teachers in research. This book will enlighten the debate considerably.

Rather than taking a position on one side or the other, the book establishes the grounds for an informed debate on the subject by defining the concepts and issues, reporting on research projects which investigate the practices and attitudes of key players in language education, and describing attempts to engage teachers in research. It is based on an extensive series of international language research projects carried out by the author over a number of years. Their purpose was to investigate teachers' attitudes towards research, the extent to which teachers currently engage with research by others or themselves, and the contextual considerations that assist or hinder this work. Extending beyond these studies on teacher research, the book demonstrates how teachers can be taught to conduct research within teacher education programs.

The book lays out the problem of teacher research in a scholarly manner, drawing upon a range of perspectives and research in general education and in language education. The overall result is a book that moves forward a topic that is not well understood, but is important in view of the fact that so many applied linguists are engaged in teacher education. Some of the data and discussions in this book will be immediately useful in informing language teacher education by, for example, providing models for research concerning teachers' attitudes and practices, and showing how to construct research projects in a teacher education program. Other aspects of the book express the clearly defined concepts and empirical data that are needed to move the field forward. We are therefore very happy to welcome this book to the Cambridge Applied Linguistics Series.

Carol A. Chapelle and Susan Hunston

Acknowledgements

This book would not have been possible without the support of a wide range of organizations and individuals and I want to warmly acknowledge this support here. I am very grateful for the contributions of the many teachers and managers who participated in my projects. I am also indebted to the many colleagues around the world who acted as intermediaries by facilitating my access to groups of respondents. A number of organizations have also supported my programme of research, either through funding or by granting access to participants. I would thus like to thank the University of Leeds, the British Council, the British Academy, English UK, TESOL International (and in particular TESOL's Research Committee), Bilkent University, International House Barcelona, the English Teachers Association of Switzerland, and the Ministry of Education in Oman.

I also want to thank Cambridge University Press for recognizing the value of this work, and in particular, Carol A. Chapelle, Joanna Garbutt and Anna Linthe for their editorial support.

Introduction: Teacher research as a paradox

The origins of this book can be traced back to 2003 and a short article called *Research in the lives of TESOL professionals* (Borg, 2003a). What stimulated (or provoked rather) this article was an item (Jarvis, 2001) in a newsletter of a leading language teaching organization which was dismissive, in a fairly unconstructive manner, of action research. My response (and two further pieces that followed in the series – Borg, 2003b, 2003c) initiated for me the process of exploring the notion of the teacher as researcher. I found of particular interest the paradox that teacher research constituted, through being potentially of huge value to teachers yet at the same time so underwhelmingly in evidence, globally speaking, in the field of language teaching. Despite much theoretical advocacy as well as practical guidance in the form of research methods manuals for language teachers, it was clear from my reading and work in a range of international contexts that, for most teachers, teacher research remained a foreign concept, or at least an unfeasible one (a point also made by Allwright, 1997). It was thus a question of either consigning teacher research to the conceptual scrapheap (as some had done) or seeking to develop a deeper understanding of what precisely the challenges were. I took the latter course.

My early contributions to this field were largely theoretical (as opposed to empirical) and it was not until 2005 that I initiated the body of research that this book is based on. There were a number of factors which motivated me in pursuing this line of inquiry. One was that the study of teacher research provided an intellectual space in which I was able to combine my existing interests in teacher education, research methods, and teacher cognition. This final interest had a particularly strong influence on the direction my investigations of teacher research took. I had since the mid 1990s been very involved in the study of language teachers' knowledge and beliefs, and a growing body of work in this area had, over a decade, established very clearly that teachers' conceptions of their work were a powerful influence on their actions. My own early work had focused on the teaching of grammar (e.g. Borg, 1998), but studies in other areas of language teaching had also shown that teachers' decisions about whether to

1

engage in particular pedagogical practices were shaped by the cognitions they had in relation to them (a review of this material is presented in Borg, 2006). Teacher cognition research thus provided me with a framework for thinking about the paradox highlighted above between the potential value and actual uptake of teacher research in language teaching. It became clear to me, at that point, that in order to better understand this paradox we needed to develop a deeper appreciation, from teachers' perspectives, of what 'research' meant and of the role teachers felt that doing research could and might play in their professional lives.

My thinking and research were also powerfully influenced by debates about the role of research in educational practice which took place in the UK from the mid 1990s (Hammersley, 2007 brings together a number of key contributions to this debate). A key argument in these debates related to the need for teaching to be evidence based, i.e. for teachers to be able use available evidence, as well as to systematically generate their own, for the purposes of more effective instructional decision making. *Teacher research engagement* became part of the discourse of evidence-based practice in education and I adopted this term to describe the focus of my unfolding programme of research.

Promoting evidence-based practice became educational policy in the UK, and one consequence of this was that significant funding was made available to support teachers in engaging both with and in research; the scale of the investment and the range of initiatives and resources that followed strongly enhanced my sense of how limited, in language teaching, attempts to understand and support teacher research engagement had been. The occasional small study examining teachers' views about research (e.g. McDonough & McDonough, 1990) was available but the theme did not feature, even in the most remote sense, a research agenda for the field.

This book represents my attempts to redress this situation. Here I draw on a programme of research and professional activity that took place over six years. The research component consists of a series of four studies involving over 1,700 language teaching professionals – both teachers and managers – from around the world. These studies address in a consistent manner a series of themes which provide the organizational framework for the book and which I outline the below. This strong empirical dimension is complemented by insights from my professional involvement in designing and facilitating teacher research projects.

Following this introduction, the book is organized into nine chapters. Chapter 1 introduces the theme of teachers and research by establishing a definition for teacher research and providing a brief overview of its origins. Different conceptualizations of teacher research are discussed, together with an analysis of both its benefits and critiques. This chapter also reviews the current status of teacher research in language teaching.

As noted above, the empirical core of this book draws on a programme of research into language teacher research engagement. Chapter 2 introduces the methodology for this work by describing in turn the four studies through which data were collected. In each case, the research questions addressed are defined, together with the contexts and participants involved and the manner in which data were collected and analyzed. For each study, I also comment briefly on particular methodological challenges that were encountered. Examples of the instruments used in the various studies are included in the appendices to the book. One consistent methodological element across the studies I describe here was the use of questionnaires; in concluding the chapter, then, I draw on my experience to present a framework which can guide the design and conduct of questionnaire-based research.

Chapters 3–7 focus on specific themes in the study of language teacher research engagement. Chapter 3 examines the conceptions of research – and of good quality research – held by teachers and managers. As I argued above, an important element in promoting teacher research engagement needs to be an understanding of how the term 'research' is conceptualized. The chapter provides insights into this issue by exploring the kinds of activities which respondents recognize as research and the criteria they refer to in making judgements about the quality of research.

Teacher research engagement, as defined above, has two dimensions: using research, mainly through reading publications, and doing research. Chapters 4 and 5 focus in turn on these two issues. Chapter 4 begins with a review of literature on the issue of teachers reading research, then presents results from my studies which shed light on how frequently language teachers say they read research, what they read (if they do, and if they do not, why), and on the impact this reading has on their practice. In Chapter 5, the focus is on the frequency with which teachers say they do research, their reasons for doing or not doing so, and the impact their research has on their work. Together, Chapters 4 and 5 provide a picture of the extent to which the language teachers in my studies were research engaged, together with insights into the factors which shaped this engagement.

Chapter 6 focuses more holistically on the views held by teachers and managers about the relationship between teacher research engagement and teaching quality. Theoretically, a link between the two has been posited and my goal here was to examine practitioners' perspectives on the nature of this link. A range of positions are highlighted here, both supportive of the contribution that research engagement can make to teaching quality as well as less positive. The arguments articulated by respondents in making their case provide further insights into the ways in which they conceive of 'research'.

The final empirical chapter in this book is Chapter 7. The theme addressed here is research cultures, and findings are reported about the extent to which participants in my studies felt that their working contexts were conducive to research engagement. The perspectives of teachers and managers are contrasted and in both cases the participants make a number of suggestions for changes in their working environments which would make research engagement more feasible.

My concerns in this book are not solely theoretical and I am committed to the idea that research should contribute to the improvement of educational practice. Chapter 8 reflects these pragmatic concerns by focusing on the facilitation of language teacher research projects. I first review evidence from a number of such projects described in the literature to highlight conditions that both facilitate and hinder their effectiveness. This is followed by a detailed analysis of two teacher research projects I have facilitated and which I consider to have been successful. The purpose of this analysis, which also draws on participant feedback, is to identify a set of conditions which give teacher research projects a greater chance of having a positive impact on teachers and their work. In this chapter I also provide some reflections on the pedagogy of teacher research courses and projects – an issue that has not been well documented and which the field of language teaching would benefit from studying more closely.

The book concludes, in Chapter 9, with a review of the key findings to emerge from the previous chapters and a discussion of practical responses to them. A list of suggestions for enhancing research cultures in language schools is presented (informed by ideas suggested earlier by teachers and managers) and a checklist is provided which can be used to assess the feasibility of teacher research projects. Some suggestions for ways of engaging teachers with research, through reading, are also provided. The chapter ends with some methodological reflections on my programme of research and outlines themes relevant to teacher research engagement which provide interesting foci for continuing study. Busy readers may want to read this chapter first before working through the detailed earlier chapters at more leisure; it has been written to provide, in a fairly standalone manner, a statement of the key messages in the book and of their implications for practice.

One point I emphasize from the outset of this book is that my argument here is not a prescriptive one – I am not suggesting that all teachers *should* be engaged in reading and doing research (although I am obviously positively disposed towards this idea). Rather, my aim here is to provide theoretical and practical insights which can inform decisions both about whether teacher research engagement is desirable and feasible in particular contexts and, if it is considered to be, how to promote it effectively. It is my sincere hope too, that this book will stimulate the kind of concrete action in our field which can begin to address the paradox which provided the stimulus for this work.

References

Allwright, D. (1997). Quality and sustainability in teacher-research. *TESOL Quarterly, 31*(2), 368–370.

Borg, S. (1998). Teachers' pedagogical systems and grammar teaching: A qualitative study. *TESOL Quarterly, 32*(1), 9–38.

Borg, S. (2003a). Research in the lives of TESOL professionals. *TESOL Matters, 13*(1), 1–5.

Borg, S. (2003b). Teachers, researchers, and research in TESOL: Seeking productive relationships. *TESOL Matters, 13*(3), 1–4.

Borg, S. (2003c). Teachers' involvement in TESOL research. *TESOL Matters, 13*(2), 1–8.

Borg, S. (2006). *Teacher cognition and language education: Research and practice*. London: Continuum.

Hammersley, M. (Ed.). (2007). *Educational research and evidence-based practice*. London: Sage.

Jarvis, S. (2001). Research in TESOL: Sunset or a new dawn? *TESOL Research Interest Section Newsletter, 8*(2), 1–7.

McDonough, J., & McDonough, S. (1990). What's the use of research? *ELT Journal, 44*(2), 102–109.

1 *Research and teachers*

1.1 Introduction

To avoid any misunderstandings about my purposes in writing this book, I will begin with two assertions. The first is that teacher research has the potential to be a powerful transformative force in the professional development of language teachers. The second is that teacher research remains a minority activity in the field of language teaching. The motivation for this book thus stems from the tension between these two assertions and my goal here is to explore the gap between what is theoretically possible and the contemporary status of teacher research in language teaching. One of my key goals here is to provide insight into the reasons for this gap and the strategy I adopt in doing so is to draw on a substantial volume of data from language teaching contexts globally which illustrate the conceptions of research held by professionals in this field. Before I start to examine the empirical data which is core to this book, I will in this chapter provide an introductory discussion of key issues relevant to the theme of teachers and research.

Before proceeding, though, there are two additional points I would like to stress, again to ensure that there is no doubt about my purposes here. The first is that in saying that teacher research is a minority activity I am not being critical of language teachers. Similar observations have been made about teachers in other subject areas (see, for example, Hancock, 2001). Additionally, readers familiar with my work will know that it focuses on understanding teachers and deploying this understanding in the support of teacher learning and professional development. My goals here are no different; this book aims to impact on the awareness and understandings of a readership – researchers, academics, policy makers, head teachers, directors, curriculum developers, teacher educators – who can be influential in making teacher research a more feasible and productive activity. The second point to clarify here is that I do not want to be prescriptive in arguing that teachers *should* be research engaged. I am very committed to the idea of teacher research and believe in its potential; however, I recognize that there are many professional development options available to language teachers (see, for example, Richards & Farrell, 2005) and that teacher research is but one of these. My argument, then, is not that teachers should be required to do research; it is that if we can understand why the relationship between teachers and research in our field is problematic, we will then be in a stronger position to promote and support teacher research, if that is considered to be a desirable activity (and there is growing evidence that this is the case). Although decisions about what is desirable can only be made locally, this book provides material which can inform this decision-making process.

The discussion that follows covers foundational issues relevant to teacher research: what it is, its origins, different conceptualizations of teacher research, an overview of the current status of teacher research in language teaching, the potential benefits of teacher research, and critiques of it. These issues collectively provide a framework against which the empirical data presented in this book can be discussed.

1.2 Defining teacher research

Various labels have been applied to the research teachers do in classrooms and schools. Roulston et al. (2005), for example, list the following: action research, practitioner research, collaborative inquiry, critical inquiry, self study, and teacher research. It is the latter term that I will use here in discussing teacher engagement in research.

The work on teacher research of Cochran-Smith & Lytle, has been very influential in education generally, particularly in North America (e.g. Cochran-Smith & Lytle, 1990, 1993; Lytle & Cochran-Smith, 1990, 1994). They see teacher research as 'all forms of practitioner inquiry that involve systematic, intentional, and self-critical inquiry about one's work ... This definition ... does not necessarily include reflection or other terms that refer to being thoughtful about one's educational work in ways that are not necessarily systematic or intentional' (Cochran-Smith & Lytle, 1999: 22). In the UK, and writing in the context of school improvement, Carter & Halsall (1998: 73–74) suggest that teacher research has the following 'essential characteristics': it involves systematic and purposeful data collection; it is conducted by teachers, alone or with the support of 'external critical friends'; its focus is teachers' professional work; and its purpose is to bring about beneficial change, ultimately, in student learning. One final definition we can consider here comes from Lankshear & Knobel (2004: 9), who define teacher researchers as 'classroom practitioners at *any* level, from preschool to tertiary, who are involved individually or collaboratively in self-motivated and self-generated systematic and informed inquiry undertaken with a view to enhancing their vocation as professional educators'.

What these and other definitions of teacher research have in common is that they refer to inquiry conducted by teachers in their own professional contexts; and, influenced by the work of Stenhouse (1975), these definitions also typically characterize such inquiry as being systematic. Lankshear & Knobel's definition stresses the self-initiated nature of teacher research (i.e. teachers themselves must want to do it and must have some control over its focus and conduct) and suggests it may be collaborative, while Cochran-Smith & Lytle distinguish, helpfully I feel, between reflection and teacher research: while teacher research is necessarily reflective, reflecting on one's practice does not automatically constitute teacher research. This is a theme I return to in several places in this book.

Returning to terms commonly associated with teacher research, practitioner research is similar in purpose and conduct to teacher research (and is often used as a synonym for it). It refers to systematic inquiry by professionals in any discipline who are investigating their own practices (so the practitioners may be, for example, nurses). Action research is a form of practitioner research which is characterized by particular procedures which broadly involve the introduction and evaluation of new practices, typically through a number of investigative cycles (in language teaching, see Burns, 2005b, 2010a; Wallace, 1998). Some definitions of action research (e.g. Kemmis & McTaggart, 1988) also stipulate that it should be collective or collaborative. Teacher research is thus a broader term than action research – while action research (when conducted by teachers) will also be teacher research, not all teacher research follows the procedures which define action research. Classroom research, a third term often mentioned in the context of teacher research, is simply systematic inquiry which is conducted in classrooms; much teacher research is classroom research, but not all classroom research is teacher research (e.g. academics may visit schools to collect data for their research). In her analysis of the relationship between teacher research, action research, and classroom research in language teaching, Bailey (2001: 491) concludes that 'the term *classroom research* refers to the location and focus of the study. *Teacher research* refers to the agents who conduct the study. *Action research* denotes a particular approach ...' I would extend the definition of teacher research provided here to refer to the purpose and context of the inquiry; not all research done by teachers is teacher research – it needs to be conducted in teachers' own professional context and with the purpose of enhancing their understanding of some aspect of their work.

Another definitional issue to consider here relates to whether teacher research needs to be made public. One argument for doing so is that dissemination is a basic characteristic of all research. Stenhouse's definition of research – 'systematic inquiry made public' (1975: 142) makes this position clear; he also notes that 'private research for our purpose does not count as research' (1981: 111). Support for this position is also evident in language teaching. Brumfit & Mitchell (1989: 7) argue that all research, including teacher research, should be 'public because it needs to be distinguished from simply improving one's own private understanding: it is not another name for personal study', while Crookes (1993: 137, drawing on Stern, 1983) says that 'research is not research unless communicated'.

From a different perspective, Allwright & Hanks (2009) also focus on the benefits of making language teacher research public; for example, they note that findings which are public can inform educational decision making. More generally I would add that the dissemination of teacher research creates greater potential for the knowledge generated by teachers through their inquiries to have influence beyond the contexts in which this knowledge originates. Conversely, as Barkhuizen (2009: 124) explains, a failure to make teacher research public 'would mean missing the opportunity and ignoring the responsibility to contribute to discussions and debates in the field of language education'. Freeman (1996: 105) similarly expresses concerns that if language teacher research is not made public, the knowledge it generates will 'dissipate in the recesses of private conversations, staff rooms, or schools'. The need for teacher research to be made public does not imply that private inquiry is not beneficial. Given its private nature though, such inquiry need not appropriate the term 'research'. It is important to stress that the argument that teacher research cannot remain a private activity is not motivated by a desire to see it as an approximation of academic research. Bartels (2003) suggests that imposing academic notions of dissemination on teacher research in this way would be 'colonialist'. Bartels' concerns are justified if formal research reports are seen as the only acceptable way of making teacher research public. My position is to promote a broad view of dissemination which directs teachers to the many varied formats, oral and written, formal and less formal, formative and summative, through which they can make their work available for public scrutiny. This stance, I believe, is in no way colonialist, and it is illustrated in the many excellent suggestions for sharing teacher research contained in texts, such as, for example, Burns (1999) and Altrichter et al. (2008).

One final element to consider briefly in defining teacher research is the data collection strategies it utilizes. Teacher research is more commonly associated with qualitative forms of inquiry and investigative strategies which are accessible to teachers, though in theory there are no limitations on the strategies that teacher researchers can deploy (and quantitative techniques are sometimes used). The many different data collection methods available to language teacher researchers are illustrated in, for example, Burns (1999), Edwards (2005) and Freeman (1998).

On the basis of the above analysis, I have defined teacher research as

> systematic inquiry, qualitative and/or quantitative, conducted by teachers in their own professional contexts, individually or collaboratively (with other teachers and/or external collaborators), and which aims to enhance teachers' understandings of some aspect of their work, is made public, has the potential to contribute to better quality teaching and learning in individual classrooms and which may also inform institutional improvement and educational policy more broadly.
>
> (Borg, 2010: 395)

1.3 Origins of teacher research

The history of teacher research has been well documented (e.g. Burns, 1999; Crookes, 1993; Elliott, 1991; Hammersley, 2004a; Hollingsworth & Sockett, 1994; McNiff & Whitehead, 2002; Noffke, 2002; Olson, 1990; Zeichner & Noffke, 2001). Action research is seen as its ancestor and accounts of the origins of teacher research thus typically begin with reference to the work of Kurt Lewin in the USA in the 1940s. Another early source was Corey (1953) though, despite this work, action research virtually disappeared from the educational landscape in the USA in the 1950s and 1960s. The more recent emergence of teacher research is traced to parallel efforts in the UK and the USA which took place in the 1970s. These efforts shared a concern for educational reform, in particular for democratizing education and making it a more participatory process. In the UK, the teacher research movement emerged in the context of curriculum reform initiatives and is most closely associated with the work of Stenhouse (1975) and Elliott (see Elliott, 1990 for brief history). In the USA, it is Schön's (1983) work on reflective practice which is seen as critical to a renewed interest in teacher research; his argument that professionals were not unthinking technicians but reflective practitioners provided impetus for initiatives which placed teachers in the role of autonomous investigators of their work. Teacher research with a strong reflective element was thus seen as an ideal way for professionals to explore and develop their own understandings of their practices.

In language teaching, attention to teacher research dates back to the 1980s, stimulated in part, as Allwright & Bailey (1991) explain, by the inconclusive results of large-scale studies aiming to identify the best way to promote language learning. These results created an awareness in the field that the search for global pedagogical prescriptions was unlikely to be productive; local, classroom-based research thus emerged as an alternative. Of course, much of the early classroom research in language teaching was not teacher research (see, for example, the review of academic classroom research in Chaudron, 1988); however, the emergence of classroom research did provide the basis for the next logical step in the evolution of language teaching research – that classroom studies would start to be conducted by teachers themselves. Distinctions between teachers and researchers, between practice and theory, would thus, it was believed, be narrowed and teaching would no longer be seen as 'something which certain people do and others research' (Freeman, 1996: 106).

Allwright & Bailey (1991) was an early attempt to promote teacher inquiry (though Allwright (2003: 116) later reflected with regret that that text 'had unintentionally made classroom research so demanding that teachers would not be able to do it unless they had extra time and extra support'); Nunan's work (1989a, 1989b) was also influential in giving teacher research prominence in language teaching. In the last 20 years, there have been a number of texts whose aim is to enable language teachers to engage in research, often from an explicitly teacher research (or action research) perspective (Burns, 1999; Burns, 2010a; Freeman, 1998; McDonough & McDonough, 1997; O'Brien & Beaumont, 2000; Wallace, 1998).

1.4 Conceptualizations of teacher research

Given its diverse historical roots, it is not surprising that contemporary forms of teacher research reflect different underlying conceptualizations of its goals. Hammersley (2004a), for example, talks about three views of action research – as a way of solving practical classroom problems, as a movement for social change, and as a form of personal professional development. In a related though not identical scheme, Cochran-Smith & Lytle (1999) also discuss three conceptualizations of teacher research: teacher research as social inquiry, as ways of knowing within communities, and as practical inquiry. The first sees teacher research – particularly in the form of action research – as a way of promoting social change. Teacher research with a social orientation is often described as emancipatory (drawing on Carr &

Kemmis, 1986). This perspective on teacher research is also referred to as critical praxis (Hollingsworth & Sockett, 1994). It adopts a socio-political stance to the study of education, which aims to disrupt and change existing inequitable social conditions.

The second view of teacher research noted above (ways of knowing within communities) sees it as a form of collaborative inquiry through which teachers improve classrooms and schools. As already noted, collaboration is core to some definitions of teacher research (in language teaching, see Burns, 1999) and the idea that teacher research can contribute not just to individual teacher development but to broader improvements in schools and classrooms is also a common one. This perspective can be seen, for example, in the papers in Halsall (1998), where teacher research is positioned as a key mechanism for school improvement. A concern for improving schools also underlies much recent state-funded teacher research in the UK, with references to research-engaged schools a common feature of the discourse in this context (e.g. CUREE, 2003; Handscomb & Macbeath, 2003; Sharp et al., 2005, 2006).

In the third conceptualization of teacher research noted above (as practical inquiry), it is seen as a vehicle for making explicit and developing teachers' practical knowledge. Here there is an often individual (and, Hammersley (2004a) suggests, instrumental) focus on solving practical classroom problems. In language teaching, Edge (2001: 5) describes this view of action research as being 'means oriented'. (He does also list a number of other possible orientations, some of which – e.g. society oriented – relate to the various conceptualizations of teacher research outlined above.)

Also in the context of language teaching, a particular conceptualization of teacher research that merits attention here is exploratory practice (EP) (Allwright, 2003, 2005). Motivated by the view that 'practitioner-research, at its worst, seems to constitute a way of getting research done badly and making the process so demanding that it is patently unsustainable and therefore soon abandoned' (Allwright, 1997: 368), EP was developed as a form of teacher research which can be integrated into teachers' everyday practices and which aims to improve the quality of classroom life for teachers and learners. EP is contrasted with action research as follows:

> Practitioner research involves two conceptually distinct processes: taking action for understanding, and taking action for change. Taking action for *change* ... is more the realm of Action Research. EP's is action for *understanding* ... why insist on two distinct processes, taking action for understanding and taking action for change? The answer lies in the 'for'.

It is a matter of intentions. AR starts out with an *intention to change* in order to solve a problem, or at least to introduce an innovation.

(Allwright & Hanks, 2009: 172)

Given this position, proponents of EP might disagree with it being described as 'a more teacher-friendly version of action research' (Dörnyei, 2007: 193). That apart, though, some justification for EP's stance to action research is found in the way that the latter is often defined as a problem-solving activity (which thus implies an intention to promote change). Richards & Farrell (2005: 171), for example, define action research as 'teacher-conducted classroom research that seeks to clarify and resolve practical teaching issues and problems'. Burns (2010a) also states that action research addresses a problem (though she does stress that this does not refer to a deficiency in teaching but rather a puzzling issue). There is evidence too that language teachers often see action research as a problem-solving activity (Rainey, 2000). However, I consider this explicit emphasis on problem-solving unnecessary as action research can be stimulated by an interest in understanding current practice even when there is no immediate problem to solve. On the back cover of Altrichter et al. (2008), it is stated that 'Action research is a method used by teachers and other professionals to improve their understanding of their practice situations, and as a way to generate knowledge about practice.' This conception of action research aligns quite well with EP's focus on understanding; thus while I fully support EP's goal of making teacher research a more feasible and productive activity for teachers and learners, I do not feel the oppositions it sets up with action research are wholly necessary. Examples of action research do exist which show how it can be integrated into language teachers' routine work; Valeri (1997: 38), for example, notes that 'the data collection soon became a part of the teaching/learning process whenever group work was done, rather than simply for the purposes of the research project'. The differences between EP and action research, then, need not be overstated.

1.5 Evidence-based practice

A further perspective on teacher research is offered by evidence-based practice (EBP). Stimulated by critiques of the quality and impact of educational research in the UK (e.g. Tooley & Darby, 1998), significant government funding has been invested in making teaching an evidence-based profession i.e. one where teachers engage in and with research (for similar concerns in the USA and Australia see

Department of Education Training and Youth Affairs, 2000; Shavelson & Towne, 2002). The thinking behind EBP in the UK has been extensively described and debated in the literature (e.g. Elliott, 2002; Hammersley, 2007; Hargreaves, 1996); one of its major premises is that when teachers engage with and in research and make pedagogical decisions based on or informed by sound research evidence, this will have a beneficial effect on both teaching and learning (Davies, 1999). While the validity of the EBP metaphor (adopted from the field of medicine) for education has been challenged (e.g. Hammersley, 2004b), it is generally accepted that more informed use of and involvement in research by teachers can have a positive impact on their work.

Numerous funded opportunities have been set up in the UK to encourage teachers to become research engaged. These have been discussed in various publications (e.g. Bell et al., 2010; CERI/OECD, 2002) and have also been reviewed extensively (e.g. Bartlett, 2002; Foster, 1999; Simons, Kushner, & James, 2003). Such initiatives have included The National Teacher Research Panel, Teacher Training Agency (TTA) school-based research consortia (funded collaborations between universities and schools), the Teacher Research Grant Scheme and Best Practice Research Scholarships, and The National College of School Leadership. According to Cordingley (2004), such activities have involved over 10,000 teachers. There have also been initiatives aimed at making published research more accessible to teachers and I discuss these in Chapter 4.

1.6 Teacher research in language teaching

A number of publications evidencing language teacher research are available. Early examples came from the *Teachers Develop Teachers Research* series of conferences organized by IATEFL (e.g. Edge & Richards, 1993; Field et al., 1997). In addition to continued publications by IATEFL (e.g. Mitchell-Schuitevoerder & Mourão, 2006), recent years have seen the publication of the *Language Teacher Research* series by TESOL, with volumes covering the Americas, Asia, the Middle East, Europe, Australia and New Zealand, and Africa (Borg, 2006b; Burns & Burton, 2007; Coombe & Barlow, 2007; Farrell, 2006; Makalela, 2009; McGarrell, 2007). There have been special issues of the *TESOL Journal* (Volume 4, Issue 1) and the journal *Canadian Modern Language Review* (Volume 54, Issue 1) dedicated to teacher research. From Australia there are eight volumes in the *Teachers' Voices* series (e.g. Burns & Hood, 1995, 1997; de Silva Joyce 2000) and the LIPT (Languages Inservice Program for

Teachers) project in South Australia (for examples of work from this project, see Appendix E in Freeman, 1998). Relevant collections of papers have come out of Asia (Hadley, 2003; Tinker Sachs, 2002) and more recently the Middle East, in Dubai (Warne et al., 2006) and the Sultanate of Oman (Borg, 2006a, 2008, 2009a; 2009b). A collection edited by Edge (2001) has also showcased action research in a range of language teaching settings internationally. Edwards & Willis (2005) is a collection of reports by language teachers research-ing the use of tasks in their classrooms, while Johnson & Golombek (2002) includes narratives written by teachers exploring their own work. There are also regional publications which have a particular focus on teacher research, such as the journal *PROFILE,* published in Colombia. The journal *Language Teaching Research* devotes regular space to exploratory practice and further examples of EP are avail-able in Allwright & Hanks, 2009. Teacher research has also appeared in journals such as *English Teaching Forum* and *ELT Journal*; Kiely's (2008) analysis indicates that there were 28 teacher research articles in *ELT Journal* Volume 57 and 27 in Volume 60 – significant num-bers (but see my comments on this analysis on page 21).The recently revived *TESOL Journal* (now in electronic form only) also dedicates a regular section to teacher research. Most recently, a collection of six teacher research papers based on a project in Australia (see Chapter 8 for more details) was published in Issue 44 (2011) of *Research Notes*, Cambridge ESOL's quarterly journal. While maintaining my position here that, globally speaking, language teacher engagement in research remains limited, the publications listed above do amount to a consid-erable body of inquiry in a range of international language teaching contexts (see Burns, 2010b for a comparative book review of some of this material).

1.7 Benefits of teacher research

An extensive list of potential benefits of teacher research has been proposed in the literature in education generally and language teaching specifically (e.g. Burns, 1999; Elliott & Sarland, 1995; Goswami & Stillman, 1987; Henson, 2001; Kemmis & McTaggart, 1988; Kincheloe, 2003). For example, it has been claimed that teacher research

- develops teachers' capacity for autonomous professional judgements (Lankshear & Knobel, 2004)
- reduces teachers feelings of frustration and isolation (Roberts, 1993)

- allows teachers to move out of a submissive position and be curriculum innovators (Gurney, 1989)
- allows teachers to become more reflective, critical, and analytical about their teaching behaviours in the classroom (Atay, 2006)
- makes teachers less vulnerable to and less dependent on external answers to the challenges they face (Donato, 2003)
- fosters connections between teachers and researchers (Crookes, 1993)
- boosts teachers' sense of status (Davies, Hamilton, & James, 2007).

Olson's (1990: 17–18) list of six benefits enhances the prospective value of teacher research even further. According to her, it

- reduces the gap between research findings and classroom practice
- creates a problem solving mindset that helps teachers when they consider other classroom dilemmas
- improves teachers' instructional decision-making processes
- increases the professional status of teachers
- helps empower teachers to influence their own profession at classroom, district, state, and national levels
- offers the overriding and ultimate advantage of providing the potential for improving the educational process.

Some of these claims do have a somewhat idealistic or lofty ring to them, particularly when seen against the unfavourable conditions, vis-à-vis teacher research, that characterize many language teaching contexts worldwide. Nonetheless, broader analyses of teacher research initiatives in the USA and the UK have reported positive findings. In the USA, Zeichner's review found evidence that teacher research supports teachers in becoming 'more confident about their ability to promote student learning, to become more proactive in dealing with difficult situations that arise in their teaching ... We have also seen evidence of direct links between conducting teacher research under particular conditions and improvements in students' attitudes, behavior and learning.' (Zeichner, 2003: 317). In her review of the work of a number of research-engaged schools in the UK, Sharp (2007: 22) offered the similarly positive conclusion that 'teacher research has the potential to make a real difference to pupils and staff, the whole school and the wider community. It is also a particularly engaging means of enabling schools to drive their own agenda for innovation and improvement.' More recently, an analysis, based on 25 studies, of the impact of practitioner research on learners concluded that 'practitioner engagement in and with research was linked to a range of positive outcomes for learners' (Bell et al., 2010: 53).

In these studies, teacher research was found to contribute to learners' knowledge and skills, behaviour for learning, and attitudes and motivation for learning.

In language teaching, Nunan (1989b: 3–4) cites (from Beasley & Riordan, 1981) a list of nine benefits of teacher-initiated research, ranging from the relatively concrete 'it sharpens teachers' critical awareness through observation, recording and analysis of classroom events and thus acts as a consciousness-raising exercise' to the more fuzzy 'it matches the subtle, organic process of classroom life'. More specific examples of the benefits of teacher research in language teaching are reported in Edwards (2005: 261), who cites the feelings of a teacher researcher (on an MA programme) as ones of 'excitement about what I've learned; satisfaction at the depth of understanding and clarity of articulation I've achieved; confidence that I can approach professional challenges in a principled way and eventually overcome them; awareness about what I'm doing'. Al-Mezeini (2009) became aware that explicitly teaching spelling rules did not necessarily improve learners' spelling, while Taylor (2006: 94) said that her study 'helped me to relax about the students' use of L1 and to see it as a useful diagnostic tool rather than as something detrimental to the students' acquisition of English'.

Reviews of research into the use of teacher research in initial teacher education in the USA (e.g. Darling-Hammond et al., 2005; Grossman, 2005) provide less conclusive evidence of its benefits. The latter, for example, states that 'although many teacher educators proclaim the value of various forms of practitioner research in preservice teacher education, we are still at the early stages of being able to bolster these claims with empirical evidence' (p. 447). In language teaching, Burns (2009) provides a review of the use of action research in teacher education, while reports of specific initiatives and their impact are provided in a number of other sources (e.g. Atay, 2008; Crookes & Chandler, 2001; McDonough, 2006; Thorne & Qiang, 1996). Collectively, this work points to ways in which teacher research can support language teacher growth and identifies the challenges this process raises, though these are issues where our empirical understandings remain emergent.

1.8 Barriers to teacher research

In terms of factors which deter teachers from doing research, it is possible to extract a wide range of points from the literature in language teaching and education generally (Allison & Carey, 2007; Atay, 2006; Barker, 2005; Barkhuizen, 2009; Borg, 2003a, 2003b; Burns, 1999; Burton & Mickan, 1993; Denny, 2005; Edwards, 2005; Elliott, 1991;

Hancock, 2001; Henson, 1996; McKay, 2009; McKernan, 1993; McNamara, 2002; Rainey, 2000; Roberts, 1993; Rust & Meyers, 2006; Sharp et al., 2005; Worrall, 2004). An analysis of these sources suggests several barriers to teacher research:

- non-collaborative school cultures
- limitations in teachers' awareness, beliefs, skills, and knowledge
- limited resources
- lack of teacher motivation
- economic matters
- unsupportive leadership
- political issues.

Most of these points are self-explanatory; two that perhaps need to be clarified briefly here are economic matters and political issues. The former recognizes that the extent to which teachers can be research engaged is shaped by (a) the type of employment contract they have (in many language teaching contexts teachers are paid only for teaching) and (b) the extent to which teachers have a stable job in one institution or whether they (often out of necessity) must have more than one job. Economic instability for teachers is not conducive to teacher research. By political issues, I mean that teacher research can be hindered by a desire (by teachers, managers, or society more generally) to maintain the status quo in education; teachers may also be required to conform to a prescribed curriculum, often for political rather than pedagogical reasons, and this too can limit the scope for teacher research. Further insights into barriers to teacher research in language teaching contexts will emerge in the findings I present in this book.

1.9 Critiques of teacher research

Despite the volume of claims presented above for the benefits of teacher research, a number of critiques have also been put forward. In education generally, Lieberman & Miller (1994: 204) note that 'there is a romantic and naïve quality ... to the entire ambiance that surrounds teacher research', while Huberman's (1996) analysis questions the reliability of the investigative methods, such as narratives, often utilized in teacher research. He also describes some claims about the benefits of teacher research as 'legitimate arguments intermeshed with spleen' (p. 127). Elliott & Sarland (1995: 373) list numerous criticisms of teacher research in relation to, for example, 'the dominance of description over analysis in many accounts [and] the tendency in many accounts to adopt a narrowly technicist stance to the problems of pedagogical change'.

More recently, Brown's (2005: 399) discussion of initiatives in the UK to promote teacher research concludes that 'a healthy scepticism has to be maintained about … some of its wilder claims for the effective resolution of educational problems'. Specific evaluations of some of the UK initiatives mentioned earlier also raise concerns about the quality of the research being conducted. Foster (1999), for example, analyzed the reports produced by teachers involved in the Teacher Research Grant Pilot Scheme and concluded that some of this work did not actually constitute research, but rather 'personal descriptions of, or justifications for, their own practice; or accounts of their efforts to improve pupil achievement, or of their involvement in staff development activities' (p. 383). He also expressed serious reservations about the validity of the findings in much of this research (but see Bartlett & Burton, 2006, for a contrasting view).

Examining teacher research in language teaching more specifically, Dörnyei's (2007: 191) view is that 'there is one big problem with action research: there is too little of it … I am still to meet a teacher who has been voluntarily involved in an action research project.' I agree that, globally speaking, engagement in research by language teachers is limited, but (as illustrated above) numerous examples of teacher (and action) research do exist and I would therefore challenge Dörnyei's somewhat dismissive summation. In relation to quality, Ellis (2010: 189) says that 'the methodological limitations that are evident in much teacher research may make its findings of little value to the academe', while another sceptical view within language teaching comes from Block (2000: 138), who, with reference to action research, notes that 'the entire enterprise is strong in theory but very difficult to carry out in practice'. The reasons for this, he suggests, are that in most teaching contexts teachers receive no compensation for the extra work that engaging in research involves. Additionally, he feels that the lack of impact on the field of the results of action research discourages teachers from engaging in it.

All criticisms of teacher research, of course, reflect particular views about the nature of research. Embedded in Block's critique is the assumption that action research should have findings that are more generally relevant for the field, but this is at odds with the view of teacher research as, primarily, a powerful strategy for local inquiry. The common criticism that teacher research is of poor quality, methodologically speaking, is also often underpinned by conventional scientific notions (e.g. of large-scale replicable quantitative research). I am not, of course, defending research by teachers which is methodologically unsound – irrespective of the purposes of inquiry, if it is to inform instructional decision making then confidence must exist in the trustworthiness of the findings.

Debates about the criteria which should be used to assess the quality of research highlight two general positions (Seale, 1999). One is a foundationalist position – that there should be one set of criteria for judging the quality of all types of research. The second is nonfoundationalist, arguing that different types of research require different criteria. Huberman (1996), for example, argues that conventional criteria – for example to do with the provision of evidence and freedom from obvious bias – should apply to teacher research too. In language teaching, Nunan (1997: 367) similarly argues that the 'key distinction should be not whether an activity is practitioner research or regular research but whether it is good research or poor research', while Brumfit & Mitchell (1989: 9) write that 'if obtaining a clearer understanding of teaching processes requires care and rigour in other modes of research, there is no good argument for action research producing less care and rigour unless it is less concerned with clear understanding, which it is not'.

Alternative criteria for assessing teacher research have been proposed. Bartlett & Burton (2006), for example, suggest that professional relevance is one criterion that enhances the validity of teacher research; I agree, but on its own this does not provide sufficient reassurance that an inquiry has been conducted in a trustworthy manner. Anderson & Herr (1999) describe several other types of validity which can be referred to in evaluating the quality of teacher research: outcome validity, process validity, democratic validity, catalytic validity, and dialogic validity. The third of these, for example, refers to 'the extent to which research is done in collaboration with all parties who have a stake in the problem under investigation' (p. 15). Again, this is valuable, but collaboration in itself does not guarantee that an inquiry has been conducted systematically. A basic level of (not necessarily 'scientific') rigour must apply to the collection and analysis of data if teacher research is to generate understandings we can have confidence in. Burns' (2005a: 250) comments on the quality of action research seem to acknowledge this and she argues that 'one of the strongest features of action research that can contribute to enhancing rigor is its iterative, or cyclical, nature … The iterative aspect becomes particularly powerful when research is conducted collaboratively, as findings and outcomes can be cross-referenced across multiple activities.'

Language teacher research can also be critiqued for its lack of a critical perspective (Crookes, 1993) – for having 'goals that are more or less instrumental and/or that lack clear connections to larger social and political agendas' (Cochran-Smith & Lytle, 1999: 20). In language teaching, despite claims that teacher research can function as a critical enterprise in which 'localized teachers' research can be conceptualized as knowledge that other teachers can draw from to understand and promote social change in their own schools and communities' (Stewart, 2006: 427), there has been scarce evidence of such critical practices. For example, based on his analysis of teacher research articles in *ELT Journal,* Kiely (2008: 26) concludes that 'The studies are very narrowly teacher-based, with little reference to the wider programme or institutional policy ... Teachers may, without engagement with *school culture*, reinforce a view in our field that teachers work in isolation in their classrooms, rather than as part of teams at programme and institutional levels.'

A closer examination of the range of collections of language teaching research discussed earlier leads to further critical observations. First, many examples of teacher research (e.g. Borg, 2006a, 2008; Edwards & Willis, 2005; Warne et al., 2006) are dissertations produced for undergraduate or Master's degree programmes. Questions arise here therefore about potential tensions between academic requirements and the principles of teacher research (I discuss this further in Chapter 8 – see also Elliott & Sarland, 1995). There is also evidence to suggest that teacher research is often conducted by university language teachers rather than school teachers. For example, the *Language Teacher Research* series published by TESOL consists of six volumes with a total of 67 chapters (not counting the editors' introductions); 52 of these are written by university language teachers or academics. And to return to the analysis of *ELT Journal* articles by Kiely (2008) mentioned earlier on page 15, of the first ten authors in Kiely's list, all from Volume 57 (2003), six had a PhD, one was a PhD candidate, one was a university lecturer with an MA, and one further paper was co-authored by a senior lecturer and a PhD candidate. The final paper was written by a teacher recently graduated from an MA programme. I am not suggesting that higher formal qualifications disqualify one from doing and reporting teacher research but one of my arguments in this book is that teacher research remains a minority activity for the bulk of the population of language teachers in schools. These individuals are likely to be similar to those in Rainey (2000), who found that over 75% of the 228 teachers she surveyed said they had never heard of action research. In the same vein, most contributions in Field et al. (1997) are by experts writing about teacher research rather than by teachers who are doing it. In reviewing the text *Voices from the Language classroom* (Bailey & Nunan, 1996), Rudby (1997: 277) makes the similar point that 'it appears somewhat ironical that some of these stories should still happen to come from the pens of well-known specialists/researchers in the field ... rather than grass roots teachers'.

Overall, then, an analysis of the relevant literature highlights a wide range of sometimes substantial criticisms of teacher research. These offer a sober contrast to the rhetoric celebrating teacher research's many goals and potential benefits affecting all levels of the educational system from individuals to broader communities and educational policy; more than 25 years on, Peeke's (1984: 24) question remains relevant to our field: 'If good reasons exist for teacher involvement in research, why is it not more common?' This is, of course, a key question that underpins this book, particularly in relation to the many language teachers who remain unaware of and/or uninvolved in teacher research.

1.10 Conclusion

The purpose of this chapter has been to provide an overview of key issues in the literature on teacher research. Clearly, there is a substantial amount of theoretical support for the notion that research engagement can be beneficial for teachers and their schools; in the field of language teaching, there is also increasing evidence of teacher research, though globally speaking it remains an activity which only a minority of language teaching professionals participate in. A number of reasons for this lack of engagement have also been extracted from the literature. With this theoretical background in place, I now move on to discuss the programme of research which generated the data that constitute the core of this book.

References

Allison, D., & Carey, J. (2007). What do university language teachers say about language teaching research? *TESL Canada Journal, 24*(2), 61–81.

Allwright, D. (1997). Quality and sustainability in teacher-research. *TESOL Quarterly, 31*(2), 368–370.

Allwright, D. (2003). Exploratory practice: Rethinking practitioner research in language teaching. *Language Teaching Research, 7*(2), 113–142.

Allwright, D. (2005). Developing principles for practitioner research: The case of exploratory practice. *Modern Language Journal, 89*(3), 353–366.

Allwright, D., & Bailey, K. M. (1991). *Focus on the language classroom: An introduction to classroom research for teachers.* Cambridge: Cambridge University Press.

Allwright, D., & Hanks, J. (2009). *The developing language learner: An introduction to exploratory practice.* Basingstoke: Palgrave Macmillan.

Al-Mezeini, H. S. (2009). Does teaching spelling rules make a difference? In S. Borg (Ed.), *Understanding English language teaching and learning in Oman* (pp. 124–130). Muscat: Ministry of Education, Oman.

Altrichter, H., Feldman, A., Posch, P., & Somekh, B. (2008). *Teachers investigate their work: An introduction to action research across the professions* 2nd ed. London: Routledge.

Anderson, G. L., & Herr, K. (1999). The new paradigm wars: Is there room for rigorous practitioner knowledge in schools and universities? *Educational Researcher, 28*(5), 12–21, 40.

Atay, D. (2006). Teachers' professional development: Partnerships in research. *TESL-EJ, 10*(2), 1–14.

Atay, D. (2008). Teacher research for professional development. *ELT Journal, 62*(2), 139–147.

Bailey, K. M. (2001). Action research, teacher research, and classroom research in language teaching. In M. Celce-Murcia (Ed.), *Teaching English as a second or foreign language* 3rd ed., (pp. 489–498). Boston, MA: Heinle & Heinle.

Bailey, K. M., & Nunan, D. (Eds.). (1996). *Voices from the language classroom*. Cambridge: Cambridge University Press.

Barker, P. (2005). *Research in schools and colleges*: National Educational Research Forum Working Paper 7.2. Retrieved 3 February, 2012, from www.eep.ac.uk/nerf/word/WP7.2withappendixe42d.doc?version=1

Barkhuizen, G. (2009). Topics, aims, and constraints in English teacher research: A Chinese case study. *TESOL Quarterly, 43*(1), 113–125.

Bartels, N. (2003). How teachers and researchers read academic articles. *Teaching and Teacher Education, 19*(7), 737–753.

Bartlett, S. (2002). An evaluation of the work of a group of best practice teacher researchers. *Journal of In-service Education, 28*(3), 527–540.

Bartlett, S., & Burton, D. (2006). Practitioner research or descriptions of classroom practice? A discussion of teachers investigating their classrooms. *Educational Action Research, 14*(3), 395–405.

Bell, M., Cordingley, P., Isham, C., & Davis, R. (2010). Report of professional practitioner use of research review: Practitioner engagement in and/or with research. Retrieved 3 February, 2012, from www.curee-paccts.com/node/2303

Block, D. (2000). Revisiting the gap between SLA researchers and language teachers. *Links & Letters, 7*, 129–143.

Borg, S. (2003a). 'Research education' as an objective for teacher learning. In B. Beaven & S. Borg (Eds.), *The role of research in teacher education* (pp. 41–48). Whitstable, Kent: IATEFL.

Borg, S. (2003b). Teachers' involvement in TESOL research. *TESOL Matters, 13*(2), 1–8.

Borg, S. (Ed.). (2006a). *Classroom research in ELT in Oman*. Muscat: Ministry of Education, Oman.

Borg, S. (Ed.). (2006b). *Language teacher research in Europe*. Alexandria, VA: TESOL.

Borg, S. (Ed.). (2008). *Investigating English language teaching and learning in Oman*. Muscat: Ministry of Education, Oman.

Borg, S. (Ed.). (2009a). *Researching English language teaching and teacher development in Oman*. Muscat: Ministry of Education, Oman.

Borg, S. (Ed.). (2009b). *Understanding English language teaching and learning in Oman*. Muscat: Ministry of Education, Oman.

Borg, S. (2010). Language teacher research engagement. *Language Teaching, 43*(4), 391–429.

Brown, S. (2005). How can research inform ideas of good practice in teaching? The contributions of some official initiatives in the UK. *Cambridge Journal of Education, 35*(3), 383–406.

Brumfit, C., & Mitchell, R. (1989). The language classroom as a focus for research. In C. Brumfit & R. Mitchell (Eds.), *Research in the language classroom* (pp. 3–15). London: Modern English Publications / The British Council.

Burns, A. (1999). *Collaborative action research for English language teachers*. Cambridge: Cambridge University Press.

Burns, A. (2005a). Action research. In E. Hinkel (Ed.), *Handbook of research in second language teaching and learning* (pp. 241–256). Mahwah, NJ: Erlbaum.

Burns, A. (2005b). Action research: An evolving paradigm? *Language Teaching, 38*(2), 57–74.

Burns, A. (2009). Action research in second language teacher education. In A. Burns & J. C. Richards (Eds.), *The Cambridge guide to second language teacher education* (pp. 289–297). Cambridge: Cambridge University Press.

Burns, A. (2010a). *Doing action research in English language teaching. A guide for practitioners*. New York: Routledge.

Burns, A. (2010b). Teacher engagement in research: Published resources for teacher researchers. *Language Teaching, 43*(4), 527–536.

Burns, A., & Burton, J. (Eds.). (2007). *Language teacher research in Australia and New Zealand*. Alexandria, VA: TESOL.

Burns, A., & Hood, S. (Eds.). (1995). *Teachers' voices: Exploring course design in a changing curriculum*. Sydney, Australia: NCELTR.

Burns, A., & Hood, S. (Eds.). (1997). *Teachers' voices 2: Teaching disparate learner groups*. Sydney, Australia: NCELTR.

Burton, J., & Mickan, P. (1993). Teachers' classroom research: Rhetoric and reality. In J. Edge & K. Richards (Eds.), *Teachers develop teachers research* (pp. 113–121). Oxford: Heinemann.

Carr, W., & Kemmis, S. (1986). *Becoming critical: Education, knowledge and action research*. London: The Falmer Press.

Carter, K., & Halsall, R. (1998). Teacher research for school improvement. In R. Halsall (Ed.), *Teacher research and school improvement: Opening doors from the inside* (pp. 71–90). Buckingham: Open University Press.

CERI/OECD (2002). *Education research and development in England. Background report*. Paris: OECD.

Chaudron, C. (1988). *Second language classrooms: Research on teaching and learning*. New York: Cambridge University Press.

Cochran-Smith, M., & Lytle, S. L. (1990). Research on teaching and teacher research: The issues that divide. *Educational Researcher, 19*(2), 2–11.

Cochran-Smith, M., & Lytle, S. L. (1993). *Inside/outside: Teacher research and knowledge*. New York: Teachers College Press.

Cochran-Smith, M., & Lytle, S. L. (1999). The teacher research movement: A decade later. *Educational Researcher, 28*(7), 15–25.

Coombe, C., & Barlow, L. (Eds.). (2007). *Language teacher research in the Middle East.* Alexandria, VA: TESOL.

Cordingley, P. (2004). Teachers using evidence: Using what we know about teaching and learning to reconceptualize evidence-based practice. In G. Thomas & R. Pring (Eds.), *Evidence-based practice in education* (pp. 77–87). Maidenhead: Open University Press.

Corey, S. M. (1953). *Action research to improve school practices.* New York: Columbia University.

Crookes, G. (1993). Action research for second language teachers: Going beyond teacher research. *Applied Linguistics, 14*(2), 130–144.

Crookes, G., & Chandler, P. (2001). Introducing action research into the education of postsecondary foreign language teachers. *Foreign Language Annals, 34*(2), 131–140.

CUREE (2003). Leading the research-engaged school: Why and how school leaders engage with educational research. Retrieved 3 February, 2012, from www.nationalcollege.org.uk/docinfo?id=17269&filename=leading-the-research-engaged-school-summary.pdf

Darling-Hammond, L., Hammerness, K., Grossman, P., Rust, F., & Shulman, L. S. (2005). The design of teacher education programs. In L. Darling-Hammond & J. Bransford (Eds.), *Preparing teachers for a changing world* (pp. 390–441). San Francisco: Jossey-Bass.

Davies, P. (1999). What is evidence-based education? *British Journal of Educational Studies, 47*(2), 108–121.

Davies, P., Hamilton, M., & James, K. (2007). *Practitioners leading research.* London: NRDC.

de Silva Joyce, H. (Ed.). (2000). *Teachers' voices 6: Teaching casual conversation.* Sydney, Australia: NCELTR.

Denny, H. (2005). Can busy classroom teachers really do action research? An action research study in an EAL tertiary setting. *New Zealand Studies in Applied Linguistics, 11*(2), 59–73.

Department of Education Training and Youth Affairs (2000). *The impact of educational research.* Canberra, Australia: DETYA.

Donato, R. (2003). Action research. Retrieved 3 February, 2012, from www.cal.org/resources/digest/digest_pdfs/0308donato.pdf

Dörnyei, Z. (2007). *Research methods in applied linguistics.* Oxford: Oxford University Press.

Edge, J. (Ed.). (2001). *Action research.* Alexandria, VA: TESOL.

Edge, J., & Richards, K. (Eds.). (1993). *Teachers develop teachers research.* Oxford: Heinemann.

Edwards, C. (2005). Teachers exploring research. In C. Edwards & J. Willis (Eds.), *Teachers exploring tasks in English language teaching* (pp. 256–279). Basingstoke: Palgrave Macmillan.

Edwards, C., & Willis, J. (Eds.). (2005). *Teachers exploring tasks in English language teaching.* Basingstoke: Palgrave Macmillan.

Elliott, J. (1990). Teachers as researchers: Implications for supervision and for teacher education. *Teaching and Teacher Education, 6*(1), 1–26.

Elliott, J. (1991). *Action research for educational change.* Milton Keynes: Open University Press.

Elliott, J. (2002). Making evidence-based practice educational. *British Educational Research Journal, 27*(5), 555–574.

Elliott, J., & Sarland, C. (1995). A study of 'teachers as researchers' in the context of award-bearing courses and research degrees. *British Educational Research Journal, 21*(3), 371–385.

Ellis, R. (2010). Second language acquisition, teacher education and language pedagogy. *Language Teaching, 43*(2), 182–201.

Farrell, T. S. C. (Ed.). (2006). *Language teacher research in Asia.* Alexandria, VA: TESOL.

Field, J., Graham, A., Griffiths, E., & Head, K. (Eds.). (1997). *Teachers develop teachers research 2.* Whistable, Kent: IATEFL.

Foster, P. (1999). 'Never mind the quality, feel the impact': A methodological assessment of teacher research sponsored by the teacher training agency. *British Journal of Educational Studies, 47*(4), 380–398.

Freeman, D. (1996). Redefining the relationship between research and what teachers know. In K. M. Bailey & D. Nunan (Eds.), *Voices from the language classroom* (pp. 88–115). New York: Cambridge University Press.

Freeman, D. (1998). *Doing teacher research.* Boston: Heinle and Heinle.

Goswami, P., & Stillman, P. (1987). *Reclaiming the classroom: Teacher research as an agency for change.* Upper Montclair, NJ: Boynton/Cook.

Grossman, P. (2005). Research on pedagogical approaches in teacher education. In M. Cochran-Smith & K. Zeichner (Eds.), *Studying teacher education: The report of the AERA panel on research and teacher education* (pp. 425–476). Mahwah, NJ: AERA/Lawrence Erlbaum.

Gurney, M. (1989). Implementor or innovator? A teacher's challenge to the restrictive paradigm of traditional research. In P. Lomax (Ed.), *The management of change* (pp. 13–28). Clevedon: Multilingual Matters.

Hadley, G. (Ed.). (2003). *Action research in action.* Singapore: Regional Language Centre.

Halsall, R. (Ed.). (1998). *Teacher research and school improvement: Opening doors from the inside.* Buckingham: Open University Press.

Hammersley, M. (2004a). Action research: A contradiction in terms? *Oxford Review of Education, 30*(2), 165–181.

Hammersley, M. (2004b). Some questions about evidence-based practice in education. In G. Thomas & R. Pring (Eds.), *Evidence-based practice in education* (pp. 133–149). Maidenhead: Open University Press.

Hammersley, M. (Ed.). (2007). *Educational research and evidence-based practice.* London: Sage.

Hancock, R. (2001). Why are classroom teachers reluctant to become researchers? In J. Soler, C. Craft & H. Burgess (Eds.), *Teacher development: Exploring our own practice* (pp. 119–132). London: Paul Chapman.

Handscomb, G., & Macbeath, J. (2003). *The research-engaged school.* Chelmsford: Essex County Council.

Hargreaves, D. (1996). Teachers, educational research and evidence-based teaching. *Education Review, 10*(2), 46–50.

Henson, K. T. (1996). Teachers as researchers. In J. Sikula, T. Buttery & E. Guyton (Eds.), *Handbook of research on teacher education* 2nd ed., (pp. 53–64). New York: Simon & Schuster.

Henson, R. K. (2001). The effects of participation in teacher research on research efficacy. *Teaching and Teacher Education, 17*(7), 819–836.

Hollingsworth, S., & Sockett, H. (1994). Positioning teacher research in educational reform: An introduction. In S. Hollingsworth & H. Sockett (Eds.), *Teacher research and educational reform* (pp. 1–20). Chicago: University of Chicago Press.

Huberman, M. (1996). Focus on research moving mainstream: Taking a closer look at teacher research. *Language Arts, 73*(2), 124–140.

Johnson, K. E., & Golombek, P. R. (Eds.). (2002). *Teachers' narrative inquiry as professional development.* New York: Cambridge University Press.

Kemmis, S., & McTaggart, R. (Eds.). (1988). *The action research planner* 3rd ed. Victoria, Australia: Deakin University Press.

Kiely, R. (2008). The purpose, promise and potential of teacher research. In M. Pawlak (Ed.), *Investigating English language learning and teaching* (pp. 11–30). Poznań & Kalisz, Poland: Faculty of Pedagogy and Fine Arts, Kalisz/Adam Mickiewicz University, Poznań.

Kincheloe, J. (2003). *Teachers as researchers: Qualitative inquiry as a path to empowerment* 2nd ed. New York: Falmer.

Lankshear, C., & Knobel, M. (2004). *A handbook for teacher research: From design to implementation.* Maidenhead: Open University Press.

Lieberman, A., & Miller, L. (1994). Problems and possibilities of institutionalizing teacher research. In S. Hollingsworth & H. Sockett (Eds.), *Teacher research and educational reform* (pp. 204–220). Chicago: University of Chicago Press.

Lytle, S. L., & Cochran-Smith, M. (1990). Learning from teacher research: A working typology. *Teachers College Record, 92*(1), 83–103.

Lytle, S. L., & Cochran-Smith, M. (1994). Inquiry, knowledge and practice. In S. Hollingsworth & H. Sockett (Eds.), *Teacher research and educational reform* (pp. 22–51). Chicago: University of Chicago Press.

Makalela, L. (Ed.). (2009). *Language teacher research in Africa.* Alexandria, VA: TESOL.

McDonough, J., & McDonough, S. (1997). *Research methods for English language teachers.* London: Hodder Arnold.

McDonough, K. (2006). Action research and the professional development of graduate teaching assistants. *The Modern Language Journal 90*(1), 33–47.

McGarrell, H. M. (Ed.). (2007). *Language teacher research in the Americas.* Alexandria, VA: TESOL.

McKay, S. L. (2009). Second language classroom research. In A. Burns & J. C. Richards (Eds.), *The Cambridge guide to second language teacher education* (pp. 281–288). Cambridge: Cambridge University Press.

McKernan, J. (1993). Varieties of curriculum action research: Constraints and typologies in American, British and Irish projects. *Journal of Curriculum Studies, 25*(5), 445–458.

McNamara, O. (2002). Evidence-based practice through practice-based evidence. In O. McNamara (Ed.), *Becoming an evidence-based practitioner* (pp. 15–26). London: Routledge Falmer.

McNiff, J., & Whitehead, J. (2002). *Action research: Principles and practice* 2nd ed. London: Routledge Falmer.

Mitchell-Schuitevoerder, R., & Mourão, S. (Eds.). (2006). *Teachers and young learners: Research in our classrooms.* Canterbury: IATEFL.

Noffke, S. E. (2002). Action research: Towards the next generation. In C. Day, J. Elliott, B. Somekh & R. Winter (Eds.), *Theory and practice in action research* (pp. 13–26). Oxford: Symposium Books.

Nunan, D. (1997). Developing standards for teacher-research in TESOL. *TESOL Quarterly, 31*(2), 365–367.

Nunan, D. (1989a). The teacher as researcher. In C. J. Brumfit & R. Mitchell (Eds.), *Research in the language classroom* (pp. 16–32). London: Modern English Publications / The British Council.

Nunan, D. (1989b). *Understanding language classrooms.* New York: Prentice Hall.

O'Brien, T., & Beaumont, M. (Eds.). (2000). *Collaborative research in second language education.* Stoke-on-Trent: Trentham Books Ltd.

Olson, M. W. (1990). The teacher as researcher: A historical perspective. In M. W. Olson (Ed.), *Opening the door to classroom research* (pp. 1–20). Newark, Delaware: International Reading Association.

Peeke, G. (1984). Teacher as researcher. *Educational Research, 26*(1), 24–26.

Rainey, I. (2000). Action research and the English as a foreign language practitioner: Time to take stock. *Educational Action Research, 8*(1), 65–91.

Richards, J. C., & Farrell, T. S. C. (2005). *Professional development for language teachers.* Cambridge: Cambridge University Press.

Roberts, J. R. (1993). Evaluating the impacts of teacher research. *System, 21*(1), 1–19.

Roulston, K., Legette, R., DeLoach, M., & Pittman, C. B. (2005). What is 'research' for teacher-researchers? *Educational Action Research, 13*(2), 169–190.

Rubdy, R. (1997). Review of K. Bailey and D. Nunan (Eds.), *Voices from the language classroom: Qualitative research in second language education. Applied Linguistics, 19*(2), 272–278.

Rust, F., & Meyers, E. (2006). The bright side: Teacher research in the context of educational reform and policy-making. *Teachers and Teaching, 12*(1), 69–86.

Schön, D. A. (1983). *The reflective practitioner: How professionals think in action.* London: Temple Smith.

Seale, C. (1999). Quality in qualitative research. *Qualitative Inquiry, 5*(4), 465–478.

Sharp, C. (2007). *Making research make a difference. Teacher research: A small-scale study to look at impact.* Chelmsford: Flare.

Sharp, C., Eames, A., Sanders, D., & Tomlinson, K. (2005). *Postcards from research-engaged schools.* Slough: NFER.

Sharp, C., Eames, A., Sanders, D., & Tomlinson, K. (2006). *Leading a research-engaged school.* Nottingham: National College for School Leadership.

Shavelson, R. J., & Towne, L. (2002). *Scientific research in education.* Washington, DC: National Academy Press.

Simons, H., Kushner, S., & James, D. (2003). From evidence-based practice to practice-based evidence: The idea of situated generalisation. *Research Papers in Education, 18*(4), 347–364.

Stenhouse, L. (1975). *An introduction to curriculum research and development.* London: Heinemann.

Stenhouse, L. (1981). What counts as research? *British Journal of Educational Studies, 29*(2), 103–114.

Stewart, T. (2006). Teacher-researcher collaboration or teachers' research? *TESOL Quarterly, 40*(2), 421–429.

Taylor, N. (2006). An investigation of mother tongue use in a monolingual EFL classroom. In R. Mitchell-Schuitevoerder & S. Mourão (Eds.), *Teachers and young learners: Research in our classrooms* (pp. 85–95). Canterbury: IATEFL.

Thorne, C., & Qiang, W. (1996). Action research in language teacher education. *ELT Journal, 50*(3), 254–262.

Tinker Sachs, G. (Ed.). (2002). *Action research in English language teaching.* Hong Kong: City University of Hong Kong.

Tooley, J., & Darby, D. (1998). *Educational research: A critique.* London: OFSTED Publications.

Valeri, L. (1997). What do students think of group work? In A. Burns & S. Hood (Eds.), *Teachers' voices 2: Teaching disparate learner groups* (pp. 37–39). Sydney, Australia: NCELTR.

Wallace, M. J. (1998). *Action research for language teachers.* Cambridge: Cambridge University Press.

Warne, A., O'Brien, M., Syed, Z., & Zuriek, M. (Eds.). (2006). *Action research in English language teaching in the UAE.* Abu Dhabi: HCT Press.

Worrall, N. (2004). Trying to build a research culture in a school: Trying to find the right questions to ask. *Teacher Development, 8*(2–3), 137–148.

Zeichner, K. M. (2003). Teacher research as professional development for P-12 educators in the USA. *Educational Action Research, 11*(2), 301–326.

Zeichner, K. M., & Noffke, S. E. (2001). Practitioner research. In V. Richardson (Ed.), *Handbook of research on teaching* 4th ed., (pp. 298–300). Washington, DC: American Educational Research Association.

2 Investigating teacher research engagement

2.1 Introduction

A key feature of this book is that it has a substantial empirical basis – the arguments I develop here are based on a programme of research involving over 1,700 language teaching professionals working in several countries around the world. The purpose of this chapter is to introduce this programme by describing in detail the individual studies which form it. In doing so, my primary aim is to explain the origins of the evidence I cite in Chapters 2–7; a secondary aim is (by including examples of research instruments and reflections on the challenges each study presented) to provide tools and ideas which may be of practical benefit to readers interested in conducting further research of this kind. (I also include specific reflections on using questionnaires in educational research.) The four individual studies that make up the programme of research are described in turn below; I will also introduce two teacher research projects which, while not sites for research, provide the basis of the more practical discussion of teacher research in Chapter 8. One final introductory point to make is that while I will in this chapter discuss the individual studies in my programme of research separately, the subsequent chapters are organized thematically and synthesize data from across studies.

2.2 Rationale

I was initially motivated to examine teachers' conceptions of research for several reasons. One was my long-standing interest in the study of teacher cognition (see Borg, 2006) i.e. in understanding the thinking, beliefs, attitudes, and knowledge that underpin teachers' professional practices; a second was my interest in teacher research and my awareness of its limited prevalence in language teaching; I had also become aware of work in mainstream education in which a key element in promoting teacher research engagement was understanding what precisely teachers felt 'research' meant (e.g. McNamara, 2002). Additionally, systematic investigations of language teachers' conceptions of and practices regarding research were, until relatively recently, scarce. Informed by the above issues, the core argument underlying my programme of research was straightforward: in order to identify productive strategies for promoting language teacher research engagement, we first need to understand teachers' (and managers') conceptions of research, of its role in and relevance to teaching, and of the factors that support and hinder teachers in being research engaged. The studies I describe below, collectively, addressed these issues.

The research was conducted with professionals specifically in the field of English language teaching, and throughout this book, I use *language teaching* to refer to this field. Without suggesting that English language teaching is representative of language teaching more generally, I would, however, argue that the major findings to emerge from these studies are relevant to promoting teacher research in language teaching generally.

2.3 Study 1: Research engagement in English language teaching

This was the initial study in the programme and given its foundational nature it merits a detailed discussion (subsequent studies which built on this work can then be presented more briefly). This study addressed the following research questions:

1   What are the characteristics of 'research' according to language teachers?
2   To what extent do teachers say they read published research?
3   What impact do they believe this reading has on their practices?
4   Where teachers do not read research, what reasons do they cite?
5   To what extent do teachers say they do research?
6   What are their reasons for engaging in research?
7   Where teachers do not do research, what reasons do they cite?
8   What are teachers' perceptions of their institutional culture in relation to research?

The design of this study reflected what Creswell (2003) calls a sequential explanatory multi-method strategy. This is a design which 'is characterized by the collection and analysis of quantitative data followed by the collection and analysis of qualitative data' (p. 215). This first study thus adopted a survey approach in which largely quantitative data were first collected through a questionnaire. A sub-sample of the teachers who completed the questionnaire then participated in a second phase of data collection through which their questionnaire responses were explored more qualitatively. I discuss these different forms of data collection below.

Questionnaires

This study utilized a cross-sectional survey. In the form of a question-naire, this allows large amounts of data to be collected efficiently, economically, and in a standardized manner (Aldridge & Levine, 2001; De Vaus, 2002; Dörnyei, 2007). Questionnaires (particularly when administered electronically) also facilitate data collection from geographically diverse samples (see Couper, 2005; Couper & Miller, 2008 for a discussion of the use of technology in survey administra-tion) and this was an important consideration in this study (which involved respondents from around the world). Equally, however, questionnaires have a number of disadvantages, particularly when used to examine respondents' beliefs. For example, they may gener-ate superficial answers and do not allow in-depth exploration of par-ticular issues. Responses may also be influenced by social desirability bias (Dörnyei, 2003) – the tendency to give answers that are felt to be acceptable rather than those which reflect respondents' actual opin-ions. Questionnaires too cannot measure what respondents do but only their reports of their actions (Babbie, 2003; Borg, 2006). To offset some of the above drawbacks, as I describe below, follow up data were collected in writing and through interviews.

The questionnaire used in this first study (see Appendix 1) had six sections, focusing in turn on respondents' background informa-tion, their conceptions of what counts as research, their views about the characteristics of good quality research, their perceptions of their institutional culture in relation to research, their engagement in read-ing research, and their engagement in doing research. This range of themes was chosen on the basis of issues raised in the literature on teacher research engagement, both in education generally and in lan-guage teaching.

Section 1 collected background data about the teachers. Informa-tion was requested which was felt to be relevant to understanding teachers' research engagement (e.g. qualifications and experience). Information on gender, for example, was not requested as there was no reason to hypothesize that this might be a relevant factor. In Section 2, the use of research scenarios was prompted by an oral elicitational technique used by Ratcliffe et al. (2004) in their study of science education teachers' views of research. Collectively, the sce-narios devised for this study aimed to portray a range of activities with different characteristics (e.g. methods, data, outputs) and which might, depending on one's definition, be called research. A pilot ver-sion of the questionnaire contained additional scenarios (e.g. one depicting a single-case qualitative study) and also asked teachers to give reasons for their choices; to keep the instrument to a reasonable length, though, and to minimize the amount of writing required of respondents, I decided to limit the number of scenarios to ten and to use additional written and oral elicitation strategies to identify the reasons for teachers' assessments (see below). Section 3 of the questionnaire investigated the characteristics respondents felt were important in determining the quality of a piece of research. The characteristics listed referred to issues of research design, data collection, analysis, and application. Section 4 examined teachers' perceptions of their institutions' attitudes to research. The lists of factors presented in Sections 5 and 6 in relation to why teachers do and do not read and do research were informed by the discussion of these issues in the literature.

In June 2005, the questionnaire was piloted with a group of 50 teachers in a language centre at a Turkish university (Borg, 2007) and between October 2005 and April 2006 was extended to involve a total of 597 teachers of English in 14 countries, distributed as in Table 2.1 below (a report based on this study appeared in Borg, 2009). In collecting this data, contacts in a number of language teaching contexts around the world played a vital facilitative role by providing access to respondents I would not have been able to reach, as well as by advising me on which mode of administering the questionnaire would work best in their particular contexts (hard copy, email attachment and

Table 2.1   Distribution of teachers in Study 1

Country	N	%
Australia	27	4.5
Mainland China	57	9.5
France	17	2.8
Hong Kong	23	3.9
Japan	33	5.5
Netherlands	92	15.4
Nigeria	26	4.4
Oman	64	10.7
Poland	39	6.5
Slovenia	31	5.2
Spain	63	10.6
Switzerland	44	7.4
Turkey	67	11.2
UAE	14	2.3
Total	597	100[1]

web-based versions of the questionnaire were prepared). As Table 2.1 shows, almost half the respondents for this study came from Europe, and over 30% from Asia, with small percentages from Australia, Africa, and the Middle East. Numerical data from the questionnaire were analyzed, with the support of SPSS 12, using descriptive and inferential statistics. Open-ended responses were subject to content analyses through which recurrent themes were identified and categorized (see Brown, 2009 for a discussion of the analysis of open-ended questionnaire responses).

Written follow-up

Teachers completing the questionnaire were asked if they would like to participate in a second phase of the study where their questionnaire responses would be explored in more detail. Two hundred and fifty-nine teachers (just over 43%) said they would be willing to. In two contexts (accounting for 50 of these 259 volunteers), interviews were conducted (see below) and thus written comments were not requested. In one further context, accounting for 20 volunteers, email addresses were not supplied. From the remaining 189 volunteers, a stratified random sample (see Bryman, 2008) of one third of the volunteers in each of the countries represented were sent follow-up questions by email. For example, if there were 30 volunteers from a country, one third of these (10) were selected randomly and followed up; if there were 15 volunteers from another country, five were selected. In total, 61 teachers were sent questions and 22 (36%) replied to these. Each follow-up question sheet was customized according to the answers teachers had given in their questionnaire. Appendix 2 provides an example of the format these prompts took. Two key issues explored through this written data were (a) teachers' reasons for feeling an activity was or was not research and (b) teachers' reasons for feeling that a particular characteristic was or was not important in making research 'good'.

Interviews

I was additionally able to conduct face-to-face interviews in two of the countries represented in this first study. In these contexts, 31 and 19 teachers respectively volunteered a follow-up contribution; 30% in each case were randomly chosen and invited to interview, and in total, 12 teachers agreed to participate. During the interviews (which lasted on average 35 minutes and were audio recorded), teachers were asked to expand on their questionnaire responses; in particular they were asked to explain why they felt certain scenarios were or were not research and to comment on their understandings of the criteria (such as 'objectivity') they had said in the questionnaire were important in making research 'good'. Interviewees were also asked about the nature and frequency of their engagement with and in research. The interviews, therefore, were similar in function to the written follow-up, though the former generated more and richer data than the written questions did. While the items in the questionnaire did provide a framework for the questions asked in the interviews, nonetheless there was also scope for semi-structured discussion (as, for example, outlined in Kvale & Brinkmann, 2008) of additional emergent themes of relevance.

The interviews were transcribed in full. The thematic analysis (see, for example, Braun & Clarke, 2006) of these transcriptions (supported by Nvivo 7) initially involved mapping teachers' interview comments onto the section of the questionnaire they related to – i.e. these sections provided the broad initial categories for analysis, such as characteristics of good quality research – and transcripts were then coded in relation to these categories. The resulting categories and subcategories were then used to elaborate on the quantitative analysis of each questionnaire section (e.g. using examples and explanations teachers provided). Thus by combining quantitative and qualitative data I was, for example, able to comment both on how many teachers felt 'objectivity' was an important characteristic of research as well as how teachers defined this characteristic and why they felt it was important.

Challenges

Given that this was the first study in my programme of research, one key challenge was developing the main instrument for data collection – the questionnaire. I addressed this challenge by spending considerable time at the design stage engaging with the relevant substantive and methodological literature as well as collecting feedback through piloting. The next key challenge was generating significant numbers of responses from a range of contexts. Three strategies facilitated this. The first was that I did not approach potential respondents directly but via contacts known to these individuals. The only way to approach teachers directly, given that I did not have their contact details, would have been by posting invitations to participate on web-based bulletins and discussion lists. However, I discounted this approach on the basis that it was too impersonal and would fail to generate sufficient interest. I was also aware of my own reactions to such unmediated invitations (which is typically not to respond to them). Approaching teachers via contacts known to them, however, worked well. My aim was to generate 25 responses from each context I collected data in and to aim for 400 responses in total. The first target was met in all but three contexts, the latter surpassed by almost 50%. Two other factors contributed to a satisfactory number of responses in this study; one is that I was able to collect data over time (ten months); the second is that the questionnaire was available electronically via the web (which is how the majority of responses were provided) and as an email attachment (an option fewer respondents preferred).

One final comment to make about this first study – and one which applies to the remaining studies below – is that it took account of key ethical concerns in educational research. Participation was always informed and voluntary and the anonymity of those contributing was protected, as was the confidentiality of the data.

2.4 Study 2: ELT directors' conceptions of research

The motivation for the second study I draw on here was the view (see, for example, Barker, 2005) that teacher research engagement may be significantly influenced by the attitudes towards research held by school leaders. There was scant existing research in education generally (e.g. Saha, Biddle, & Anderson, 1995) and none at all in language teaching, which had examined the perspectives on research engagement of school leaders. This second study, which ran from December 2006 until June 2008, thus addressed the following questions:

1   What are the conceptions of research held by directors in recognized ELT centres in the UK?
2   What is the extent and nature of directors' own reported research engagement?
3   To what extent do directors believe that research engagement by teachers contributes to more effective teaching?
4   To what extent do directors feel that their institutions are research engaged?
5   According to directors, what factors, both institutional and personal to teachers, support or hinder teacher research engagement?

Questionnaires

The study had two phases. In Phase 1, the directors of all recognized English Language schools in the UK were invited to complete a questionnaire. 'Recognized' here was taken to mean that they were officially accredited by English UK and/or the British Council. These schools are in their majority private EFL schools, though a good proportion are language centres in universities and further education colleges.

The questionnaire (Appendix 3) used in this study had three sections. Section 1 focused on characteristics of the school and asked respondents about their engagement in reading and doing research. Section 2 asked respondents for their views on the value of research for their teachers. A key question here elicited their views on the relationship between doing research and the quality of teachers' work in the classroom. Section 3 examined directors' perceptions of the research culture in their schools.

Questionnaires were collected between January and March 2007. The administration of questionnaires involved an initial postal mailing to all schools, supported by requests via electronic bulletins sent out to directors by English UK and the British Council. I also sent all schools two further postal reminders. In addition to the hard copies of the questionnaire posted to all schools (all of which included postage-paid return envelopes), the questionnaire was also made available electronically, both in web-based format and as an email attachment.

Table 2.2 summarizes the response rate for the first phase of this study. As this shows, 208 questionnaires were returned (of 397 distributed), giving a response rate of 52.5%. Descriptive and inferential statistical analyses were once again carried out, supported by SPSS 15.

Table 2.2   Responses for Study 2

Type of school	N	%
Language school	133	63.9
Further/Higher education college	35	16.8
University	24	11.5
International school/college	10	4.8
Other	6	2.9
Total	208	100

Interviews

Questionnaire respondents were invited to volunteer for a follow-up interview, and 100 did so. I had anticipated doing around 20 interviews, but given the interest I increased my target to 50. Interviewees were chosen using random stratified sampling so that the proportion of directors interviewed from each type of school reflected the proportions in the overall sample as shown in Table 2.2 (for example, 63.9% of the overall sample were directors from private language schools; 66% of the interview sample were from such schools). The purpose of these semi-structured interviews (which lasted on average 15 minutes – see Appendix 4 for interview prompts) was to explore in more detail directors' questionnaire responses. For example, in the questionnaire respondents expressed a view on whether doing research made teachers more effective in the classroom; in the interview I asked them to comment on the kinds of activities they had in mind (i.e. what 'research' meant to them) when they were answering this question. In response to the generally negative way (in their questionnaires) that respondents rated the research culture of their institutions, in the interview I also asked them why they felt the existing culture was not strong. Forty-three interviews were eventually conducted by telephone in April and May 2007 (seven individuals who had agreed to do an interview either did not respond when contacted to make arrangements or were not able to keep our appointment due to unforeseen circumstances). Interviews (except one where the respondent did not give consent) were recorded and transcribed in full.

The interviews were analyzed qualitatively, following a pattern similar to that described for Study 1 above (see also, for example, Newby, 2010: 459–60 for a discussion of the process of qualitative data analysis). Key categories in the interviews were identified and used to elaborate on and extend the basic quantitative analysis of the questionnaire. Particular insights emerged from these interviews relevant to directors' views about (a) the relationship between research engagement and teaching quality; (b) the extent to which their schools constituted a positive research culture; (c) factors which support and hinder positive research cultures; and (d) the desirability and feasibility of promoting research engagement in their schools.

Emails

As noted above, only 50 of the 100 volunteers for interview were followed up. I did, however, invite the remaining 50 to provide a written response via email to this question:

> In the questionnaire, you gave your opinion about how important it is for English language teachers in your institution to do research. Could you expand on this by commenting briefly on what 'research' means for you here? In other words, what kind of activity did you have in mind when you were saying that it is or is not important for teachers to do?

Twenty-four directors responded to this question. The qualitative analysis of these email responses provided deeper insight into the conceptions of research held by directors of ELT schools in the UK.

Challenges

The key challenge in this study was generating a sufficient level of response. First, while a list of recognized ELT schools in the UK is available online, there is no publicly available list of directors of these schools. Such lists are held by English UK and the British Council but for data protection reasons these could not be released. I was, therefore, not able to address postal questionnaires personally and this may have meant that some of these never made it to their intended recipients.

Second, although I have been involved in language teaching for many years, I could not assume that the directors I was targeting would see me as an insider within the UK ELT sector. Rather, my invitation for them to participate in the study could easily have been seen as an academic wanting to exploit their input for his own advancement. It was important, therefore, for me to enter the field very cautiously and with a view to not generating negative reactions to my work which would lower the response rate.

Initially, my fears about a lack of interest in the project seemed justified; prior to the administration of the questionnaire, I engaged in a preliminary consultation phase in which 15 randomly chosen directors were asked (via an intermediary who held their contact details) to comment on a document outlining the goals of the study. None of them replied.

However, as reported above, a good level of response (over 52%) was ultimately achieved. A number of factors contributed to this: (a) the questionnaire was very short (two sides of A4) and could be completed in five minutes; (b) it was available in hard copy, web-based format (the most popular option) and as an attachment (the least popular option in this case); (c) potential respondents received three postal communications from me (an initial invitation, and two thank you / reminder letters); (d) additional reminders and updates were sent to directors via English UK and British Council electronic bulletins (the endorsement of the project by these bodies also gave it added credibility); and (e) cover letters for all communications were carefully crafted to appeal to directors' expertise and to signal the value of their contributions to the project (Appendix 5 shows the initial cover letter). Even with all these measures in place, almost half of the questionnaires sent out (189) were not returned, although the final response rate was much better than originally expected.

Conducting the interviews also presented logistical challenges; a large number of interviews needed to be scheduled and conducted within a relatively short period of two weeks. Additionally, because face-to-face interviews were not feasible given the national nature of the sample, it was necessary to identify a package for obtaining good quality recordings of the telephone interviews. While a cost was associated with obtaining this package (ReTell's 957adv), this was more than offset by the fact that it allowed interviews to be done remotely (saving time and eliminating travel costs) and generated digital quality recordings of the interviews.

2.5 Study 3: Research cultures in English language schools

The third study involved both managers and teachers working in private English language schools in 15 countries around the world (see Table 2.3). The range of questions covered here was quite extensive:

1 What are the conceptions of research held by respondents?
2 To what extent do respondents say they read published research?
3 To what extent do respondents say they do research?
4 What are teachers' perceptions of their institutional culture in relation to research?
5 How do these perceptions relate to teachers' research engagement?
6 To what extent do managers see research engagement as a desirable goal for their schools?
7 According to managers, what factors, both institutional and personal to teachers, support or hinder teacher research engagement?

Table 2.3   Respondents for Study 3

Regions	Directors	Teachers	Total	%
Europe	12	31	43	32.3
Asia	12	28	40	30.1
Middle East	5	21	26	19.5
Africa	3	6	9	6.8
South America	1	6	7	5.3
Unspecified	0	8	8	6.0
Total	33	100	133	100

Questionnaires and interviews

The design of the study followed the questionnaire-plus-interview format described for Study 2. The managers' questionnaire was slightly modified (after piloting) from that used in Study 2. Thirty-three managers (in different schools) completed the questionnaire and 16 were interviewed. The teacher's questionnaire was based on that in Study 1. One hundred teachers (working in the same schools as the directors) completed the questionnaire and 16 of these were interviewed (these were chosen randomly out of 40 who volunteered). Both versions of the questionnaire were made available electronically and in hard copy. All interviews (which lasted on average 35 minutes) were done by telephone, recorded, and then transcribed in full.

Initial access to participants was again handled through a mediator; managers received an invitation to participate in the study via a senior manager working for their organization. Managers who agreed to participate then invited the teachers in their schools to do so too. Managers and teachers who completed the questionnaire and agreed to be interviewed also provided an email address, at which point I was able to contact them directly.

Data analysis followed the patterns already described. The numerical data were processed statistically using a range of descriptive, correlational and inferential measures; open-ended responses and interview data were analyzed qualitatively via content analysis.

Challenges

The experience of the first two studies enabled this one to proceed relatively smoothly. Logistically, scheduling and conducting the telephone interviews did present a challenge, given the international nature of the sample, time differences, and the unreliability of long-distance telephone connections to certain countries. Teachers were also subject to last-minute changes in their teaching schedules, meaning that interviews in some cases had to be rescheduled. One additional challenge, similar to Study 2, stemmed from the fact that I did not have direct access to the population of target respondents and was reliant on mediators for access. While this had advantages (e.g. respondents were initially contacted by someone they knew, rather than myself), it did also reduce the amount of direct control I had over following up non-respondents.

2.6 Study 4: ELT professionals' views of research

The final study I draw on here was based wholly on a questionnaire and the instrument used was a modified version of that used in Study 1.

Similar to the earlier studies, it asked how often respondents read and did research and why or why not they engaged in these activities; it also elicited their views of their institutional research cultures and explored their conceptions of what counts as research.

Participants in this study were members of an international language teaching organization. With the permission and support of this organization, in February 2007 all members were invited by email to complete a web-based questionnaire (hard copy or email attachment versions were not made available on this occasion). For ethical reasons, the invitation made it clear that while responses would be used by the organization to inform its own policies relating to research, these responses would also be used as part of my programme of research. The questionnaire was available online for two weeks and at the end of this period 1,950 responses had been submitted. Of the 1,608 who identified their professional role, 666 (41.4%) described themselves as language teachers. As Table 2.4 shows, over 74% of these worked in North America. Of the 126 managers in this study, 92 (73%) also worked in the USA. The numerical data for this study were analyzed statistically using SPSS 16, but additionally there were substantial volumes of open-ended data here too, with teachers explaining in detail their views about research and, very often, the frustrations they felt because their working conditions did not make research engagement a viable option. These data were analyzed qualitatively, via content analysis, as described for Study 1.

Table 2.4   Teachers in Study 4

Regions	N	%
North America	494	74.2
Asia	84	12.6
South America	37	5.6
Unspecified	21	3.2
Middle East	14	2.1
Europe	12	1.8
Africa	4	0.6
Total	666	100

Challenges

In terms of respondents, this was the largest study in my programme; in terms of administration, though, it was the most straightforward. The content of the web-based questionnaire was largely already available from instruments used in previous studies, and access to potential respondents was facilitated by an organization of which they were members. One major administrative issue to address though, was obtaining clearance from the organization for their members' data to be incorporated into my own research. This was obtained on the basis that the invitation would be sent out centrally (i.e. I would not have access to respondents' email addresses), that it was made clear in the invitation that the data would be used for research purposes, and that in reporting the data, I would not write specifically about the organization and its members. These conditions were all feasible and certainly worth agreeing to, given the benefits of having access to such a large pool of respondents.

2.7 Teacher research projects

The four studies described above (which from now on will be referred to as Study 1, Study 2, Study 3, and Study 4) provide the data that I draw on in Chapters 3–7 of this book. Chapter 8, though, is informed not by a specific piece of research but by my practical involvement in two teacher research projects. I discuss these projects in detail later in this book, and at this stage I am just signalling that they are an additional source of input that I draw on in shaping the arguments I develop here. The two projects, one in the Middle East and one in South-east Asia, were set up as professional development initiatives rather than as sites for research, and in both cases my primary role was to facilitate teacher research rather than to research it. Nonetheless, an analysis of both projects, including feedback from participants, provides additional practical insight into the process of supporting teacher research which complements (and provides an interesting contrast with, as will become evident) the empirical findings presented in this text.

2.8 Working with questionnaires

Much of the data generated by my programme of research was derived through questionnaire responses. Before ending this chapter, then, I would like to reflect briefly on my experiences to examine what they imply about the effective use of questionnaires in language teaching research. Questionnaire design and administration is, of course, a topic on which vast amounts of theoretical and practical literature exist (e.g. De Vaus, 2002; Fowler, 2002; Gillham, 2000; Oppenheim, 1992) and it is not my goal here to repeat this; rather, I would like to suggest a simple framework of considerations which I have found useful in enabling me to maximize the value of questionnaires in

Substantive considerations

- Does the questionnaire have a clear purpose?
- Are all items relevant to this purpose?
- Is the questionnaire comprehensive in its treatment of the theme(s) covered?
- Are issues covered in sufficient depth?

Technical considerations

- Has the instrument been through extensive development, piloting and revision?
- Are instructions clear and precise?
- Are a range of item types used?
- Has the potential for ambiguity in questions been minimized?
- Have common design problems been avoided?

Logistical considerations

- Have a range of (appropriate) delivery/return mechanisms been considered?
- Has a timetable for the development and administration of the survey been defined?
- Is there a clear strategy for maximizing response rates?
- If relevant, have gatekeepers been identified and contacted?

User considerations

- Does the questionnaire look good?
- Is the topic likely to interest the target respondents?
- Are the demands on the target users – cognitively, emotionally, and time-wise – realistic?
- Is the questionnaire easy to follow, complete, and return?

Figure 2.1   Key considerations in questionnaire design and administration

my work. This framework is summarized in Figure 2.1; it consists of four components – substantive, technical, logistical and user – and for each a set of key questions is provided. At the design and administration stage of a questionnaire, ensuring that as many of these as possible can be answered affirmatively can, my experience suggests, enhance both response rates and the quality of the data. It is particularly important to stress the role that user considerations play in determining whether target respondents decide to complete an instrument; a questionnaire may be technically competent, purposeful, and strategically administered, but if it is not user-friendly (e.g. if it is too long, too complicated, too demanding) respondents are less likely to engage with it. Of course, I am aware that tensions may arise in seeking to address all four components of this framework; for example, the need for comprehensive treatment of an issue may be at odds with the demand for an instrument which is quick to complete. In such cases, as researchers we need to make judgements about which component we want to give more weight to, and this decision will be influenced by our understanding of our target respondents. For example, the teacher questionnaires described above were quite challenging to complete; however, the population was large enough to mean that I was confident that a substantial volume of responses could, over time, be obtained. In the studies with the managers though, the populations were smaller, and the respondents very busy and in many cases possibly not well disposed to academics and to research; for those reasons a shorter questionnaire was desirable, with the option of subsequent interviews. My experience of studying teachers' and managers' conceptions of research suggests that this framework of four considerations (which combines advice from the research methods literature and insights from my own practical experience) can support the productive use of questionnaires in educational research.

2.9 Conclusion

As Table 2.5 shows, the programme of research I have presented here involved a non-probability sample of 1,730 language teaching professionals from all over the world. The majority of these individuals worked in North America, Europe, and Asia, with input also coming to a lesser extent from Australia & New Zealand, Africa, the Middle East, and South America. Teachers worked in a range of private and state sector contexts (although most of the qualitative data came from

Table 2.5 Participants in research programme by region

Regions	Study 1	Study 2	Study 3	Study 4	Total	%
Africa	26	0	9	5	40	2.3
Asia	180	0	40	90	310	17.9
Australia & NZ	27	0	0	3	30	1.7
Europe	286	208	43	15	552	31.9
Middle East	78	0	26	16	120	6.9
North America	0	0	0	588	588	34.0
South America	0	0	7	52	59	3.4
Unspecified	0	0	8	23	31	1.8
Total	597	208	133	792	1730	100

Table 2.6 Teachers in research programme, by ages taught

Age group	N	%
12 or younger	200	14.7
13–19	439	32.2
20–25	371	27.2
26+	238	17.5
Not specified	115	8.4
Total	1363	100.0

respondents in the private sector), teaching learners at all levels (see Table 2.6) and were both native and non-native speakers of English.

This research can thus justifiably be referred to as international in nature. The non-probability nature of the sample (i.e. comprising volunteers and not defined through random sampling) together with the variability that exists in language teaching contexts around the world, though, mean that caution is needed in suggesting that the findings that emerge here reflect global trends in the field. Nonetheless, this work does provide a substantial evidence base on which informed decisions about promoting teacher research in language teaching can be made. The fact that the arguments I advance in the rest of this book are grounded in extensive empirical evidence is significant and provides a contrast to the predominantly theoretical nature of the debate through which the relevance of research to teachers in language teaching has been conducted. In the five chapters that follow I synthesize the results from the different studies to address the following series of research questions:

1 What conceptions of research are held by language teachers and managers? (From now on, I use *managers* to include both the directors from Study 2 and the managers from Studies 3 and 4.) (Chapter 3)
2 What is the nature of language teachers' engagement with research – i.e. through reading it? (Chapter 4)
3 What is the nature of language teachers' engagement in research – i.e. through doing it? (Chapter 5)
4 What is the relationship, according to language teachers and managers, between research engagement and teaching quality? (Chapter 6)
5 To what extent do teachers and managers feel that their working contexts are positive research cultures? (Chapter 7)

Notes

1 Please note that in this and other tables in the book, although figures are presented to one decimal place, the total is rounded up to 100%.

References

Aldridge, A., & Levine, K. (2001). *Surveying the social world: Principles and practice in survey research*. Buckingham: Open University Press.

Babbie, E. (2003). *The practice of social research* 10th ed. Belmont: Thomson/ Wadsworth.

Barker, P. (2005). *Research in schools and colleges*: National Educational Research Forum Working Paper 7.2. Retrieved 3 February, 2012, from www.eep.ac.uk/nerf/word/WP7.2withappendixe42d.doc?version=1

Borg, S. (2006). *Teacher cognition and language education: Research and practice*. London: Continuum.

Borg, S. (2007). Research engagement in English language teaching. *Teaching and Teacher Education, 23*(5), 731–747.

Borg, S. (2009). English language teachers' conceptions of research. *Applied Linguistics, 30*(3), 355–388.

Braun, V., & Clarke, V. (2006). Using thematic analysis in psychology. *Qualitative Research in Psychology, 3*(2), 77–101.

Brown, J. D. (2009). Open-response items in questionnaires. In J. Heigham & R. A. Croker (Eds.), *Qualitative research in applied linguistics* (pp. 200–219). Basingstoke: Palgrave Macmillan.

Bryman, A. (2008). *Social research methods* 3rd ed. Oxford: Oxford University Press.

Couper, M. P. (2005). Technology trends in survey data collection. *Social Science Computer Review, 23*(4), 486–501.

Couper, M. P., & Miller, P. V. (2008). Web survey methods: Introduction. *Public Opinion Quarterly, 72*(5), 831–835.

Creswell, J. (2003). *Research design: Qualitative, quantitative, and mixed methods approaches* 2nd ed. Thousand Oaks, CA: Sage.

De Vaus, D. (2002). *Surveys in social research* 5th ed. London: Routledge.

Dörnyei, Z. (2003). *Questionnaires in second language research: Construction, administration and processing*. New York: Lawrence Erlbaum Associates.

Dörnyei, Z. (2007). *Research methods in applied linguistics*. Oxford: Oxford University Press.

Fowler, F. J. (2002). *Survey research methods* 3rd ed. Thousand Oaks: Sage.

Gillham, B. (2000). *Developing a questionnaire*. London: Continuum

Kvale, S., & Brinkmann, S. (2008). *Interviews: Learning the craft of qualitative research interviewing* 2nd ed. Thousand Oaks: Sage.

McNamara, O. (2002). Evidence-based practice through practice-based evidence. In O. McNamara (Ed.), *Becoming an evidence-based practitioner* (pp. 15–26). London: Routledge Falmer.

Newby, P. (2010). *Research methods for education*. Harlow: Pearson Education Limited.

Oppenheim, A. N. (1992). *Questionnaire design, interviewing and attitude measurement* 2nd ed. London: Continuum.

Ratcliffe, M., Bartholomew, H., Hames, V., Hind, A., Leach, J., & Millar, R. (2004). *Science education practitioners' views of research and its influence on their practice*. York: Department of Educational Studies, University of York.

Saha, L. J., Biddle, B. J., & Anderson, D. S. (1995). Attitudes towards education research knowledge and policy making among American and Australian school principals. *International Journal of Educational Research, 23*(2), 113–126.

3 Conceptions of research in language teaching

3.1 Introduction

The relationship between language teachers' beliefs and their actions has been the focus of a substantial volume of research in the last 15 years (Borg, 2009b). This work has established that while what teachers do is not always determined by their beliefs, these have a powerful influence on teachers' decisions. This premise underpins the focus of this chapter, which examines the conceptions of research held by language teachers and managers. Insights into these conceptions can inform our understandings of how language teaching professionals respond (often negatively) to calls for them to be research engaged. Such insights also have clear potential to contribute to the design of initiatives which seek to promote teacher research (see Chapter 9 for further discussion). I will begin by reviewing what is currently known about teachers' conceptions of research in education generally and specifically in the field of language teaching. Then I will draw on data from across the studies in my programme of research to analyze the conceptions of research held by teachers and managers from a range of language teaching contexts worldwide.

3.2 Prior research

Education studies

Within the framework of evidence-based practice (EBP) discussed in Chapter 1, one strand of research has focused on examining what teachers actually think about research. The rationale for such inquiry (and a key premise in this book) is that initiatives to encourage teachers to do research are more likely to have an impact if they are based on an understanding of teachers' beliefs about research and its relevance to their work. I now discuss the findings from this research, which, unless otherwise stated, has been conducted in the UK.

Everton, Galton and Pell (2002) surveyed 572 teachers. Respondents were asked, amongst other issues, whether research had influenced their teaching and whether they were interested in engaging in research themselves. In McNamara's (2002) study, 100 teachers were surveyed on issues such as what image educational research held for them and whether they felt research might have an impact on their work. Both these studies suggested that teachers acknowledged the potential positive impact of research on various aspects of professional practice. The two studies above, plus that by Shkedi (1998), in Israel, also explored what associations the word 'research' had for teachers. Two prominent images in McNamara (2002: 16–17) were that research is academic and that it involves statistics, and teachers' often negative characterizations of research were reflected in comments referring to

- 'professors undertaking tests and surveys and making reports'
- 'academia' as 'utopia irrelevant to actual classroom situations'
- 'dry facts' that 'failed to influence practice'
- statistics 'telling us how bad we are with no ideas of how to improve'.

Shkedi's study highlighted, via interviews with 47 teachers, similar views of research, showing that it was associated with

- quantitative-objective tools
- theory and hypotheses
- representativeness
- generalizability.

The study by Ratcliffe et al. (2004), based on interviews with over 60 science educators, found that respondents, unless already experienced in research, had limited understandings of the nature of and the processes involved in social science research.

While in the UK there has been substantial interest in the way school managers can promote research engagement (e.g. Sharp et al., 2006), there has been little specific investigation of the conceptions of research held by these individuals. Yet one of my arguments here is that managers can exert a significant influence on the extent to which teachers engage in research and thus 'an important aspect of many practitioner-research programmes is to also engage the senior management of organisations in the programme' (Davies, Hamilton, & James, 2007: 6). In the work that does exist, Saha, Biddle, & Anderson (1995) studied the attitudes towards educational research of 120 American and Australian school principals, concluding that these attitudes were generally positive.

Language teaching studies

Recent years have seen an increasing, though still emergent, interest in the conceptions of research held by language teachers. In early studies, McDonough & McDonough (1990) surveyed the views of research of 34 teachers of English as a foreign language, while Brown et al. (1992) reports a survey of 607 members of an international association for ELT professionals[1]. These studies, echoing those in mainstream education, reported notions of research closely tied to quantitative and statistical methods and a general ambivalence about the role of educational research in teachers' professional lives. For example, respondents in Brown et al. (1992: 22) defined research as (amongst others) 'hypothesis testing', 'controlled study of a problem', 'use of scientific method to test a theory', and 'scientifically controlled study to test a hypothesis'. Rainey (2000) conducted a survey of the views EFL classroom teachers held specifically about action research (AR). Based on responses from 228 respondents in 10 countries, she found that over 75% of the teachers had never heard of AR; those who had, though, had positive views about it and defined it primarily as a problem-solving activity; for example, a teacher from Thailand said AR was 'what one tries to find any problems in our work, then analyse why the problems happen and then tries to find out how to solve the problems' (p. 73).

More recent work by Allison & Carey (2007) examined the views of language teachers at a university in Canada about research; lack of encouragement and motivation to do research were commonly cited as challenges to teachers' efforts to engage in research, and one teacher was quoted as saying they were explicitly discouraged by 'high ranking members of the university' from 'acting like professors and publishing research' (p. 70). Clear views emerge in this study of what is described as a 'feudal scenario' in which teachers are 'working the land, but not owning it' (p. 73). Such metaphors reveal frustrations among teachers about the manner in which research on teaching is dominated by academics while teachers' own potential role as researchers in their own contexts is minimized.

Various papers of my own, drawing on aspects of the programme of research I report on more fully in this book, have also added in recent years to the literature on language teachers' conceptions of research (Borg, 2006a, 2007a, 2007b, 2007c, 2009a). Two studies which build on this work involved groups of teachers of English in China. Barkhuizen (2009) used a narrative frame to elicit 83 College English Teachers' (CETs) accounts of issues in their teaching they would like to research, how they might go about such research, and what obstacles they would anticipate facing. One recurrent concern teachers wanted to investigate related to increasing student participation during communicative activities (especially in relation to speaking). In terms of how teachers said they would conduct their projects, qualitative strategies such as interviews and observations were those most frequently cited. Finally, the CETs in this study identified a range of constraints on their ability to do the envisaged projects: lack of time, lack of research methodology knowledge and skills, lack of student co-operation, and lack of resources. Gao, Barkhuizen & Chow (2011a) used a questionnaire and focus group interviews to study the conceptions of and motivations to do research of 33 primary school teachers of English in China. In this study teachers held conceptions of research associated with experiments, though their use of this term referred to experimenting with pedagogical strategies in class rather than systematic comparative studies involving control and treatment groups (see also Gao, Barkhuizen, & Chow, 2011b for another paper from this project). Two additional recent studies conducted in the Chinese context (Bai & Hudson, 2011; Bai & Millwater, 2011) will be discussed in subsequent chapters.

Other than in my own work, the conceptions of research held by managers in language education have not been studied. Given, though, that there is evidence that teachers are better able to engage in and with research when their institution, and its administration, are sympathetic to such activity (e.g. Roberts, 1993), in understanding teachers' attitudes to research it is also important to investigate those of their managers.

I will now proceed to present the insights emerging from my work into the conceptions of research held by language teachers and managers. As explained in Chapter 2, these conceptions were elicited through questionnaires, interviews, and open-ended writing in which respondents articulated their views about what counts as research and about the characteristics of good quality research.

3.3 Conceptions of research

Teachers' assessments of scenarios

Teachers in Studies 1, 3 and 4 in my programme of research (see Chapter 2) were asked to consider a set of scenarios (see Figure 3.1), all involving some form of inquiry, and to indicate to what extent they felt each was research. The findings for this question are summarized in Table 3.1, which shows the number of teachers who commented on each scenario (N) and the percentage of teachers selecting each of the four possible ratings for the individual scenarios.

1 A teacher noticed that an activity she used in class did not work well. She thought about this after the lesson and made some notes in her diary. She tried something different in her next lesson. This time the activity was more successful.

2 A teacher read about a new approach to teaching writing and decided to try it out in his class over a period of two weeks. He video recorded some of his lessons and collected samples of learners' written work. He analyzed this information, then presented the results to his colleagues at a staff meeting.

3 A teacher was doing an MA course. She read several books and articles about grammar teaching, then wrote an essay of 6,000 words in which she discussed the main points in those readings.

4 A university lecturer gave a questionnaire about the use of computers in language teaching to 500 teachers. Statistics were used to analyze the questionnaires. The lecturer wrote an article about the work in an academic journal.

5 Two teachers were both interested in discipline. They observed each other's lessons once a week for three months and made notes about how they controlled their classes. They discussed their notes and wrote a short article about what they learned for the newsletter of the national language teachers' association.

6 To find out which of two methods for teaching vocabulary was more effective, a teacher first tested two classes. Then for four weeks she taught vocabulary to each class using a different method. After that she tested both groups again and compared the results to the first test. She decided to use the method which worked best in her own teaching.

7 A head teacher met every teacher individually and asked them about their working conditions. The head made notes about the teachers' answers. He used his notes to write a report which he submitted to the Ministry of Education.

8 Midway through a course, a teacher gave a class of 30 students a feedback form. The next day, five students handed in their completed forms. The teacher read these and used the information to decide what to do in the second part of the course.

9 A teacher trainer asked his trainees to write an essay about ways of motivating teenage learners of English. After reading the assignments, the trainer decided to write an article on the trainees' ideas about motivation. He submitted his article to a professional journal.

10 The Head of the English department wanted to know what teachers thought of the new course book. She gave all teachers a questionnaire to complete, studied their responses, then presented the results at a staff meeting.

Figure 3.1   Ten scenarios

Table 3.1   Teachers' assessment of ten scenarios

Scenario	N	Definitely not research (%)	Probably not research (%)	Probably research (%)	Definitely research (%)
1	1355	19.6	29.2	36.4	14.8
2	1353	1.8	5.8	33.1	59.3
3	1348	14.2	23.6	32.2	30.0
4	1350	0.9	5.0	25.1	69.0
5	1165	2.9	13.2	37.4	46.4
6	1348	2.2	6.2	27.2	64.4
7	1165	13.8	26.8	33.2	26.2
8	1350	26.8	37.3	22.7	13.2
9	1164	16.0	30.8	32.5	20.7
10	1167	11.9	23.9	38.0	26.2

Figure 3.2 collapses these results into two categories for each scenario – 'not research' (made up of 'definitely not research' and 'probably not research') and 'research' (which includes 'probably research' and 'definitely research'). This allows the overall direction of the teachers' responses to emerge more clearly. While defining research is in itself not a straightforward issue, it is possible to extract from the educational research methodology literature (e.g. Babbie, 2003; Cohen, Manion, & Morrison, 2000; Robson, 2002; Wiersma, 1991) a number of commonly cited minimal elements – a problem or question, data, analysis, and interpretation. Characteristics of the process, such as systematicity and rigour, are also commonly cited. Additionally, it has been argued (as discussed in Chapter 1) that to qualify as research, inquiry needs to be made public (Freeman, 1996; Stenhouse, 1975). These factors will be borne in mind in the following discussion of teachers' assessments of the research scenarios.

As Table 3.1 and Figure 3.2 show, the three scenarios most highly rated as research by the teachers were numbers 4 (94.1% said this was research), 2 (92.4%), and 6 (91.6%). Scenario 4 includes a number of elements commonly associated with 'scientific' approaches to research – e.g. a large sample and statistics. The researcher in this scenario was also an academic and the output took the form of a research article. Scenarios 2 and 6 are, in contrast, both examples of teacher research, although the particular research methods adopted by the teachers in each case varied. In scenario 2, for example, a teacher studied a new approach to teaching writing by collecting

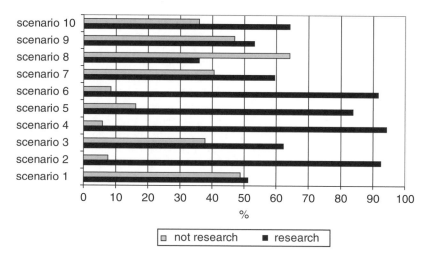

Figure 3.2   Teachers' assessments of ten scenarios

video data and learners' work, then presented the results to colleagues (in this case, the words *samples, analyzed,* and *results* in the scenario may have influenced teachers' judgements). Scenario 6 also reflected characteristics (e.g. pre- and post-tests) commonly associated with research.

Scenarios 8, 1 and 9 were the three least highly rated by teachers as research. Only 35.6% of the teachers felt the library-based inquiry described in number 8 was research (and using common definitions of educational research, this low assessment is justified). In scenario 9 a teacher trainer used trainees' essays as data for an article, while scenario 1 described a teacher reflecting on their practice and modifying their teaching as a result.

While the statistical analysis of these scenarios is in itself of interest, the questionnaire data alone do not provide any insight into teachers' reasons for their assessments. For this we must turn to the follow-up data obtained, as discussed in Chapter 2, in writing (for Study 1) and through interviews (for Studies 1 and 3).

As noted above, the most highly rated scenario was number 4. Teachers who provided written follow-up data and who said this was definitely research were asked to explain their choice. A number of common influences on their assessments are highlighted in the following written comments:

> This is classic quantitative research: large sample, statistical data analysis, and a very public report. (Japan)

> Because the large number of teachers were taking part in the research and because of the feedback that was published. (Slovenia)

> Using statistics also suggests that the approach was objective. I also assume, rightly or wrongly, that an academic journal would only publish results that were worthwhile. (Switzerland)

> ... the use of statistics represents a scientific attempt to analyse and quantify a large body of data. The resulting article is an attempt to present the findings of the study to academic peers. The findings of the paper may then be either accepted or refuted along the usual lines of reliability/validity etc. (Japan)

Similar themes were reflected in the interview data when teachers were asked to discuss why they felt scenario 4 was definitely research:

> The sample – 500 people. Statistics were used, writing an article in an academic journal – what more could you want! (Turkey)

> ... because the university lecturer first of all he or she uses a tool to collect the information. And the collected information is systematically analysed with the help of using statistical methods, and then the lecturer, by using the statistics or the data, writes an article for an academic journal. Writing to an academic journal means the information gathered should be put together in a very systematic way. (Turkey)

References to large samples, statistics, and academic outputs recur here and clearly influenced teachers' assessments of this scenario. In addition, there were also references to other aspects of research such as objectivity, systematicity, and hypothesis. The first of these, as we see later, was another powerful influence on this sample of teachers' conceptions of good quality research.

As noted above, scenario 8 was the least highly rated as research. Teachers' critiques of it centred around limitations in the number of participants, the volume of data, and the representativeness of the conclusions:

> The number of the completed questionnaires and studied by the teacher is too low. (Slovenia)

> ... because the teacher used only student feedback without any objective results and it was only a single instance of gathering information. (Australia)

> The information he collects is not an overall reflection of the students' ideas. (China)

> Although possibly of some small use for the teacher, such a feedback form is not very useful as research, as it only included a small sampling of the

students and was only intended to gear the course to suit a particular group of students. (Switzerland)

... the data collection process is flawed (you cannot draw reliable conclusions from such a small sample). (France)

Getting feedback from students seems like normal ' teaching' work to me. (Switzerland)

I'm really sorry. This is definitely not a research. Data collection is invalid since they're just five out of thirty. (UAE)

Observations of this kind recurred in teachers' comments on this particular scenario. They reflect conceptions of good research in which the number of participants and representativeness of the sample are key elements; critiques of this scenario also referred to the limited local relevance of the exercise (i.e. no generalizability) and to the fact that collecting feedback from students was a normal teaching activity rather than research. This distinction between routine teaching and research surfaced more than once and seemed to underpin at least some teachers' conceptions of what research is. This was clearly true for the teacher who wrote that 'much of what you ask [in the questionnaire] is what we normally do as part of our teaching and we do not call it research!' (Switzerland). Also evident in some teachers' comments was a broad view of research which saw it as 'anything we do in the classroom with the view to making our own teaching better and then sharing it with our colleagues' (Spain).

References to reflection were also common in critiques of scenario 1 (the second least highly rated as research). One teacher wrote that 'it is part of the teaching workload and something we do all the time without even thinking of it as something extra' (Switzerland) while another said, 'This is what a teacher does almost everyday, isn't it? It may be a starting point of research but I would call it reflective teaching' (Japan). Research, then, is here being contrasted with the more regular and routine thinking about their work which teachers engage in.

Managers' conceptions of research

In Study 4, language teaching managers were also asked to rate the scenarios discussed above and their ratings reflected those of the teachers. For example, the scenarios most highly rated as research by 126 managers, mainly from North America, were 4 (96.7% said it was research), 2 (93.6%) and 6 (92.7%) respectively. The same order was seen in the ratings of another sub-sample of 33 managers working for a global language teaching organization: 96.7% said scenario 4 was research, 93.6% scenario 2 and 92.7% scenario 6. The assessments of the scenarios by teachers and managers across a wide range of international language teaching contexts thus displayed a high degree of congruence.

Further insight into what research means to language teaching managers emerged from a series of 59 interviews conducted in two of my projects. In the first set of interviews (Study 3), 16 managers were asked to elaborate on the thinking behind the way they assessed various scenarios. In relation to scenario 6 (one of the two most highly rated), these managers explained their positive views with reference to its methodological rigour. For example, one said:

> I just I found it to be quite what's the word? More methodologically sound from a scientific point of view where the person is actually trying to analyse and compare. (Kuwait)

Scenario 1, in comparison, was not seen to be research because it lacked a systematic approach and was a largely private and personal endeavour:

> I think it has to be systematic doesn't it, I mean there has to be something that definitely comes out of it that goes beyond a personal objective, which is what that first one [scenario] seems to be. If that was then disseminated to some other people then I think it would be quite different. (Bahrain)

Manager comments on the scenarios also illustrated the often inclusive way in which research was defined. One manager, for example, said, 'I would have thought that research was finding out something that you didn't know' (Ukraine). Similarly broad views about research were reflected in the following comments too:

> My understanding of research is basically when you read something, you observe something, you reflect on something and then you try something different as a result of that kind of input, for me that's research. (Czech Republic)

> I think it's really anything you do to investigate, whether you're sort of testing your own understanding of a learning theory or whether you're trying to find out specific learners' needs, whether you're testing a new course book, I think it has to be quite a broad definition. (Jordan)

Interviews were also conducted with 43 managers of ELT schools in the UK (Study 2). Prior to the interviews the managers had completed a questionnaire and one of the items there asked them how important they felt it was for their teachers to do research (I discuss this question in Chapter 6). In the follow-up interviews with these managers, I then asked them to provide examples of the kinds of activities they had in mind when answering this question. In addition to these interview responses, a further 24 managers responded in writing to explain what activities they considered to be research. An analysis of these interviews and written comments sheds light on what research means for these individuals.

Table 3.2 lists, in descending order of frequency, the activities which managers most commonly referred to in explaining what research meant for them. Professional development activities, particularly those involving reflection, were those most commonly cited here. Several managers illustrated this point with reference to the manner in which, through research, teachers could critically think about what happens in their classrooms and adjust their teaching accordingly. For example:

> It may not be formal research, it may not actually be sort of written down and you know, reported back although it might be in some cases, but they need to be thinking about what's going on in their classrooms and adjusting their, you know their planning their preparation and delivery in accordance with what they discover about their groups as they go on. (UK)

Another manager explained the same idea as follows:

> ... they're actively reflecting on what they're doing by sort of critically looking at it in terms of improving the learning of the student, and thinking about the contribution that the teacher makes to that outcome. (UK)

The belief that reflective practice is necessarily a form of research conflicts both with formal definitions of research as well as with widely

Table 3.2 Activities described as 'research' by managers

Activity	N
Professional development and reflection	39
Materials and test evaluation	13
Action research	13
Trying out new things	12
Materials and test development	9
Needs analysis and course design	5

cited definitions of teacher research. That by Cochran-Smith & Lytle (1999) cited in Chapter 1, for example, is explicit in the view that teacher research extends beyond thoughtful teaching of a reflective nature. The first manager quote above also highlights, once again, informal views of research as an activity which does not have to be documented. My position on this matter has already been made clear (see Chapter 1) – without a record which is shared in some way with others, it is unhelpful to describe teachers' reflections on their work as research.

Table 3.2 highlights a range of other activities which managers referred to in explaining their views of what research is. Several saw the evaluation of tests and materials as research, as in the example below:

> I've also encouraged teachers to do, you know, self analytical tasks where they take a new text book into the class ... try it out for a week and then present it to their peers and discuss what results they found and how effective it's been as a teaching tool. (UK)

Action research was also mentioned a number of times by managers, as in the next comment:

> I was thinking of action research, classroom research where they're asking questions about their own learners and about their own teaching process, they're asking questions about what works, what doesn't, why does it, has anyone else asked this question, where they're looking at problems as potential research topics rather than as something they grapple with on their own, they're seeing problems as enquiries, so if something isn't working, how does it fit into the literature, what are other teachers saying about this? Is this a common trend? You know, is there something here where there are answers in the field, or the same questions at least being asked? (UK)

On closer analysis, this explanation of action research does not explicitly link this form of inquiry to the introduction, monitoring, and evaluation of new practices (which is what action research typically involves – see, for example, Kemmis & McTaggart, 1988). Rather, action research is explained here in terms of teachers' awareness of their own practices and of their ability to seek answers, or at least parallels, to their problems in existing literature. Clearly, although many managers referred to action research in articulating their views of what research is, it is likely that they held various understandings of what this activity entailed. Thus while one manager explained that action research was 'things like recording themselves and evaluating it without necessarily seeing me or anyone else about it' (UK), another emphasized it as a process of introducing and evaluating change:

> ... action research projects with the groups of students that they teach. These projects involve looking at an aspect of their teaching – perhaps a problem area or an area of interest, researching this with students and colleagues via questionnaires or discussions, thinking about a solution and implementing a change within their normal practice, and following the action up with an evaluation. (UK)

Returning to Table 3.2, several managers also referred to research as doing something innovative, experimenting or trying out something new. The next quote equates doing research with teachers putting themselves 'on trial':

> I think it's a much healthier situation to try and encourage people to expand their repertoire particularly in terms of incorporating new technology into classes and that kind of thing by, you know, just almost putting themselves on trial ... try something trial and error and self reflection afterwards to sort of say yes I tried this ... this worked, this didn't work and you know how can we do this better next time? That kind of thing. (UK)

Reflection is once again seen to be part of the process here, though the central idea is that research involves doing something new and monitoring how it works. Finally, research was also described both in terms of materials and test development and with reference to needs analysis and course design. Regarding the former, one manager explained his views of research as follows:

> Well I suppose I'm immediately thinking perhaps of people doing things like developing course materials and leading eventually I suppose to producing course books or skills books, that sort of thing. I suppose probably that's immediately where my mind goes if people are talking about research. (UK)

And in terms of research as the development of new courses, another manager noted that

> [we are] constantly sort of looking for niche markets to try and sort of get ahead of the game, in other words, any area that we're not sort of covered by, and somebody would want to look into it, we would be willing to sponsor, by which I mean you know, as you know, if somebody came in the door asking to do English with golf, or whatever it was, you know, we would always say yes to doing the course, and send somebody off to do some research about it afterwards. (UK)

In addition to the specific types of activities mentioned above, a number of managers explained that for them research had academic connotations. Examples of comments in this vein make this orientation clear:

> I was viewing research as being more along the lines of academic research. I see this as something which can be useful and motivating for some teachers, but not essential in day to day practice within our environment. (UK)

> 'Academic research' is a systematic approach to investigating an academic hypothesis e.g. how languages are learned, how language is patterned (grammar, text patterns, discourse patterns etc.). Few teachers will ever do this unless they take a research degree. (UK)

> I interpreted research as being coming up with a hypothesis and then testing it. Not in terms of kind of reflective teaching, experimenting with a slightly different classroom technique or, but as in terms of doing rigorous, properly controlled scientific testing. (UK)

> I don't think that it is important for teachers to do original research, developing new theories about language learning, or to develop new ideas on language acquisition, by, for example, conducting quantitative or qualitative original research. (UK)

Generally, managers did not see this academic orientation to research as having much potential for teachers; the kinds of activities highlighted in Table 3.2 were seen to be more realistic targets which nonetheless involved research. Overall, then, although several managers did acknowledge the scientific perspective on research, in most cases the forms of research which they immediately thought of in relation to their teachers consisted of more informal activities with clear links to teachers' daily practices and to their professional development. In many cases, the kinds of activities managers saw as research (e.g. writing materials) did involve searching for information but lacked the purposeful and systematic empirical elements which research must have.

3.4 Characteristics of good quality research

In addition to expressing their views on what counts as research, teachers and managers were also asked to comment on the characteristics of good quality research by (a) rating the importance of a list of criteria for determining research quality and (b) suggesting additional criteria for doing so. I will now report on the responses these tasks elicited.

Teachers' perspectives

Teachers' ratings of a list of 11 potential characteristics of good quality research are presented in Table 3.3. In this table, 'more important' constitutes 'important' and 'very important' ratings for each characteristic, while 'less important' includes 'unimportant' and 'moderately important' responses. The responses are listed in descending order according to the percentage of teachers who indicated that a characteristic was 'more important'.

As Table 3.3 shows, the characteristic most highly rated was 'the researcher is objective', followed by 'hypotheses are tested'. Together these responses provide further support for the view that teachers' conceptions of research are aligned with more scientific notions of inquiry; having said that, the third most highly rated characteristic was 'the results give teachers results they can use', which reflects a more pragmatic perspective on research quality. Other points worth noting here are that 'the results apply to many ELT contexts' was the characteristic which generated the largest number of 'unsure' answers (this reflects uncertainties about the notion of 'generalizability' in

Table 3.3   Features of good research, according to teachers

Characteristic	N	More important %	Less important %	Unsure %
The researcher is objective	1245	84.7	8.7	6.6
Hypotheses are tested	1246	79.3	14.4	6.3
The results give teachers ideas they can use	1248	77.4	16.3	6.3
Variables are controlled	1203	71.2	14.6	14.1
Information is analyzed statistically	1251	61.9	27.7	10.4
A large number of people are studied	1253	58.4	35.0	6.6
Experiments are used	1247	52.1	33.3	14.6
The results are made public	1248	51.8	35.4	12.8
A large volume of information is collected	1245	51.5	36.5	12.0
The results apply to many ELT contexts	1237	38.7	42.8	18.5
Questionnaires are used	1238	37.4	47.0	15.6

research), while over 35% of the teachers did not actually feel that public dissemination was important in determining research quality. As one teacher explained, 'Small-scale research is within the reach of all teachers; if we consider good research only that which is published, then we exclude the possibility of non-academics doing good research' (USA). Such perspectives are often based on the view that making research public means writing a long, academic journal article; as I argue in various places in this book, though, a wide range of more feasible ways for teachers to share their research findings does exist (for an excellent discussion, see Burns, 2010). If teachers prefer not to share their work, that does not diminish its personal value for them; but in such cases there is no need to call the activity research.

Through interviews and written responses teachers were encouraged to articulate why they felt particular characteristics were or were not important in defining the quality of research. I will limit my focus here to teachers' comments on the characteristic most highly rated, objectivity. Here are some written comments explaining why teachers rated objectivity so highly:

> Well you don't want to make your research and results fit your hypothesis just to make it look as though you have an excellent result and it is a neat and tidy piece of research. (Australia)

> The research he is doing must reflect the situation and the problems existing in present teaching practice. The research shouldn't put any assumption or personal preference in it. (China)

> When you do research, first you have your hypotheses and then you have to prove whether your hypotheses are right or wrong ... Next, you have to convince others that what you have done has some merits. To convince others, you cannot use your 'belief'. You have to give some evidence to convince others. The results should be supported by some scientific measures. (Japan)

> Total lack of subjectivism, trying to keep your opinions as far away from the project. I believe sometimes researchers from another country can be more objective than a native one, because he is researching in a field, which he hasn't been connected to until then. (Slovenia)

Interview data highlighted similar conceptions:

> Objective, being objective I think is very important ... I mean there are people in the field who support what you're saying and who are against, and that you don't choose sources which are very biased ... Because, you know, you may start with your own idea and then you just go and read the people who are on the same wavelength as you are and you just ignore the others and you say that you have reached the truth, which is not the truth at all, who are you trying to fool? (Turkey)

Objective is that you try to some extent to distance yourself from your immediate emotional gut feeling about something. (Spain)

I think, any researcher who wants true and valid results needs to be objective. They may have an idea of what they think the results might be, for me the purpose of research is to test and analyse to see if that's true, not to say, I want to prove this, let's see if I can do it, let's do what I can to prove it ... they may have an idea what they think but they can't say this is it and let's work backwards from that point to prove it. (Spain)

These comments highlight several different components of objectivity as a criterion of good research. Teachers consider objectivity to be an important characteristic of research because it minimizes researcher bias, allows the researcher to detach themselves from the study, enhances the integrity of research, leads to a more balanced analysis of arguments, and requires conclusions to be grounded in evidence rather than in opinion, belief or instinct. Such notions of what counts as good research may shed light on why, for many teachers, research is not an activity they feel they can engage in. For if good research needs to be objective in the ways suggested here, this then excludes as a legitimate form of inquiry the personally motivated and intro-spective study of immediate first-hand experience which often char-acterizes teacher research. This is not to say that teacher researchers should not be able to stand back from their inquiries; but ultimately they are part of these inquiries and it may thus be more useful to talk about the need for 'disciplined subjectivity' (self-monitoring that involves constant questioning – see LeCompte & Goetz, 1982) rather than about rigid notions of objectivity derived from scien-tific research. There was not much awareness of this perspective on objectivity in the teachers' comments about good quality research; one exception was the teacher who wrote that objectivity is when 'the researcher is distant and detached, but this is quite impossible even in empirical study' (UAE). This was the only comment which reflected critically on the feasibility of 'scientific' objectivity in social science research.

OTHER CHARACTERISTICS OF 'GOOD' RESEARCH

A total of 251 teachers suggested additional characteristics of good quality research and Table 3.4 presents (based on a thematic analysis of these open-ended responses) the six most commonly cited char-acteristics with illustrative quotes. As this table shows, the most recurrent additional characteristic of good research mentioned by respondents was that it should refer to or build on existing litera-ture, typically through a literature review. This is an interesting point because getting access to and analyzing the literature can be major challenges that teachers face in doing research. Bell et al. (2010), in their analysis of 25 teacher research projects, did in fact note that in some cases the reports of these projects did not make any connections at all to the existing literature.

A second additional characteristic of good quality research noted by teachers was that it needed to have practical value. In addition to the quotes in the table, here are two more extended perspectives on this issue:

> If it can't be used in the classroom, I'm not interested – research for the sake of research, or into aspects of SLA that could not be applied in the classroom are of little interest to the classroom teacher. (USA)

> Since I am a teacher, I believe a good research should provide some insight for me to solve the real problems in teaching. Quite a number of the published articles I read gave suggestions about teaching, which is impossible to apply in a normal classroom. (China)

Given the practical nature of teaching, these teacher perspectives are understandable; they do, however, imply the kind of direct relationship between research and teaching that may only be feasible in the context of action research or other forms of teacher inquiry which focus very directly on pedagogical practice. The expectation by teachers that published research should always have direct implications for the classroom is one reason for the gap between teaching and research that teachers are often critical of (often unjustifiably so). I discuss this point further in Chapter 4.

Other characteristics highlighted in Table 3.4 are that good research is ethical, makes a contribution to knowledge, is replicable, and is accessible. These criteria relate to various dimensions of research: ethics and replicability are technical features (i.e. to do with the process), the need for a contribution relates to research outcomes, while accessibility is to do with the communication of research. This latter point is one that I will explore in detail in Chapter 4.

Before moving on to discuss managers' perspectives on good quality research, I would also like to comment on one final individual comment made by a teacher in their open-ended response about research quality:

> From what I can tell, research is not good if it is done by anyone who is not important. That is, your work is as good as your reputation, your university, the number of your publications. While that is not the answer you want, that is the truth in the actual world. This study for example, is

Table 3.4   Other characteristics of good quality research, according to teachers (N=251)

Characteristic	N	Illustrative quotes
Based on existing literature	27	'Background information and previous studies are taken into account or at least presented.' 'The researcher must do a thorough literature review of similar studies.'
Has practical value	17	'"Good" research is one used to implement a positive change in an area.' 'It must have a practical purpose, rather than simply being "academic" from start to finish.'
Ethical	13	'… facts are not manipulated to suit the outcomes.' '"Good" research follows the highest possible ethical standards. ESL students are not guinea pigs.'
Makes a new contribution to knowledge	11	'… contribution to the existing pool of research.' 'The information ascertained adds to the body of knowledge on the subject of inquiry.'
Replicable	9	'… follow a procedure that can be duplicated by others.' 'TESOL research that is considered "good" should be easily replicated by others.'
Presented in accessible manner	7	'It's important that research is conveyed to teachers in ways they can understand.' 'The results must be readable and comprehensible to the average instructor.'

research. My polling all 125 teachers of my school to find out what they were looking for as language tasks was an annoyance to all concerned, and NOBODY cared about it. (USA)

There is a certain frustration evident in this comment, stemming from, it seems, challenges this teacher experienced in getting colleagues to participate in a research project. The perspective here that the quality of research is defined by who does it may not be an isolated one though; another teacher, reflecting similar concerns, wrote that in their country 'if you are a big name researcher, you can publish almost anything in an academic journal'. The publication of research in reputable journals is, though, regulated by systems of blind peer review which seek to assess research quality independently of who the author is. This means (and novice researchers who I explain this to are typically surprised) that even researchers with a good track record are likely from time to time to have their manuscripts negatively critiqued and even rejected. I am, of course, not suggesting that peer review is a perfect system, and there are variations of course across journals in the rigour with which the principles of blind peer review are applied; overall, though, it is a system that gives a certain level of objectivity to the processes through which research quality is assessed. To counter the kinds of concerns highlighted in the comments above, teachers interested in research may benefit from some understanding of how this system works.

Managers' perspectives

Managers in Study 4 (N=126) were also asked to assess the importance in determining the quality of research of the same set of 11 criteria discussed above. Their responses were highly congruent with those of the teachers. (The four criteria rated most highly in each case were the same.) Thus, 'the researcher is objective' was seen to be an important criterion by 89.5% of the managers and 'variables are controlled' by 78.4%. 'Hypotheses are tested' was the criterion rated third highest (75.8% approval). I did not have the opportunity to explore through interviews the precise understandings these managers held of these criteria, but given the high levels of congruence reported in this chapter between the conceptions held by teachers and managers it would seem reasonable to suggest that managers' rationales for valuing particular criteria would not be too different to those of teachers and which were discussed above.

These managers, too, were invited to suggest additional characteristics of good quality research. There were no strong trends in the 28 open-ended responses that were provided and Table 3.5 uses extracts from these responses to give a sense of the range of issues that were mentioned.

Thus we can see that practical value, the use of the literature, research questions and procedural matters (such as using experiments and controlling variables) were all cited as being of importance in determining the quality of research. One additional comment of interest made by a manager was that

Table 3.5   Other characteristics of good quality research, according to managers (N=28)

- 'useful to teachers, learners and/or administrators'
- 'acknowledges and builds upon existing research'
- 'clearly describes procedures'
- 'good research questions – questions to which the answers are not known and which are important'
- 'experiments can be repeated with same/similar results'
- 'variables are controlled is a must and also to avoid contamination of other unexpected variables'

> Classroom based 'research' does not apply to many of these items [i.e. the characteristics of research listed in the questionnaire] and yet is very valuable in changing practices. However true research for public use must have most of these qualities. (USA)

The contrast made here between classroom-based research (presumably as done by teachers) and 'real' research (which is for public use) is both simplistic and, I would argue, common. It does, however, force us to confront one of the challenges that arise in relation to teacher research: how can we define it in a way that does not obviate the need for rigour and quality without, at the same time, making it an undertaking which most practitioners perceive to be unfeasible? This is a dilemma I will continue to dwell on as we proceed through this book, with a view to commenting more concretely on it in the final chapter. Even at this early stage, though, I am quite firm in my view that quality is essential in any form of research and cannot be compromised if teacher research is to be both credible and of practical value in informing practice and policy.

3.5 Conclusion

The evidence presented in this chapter suggests that language teachers' conceptions of research are predominantly associated with what has been called a 'standard' view of scientific research (Robson, 2002: 19) – i.e. one associated with statistics, objectivity, and hypothesis testing. Similar views were expressed by managers in the questionnaires, though the interviews with these managers highlighted a broader range of conceptions of research. Thus they did refer to activities that were formally academic but gave more prominence to reflective, analytical, and evaluative activities whose focus was on professional development, improving classroom practice and enhancing student learning. The status as research of many activities highlighted by the managers – such as materials evaluation and needs analysis – is of course not unproblematic. This is not to question the value of such activities – they clearly have potential to enhance teachers profession-ally; the issue is whether they should be called research and indeed whether there is any benefit to teachers in doing so. On both accounts, I have serious reservations. The distinction between reflective practice and research was also one that emerged in this chapter; while teachers often recognized the distinction between routine reflective activities and research, managers were typically more inclusive in citing reflec-tive practice as a form of research. Reflection is a powerful strategy for professional development and there is an extensive literature on the subject which supports this view (for a discussion in language teaching, see Farrell, 2007). Private reflective practice and language teaching research, though, are not synonymous (McIntyre, 2005 also distinguishes between reflective thinking and research).

Understanding the conceptions of research held by teachers is important in attempts to engage them with and in research. If, for example, large samples and statistics are considered by teachers to be key characteristics of research, then this may become a less viable activity for many teachers who either do not have access to large samples or do not have the knowledge of statistics they feel is required. Alternatively, the impact of such conceptions on teachers may be that they only consider a limited range of approaches when they do decide to do research themselves (e.g. discounting forms of inquiry which are more small-scale and qualitative in nature but which may actually be more amenable to the kind of research teach-ers are well-placed to conduct). Additionally, very rigid definitions of objectivity as a criterion for good quality research may delegitimize teacher research – given its inevitably personal nature – as a valuable and valid form of inquiry.

A substantial number of teachers also said that a characteristic of good quality research is that it gives teachers ideas they can use. This is a view which recurs in studies of teachers' research engagement in and outside language teaching (e.g. McDonough & McDonough, 1990; McNamara, 2002). Teachers are commonly found to report that they see more value in published research which has concrete implications for their practice. Of course, the instrumental value to teachers of educational research should not be presented as a neces-sary criterion for judging its value (Goldstein, 1998). However, it is clear that if our goal is to encourage teachers to engage with pub-lished research, and that teachers consistently report that one reason they do not is because they are unable to see its relevance to their work, then this is clearly an issue that merits attention. It has, though, not been the focus of any empirical work in our field, once again, in contrast to work in education generally (see, for example, Cordingley et al., 2005). We thus lack insights into teachers' perceptions of published research in our field, whether this work is seen by teachers to address their concerns, and how it impacts on what happens in classrooms (in science education, Ratcliffe, et al., 2004 suggest this impact may be more indirect than direct). This is an issue I return to in Chapter 4.

Overall, what emerges here in relation to teachers' conceptions of research suggests that initiatives to further teacher research engagement in language teaching could benefit from giving teachers ongoing opportunities to discuss and clarify their understandings of what research is and how its worth can be judged, of the range of forms it may legitimately take, and of the ways that research and classroom practice may interact in the lives of teachers. Teachers' understandings of these issues are central to the extent to which they can be productively research engaged. On the basis of this chapter then, one reason why teacher research is a minority activity in language teaching is that many teachers are unfamiliar with its defining characteristics and incorrectly assume that these are the same characteristics (e.g. large scale and hypothesis-testing) which conventionally define scientific forms of inquiry. At the same time it is clear that managers may be encompassing too broad a definition of research by including under this label a whole range of professional development and more routine pedagogical activities that may not need to (and should not) be referred to as research. This once again confirms the need in our field for greater clarity about what precisely research means in the context of teacher research engagement.

One final issue to comment on here is a methodological one, particularly in relation to the questionnaire item in which teachers and managers were asked to rate the importance in determining research quality of 11 criteria. It could be argued that a tendency among respondents to value more 'scientific' criteria was the product of a bias towards such criteria in the list they were asked to comment on. I accept this, although of course respondents had the freedom to say that particular criteria were not important. Nonetheless, designing a more effective way of eliciting teachers' views about what counts as good quality research is a methodological issue I continue to explore. For example, in a recent additional study conducted with college English teachers in China (Borg & Liu, forthcoming), I drew on the further characteristics of good quality research highlighted by respondents above to expand the list included in the questionnaire from 11 to 20 items. The outcome in this case was still not wholly satisfactory, given that hardly any of the items were rated as being unimportant. Some studies of academics' views of good quality research (e.g. Bills, 2004) have relied on an open-ended question (i.e. without a pre-determined list of characteristics which respondents then rank). While this counters the dangers of bias, it does also increase the demands made on respondents and may not be productive in the context of a survey instrument which is already quite demanding (as the one I used was); it might work well, though, in a shorter, more focused questionnaire or interview. On the basis of my experience to date, in eliciting teachers' views about good quality research, I would suggest that: (a) an extended and varied pre-determined list of characteristics for them to rate is valuable; (b) it may be preferable for the rating scale used not to include 'unimportant' options but rather to focus more positively on various degrees of importance; and (c) it is important to give respondents space to suggest additional qualities of good research. I will provide further methodological reflections on my programme of research in Chapter 9.

Notes

1 It is unclear in this study how many participants were actually teachers and the authors do acknowledge that there may have actually been more academics.

References

Allison, D., & Carey, J. (2007). What do university language teachers say about language teaching research? *TESL Canada Journal, 24*(2), 61–81.

Babbie, E. (2003). *The practice of social research* 10th ed. Belmont: Thomson/Wadsworth.

Bai, L., & Hudson, P. (2011). Understanding Chinese TEFL academics' capacity for research. *Journal of Further and Higher Education, 35*(3), 391–407.

Bai, L., & Millwater, J. (2011). Chinese TEFL academics' perceptions about research: An institutional case study. *Higher Education Research and Development, 30*(2), 233–246.

Barkhuizen, G. (2009). Topics, aims, and constraints in English teacher research: A Chinese case study. *TESOL Quarterly, 43*(1), 113–125.

Bell, M., Cordingley, P., Isham, C., & Davis, R. (2010). Report of professional practitioner use of research review: Practitioner engagement in and/or with research. Retrieved 6 February, 2012, from www.curee-paccts.com/node/2303

Bills, D. (2004). Supervisors' conceptions of research and the implications for supervisor development. *International Journal for Academic Development, 9*(1), 85–97.

Borg, S. (2006). Conditions for teacher research. *English Teaching Forum, 44*(4), 22–27.

Borg, S. (2007a). Research engagement in English language teaching. *Teaching and Teacher Education, 23*(5), 731–747.

Borg, S. (2007b). English language teachers' views of research: Some insights from Switzerland. *ETAS Newsletter, 24*(2), 15–18.

Borg, S. (2007c). Understanding what teachers think about research. *The Teacher Trainer, 21*(2), 2–4.

Borg, S. (2009a). English language teachers' conceptions of research. *Applied Linguistics, 30*(3), 355–388.

Borg, S. (2009b). Language teacher cognition. In A. Burns & J. C. Richards (Eds.), *The Cambridge guide to second language teacher education* (pp. 163–171). Cambridge: Cambridge University Press.

Borg, S. & Liu, Y. (forthcoming) Chinese college English teacher's research engagement. *TESOL Quarterly*.

Brown, J. D., Knowles, M., Murray, D., Neu, J., & Violand-Sanchez, E. (1992). *The place of research within the TESOL organization*. Alexandria, VA: TESOL.

Burns, A. (2010). *Doing action research in English language teaching. A guide for practitioners*. New York: Routledge.

Cochran-Smith, M., & Lytle, S. L. (1999). The teacher research movement: A decade later. *Educational Researcher, 28*(7), 15–25.

Cohen, L., Manion, L., & Morrison, K. (2000). *Research methods in education* 5th ed. London: Routledge.

Cordingley, P., Bell, M., Evans, D., & Holdich, K. (2–5 January 2005). *Engaging with research and evidence: What do teachers want and are they getting it? A summary*. Paper presented at the International Congress for School Effectiveness and Improvement, Barcelona.

Davies, P., Hamilton, M., & James, K. (2007). *Maximising the impact of practitioner research: A handbook of practical advice*. London: NRDC.

Everton, T., Galton, M., & Pell, T. (2002). Educational research and the teacher. *Research Papers in Education, 17*(4), 373–402.

Farrell, T. S. C. (2007). *Reflective language teaching: From research to practice*. London: Continuum.

Freeman, D. (1996). Redefining the relationship between research and what teachers know. In K. M. Bailey & D. Nunan (Eds.), *Voices from the language classroom* (pp. 88–115). New York: Cambridge University Press.

Gao, X., Barkhuizen, G., & Chow, A. W. K. (2011a). 'Nowadays teachers are relatively obedient': Understanding primary school English teachers' conceptions of and drives for research in China. *Language Teaching Research, 15*(1), 61–81.

Gao, X., Barkhuizen, G., & Chow, A. W. K. (2011b). Research engagement and educational decentralisation: Problematising primary school English teachers' research experiences in China. *Educational Studies, 37*(2), 207–219.

Goldstein, H. (1998). Excellence in research on schools – a commentary. Retrieved 6 February, 2012, from www.bristol.ac.uk/cmm/team/hg/excelres.pdf

Kemmis, S., & McTaggart, R. (Eds.). (1988). *The action research planner* 3rd ed. Victoria, Australia: Deakin University Press.

LeCompte, M., & Goetz, J. (1982). Problems of reliability and validity in ethnographic research. *Review of Educational Research, 52*(1), 31–60.

McDonough, J., & McDonough, S. (1990). What's the use of research? *ELT Journal, 44*(2), 102–109.

McIntyre, D. (2005). Bridging the gap between research and practice. *Cambridge Journal of Education, 35*(3), 357–382.

McNamara, O. (2002). Evidence-based practice through practice-based evidence. In O. McNamara (Ed.), *Becoming an evidence-based practitioner* (pp. 15–26). London: Routledge Falmer.

Rainey, I. (2000). Action research and the English as a foreign language practitioner: Time to take stock. *Educational Action Research, 8*(1), 65–91.

Ratcliffe, M., Bartholomew, H., Hames, V., Hind, A., Leach, J., & Millar, R. (2004). *Science education practitioners' views of research and its influence on their practice.* York: Department of Educational Studies, University of York.

Roberts, J. R. (1993). Evaluating the impacts of teacher research. *System, 21*(1), 1–19.

Robson, C. (2002). *Real world research* 2nd ed. Oxford: Blackwell.

Saha, L. J., Biddle, B. J., & Anderson, D. S. (1995). Attitudes towards education research knowledge and policy making among American and Australian school principals. *International Journal of Educational Research, 23*(2), 113–126.

Sharp, C., Eames, A., Sanders, D., & Tomlinson, K. (2006). *Leading a research-engaged school.* Nottingham: National College for School Leadership.

Shkedi, A. (1998). Teachers' attitudes towards research: A challenge for qualitative researchers. *International Journal of Qualitative Studies in Education, 11*(4), 559–578.

Stenhouse, L. (1975). *An introduction to curriculum research and development.* London: Heinemann.

Wiersma, W. (1991). *Research methods in education: An introduction* 5th ed. London: Allyn and Bacon.

4 Teacher engagement with research

4.1 Introduction

As explained in Chapter 1, teacher research engagement can take two forms – engagement *with* research, primarily through reading published work and engagement *in* research, by actually doing it. These two dimensions of research engagement provide the focus of the next two chapters, starting here with a focus on the former. I begin by reviewing the literature relevant to teachers reading research then draw on the series of studies described in Chapter 2 to provide some insights into the nature of language teachers' engagement with research.

4.2 Teachers' reading and use of research

Teachers as consumers

A key argument in evidence-based practice (EBP – see Chapter 1) is that teachers should be critical consumers of educational research, using it to inform their instructional decisions. In education generally, Shank & Brown (2007: 6) advise teachers that 'educational research is for the benefit of the field as a whole, not just for a handful of specialists. That is why it is important for you to improve your skills as a consumer of research.' McMillan & Wergin (2010) also have as their focus engagement with research, and their rationale is that teachers 'should not have to depend on others' assessments of the credibility or usefulness of research; they should be able to read, critique, and evaluate research information themselves' (p. v).

In language teaching, Perry (2005) argues that teachers 'and others on whom research in applied linguistics has an impact need to be able to understand it to the point where they are able to evaluate recommendations based on such research' (p. xi), while Brown (1988) and Porte (2002) both focus on developing language teachers' ability to engage with quantitative research. Porte's book, for example, 'seeks to answer a current need in the literature for a set of procedures that can be applied to the reading of quantitative research' (back jacket).

One orientation shared by the texts mentioned so far is that they conceive of the process of reading research as a largely technical one. Thus they seek to facilitate engagement with research by promoting the knowledge and skills that teachers require in order to be critical consumers. However, while certain core competencies are clearly required when reading research, conceptualizing engagement with research in largely technical terms makes four erroneous assumptions. These are: (1) teachers have access to published research; (2) teachers want to read published research; (3) teachers need to read published research; and (4) teachers have the time to read such material. All four assumptions apply to teachers engaged in formal study (and this is the audience the texts above will appeal to) but they do not hold true for the majority of language teachers around the world. I discuss reasons why teachers do not read research below, but attitudinal barriers will constitute a major obstacle. And where this is the case, books which give teachers technical solutions to becoming better consumers of research (without addressing the attitudinal barriers) are not likely to make much difference. Even in supportive, collegial and structured contexts where teachers are committed to professional development, fostering dispositions in teachers that enable them to engage with research in ways that they find meaningful and of value presents significant challenges (see Kiely & Davis, 2010).

Research knowledge and classroom practice

Critiques of EBP (evidence-based practice) have claimed that it assumes (incorrectly) that when teachers read research it will have a direct impact on their teaching. Hammersley (2004: 138), for example, argues that 'there are substantial limitations on what research can offer to policy making and practice', and develops his position with reference to three points (see also Pachler, 2003 for critique from language teaching). First, he argues that research knowledge is always fallible; second, that research knowledge usually takes the form of generalizations (but teachers need to make decisions in specific contexts); and third, factual knowledge is never a sufficient determinant of good practice. He concludes that 'professional practice cannot for the most part be governed by research findings – because it necessarily relies on multiple values, tacit judgement, local knowledge, and skills' (p. 138). Cordingley (2004: 83) also notes that, given the context-specific nature of instructional decision making, 'there will always be a skilled professional job to do in interpreting the relevance of and implications of evidence for a practitioner's own setting'. In response to such critiques, the term evidence-*informed* practice is often preferred; it still allows for research knowledge to contribute to classroom practice without implying that this contribution is an unmediated one.

In language teaching, the work of Freeman (e.g. Freeman, 1996; Freeman & Johnson, 1998) is often cited (see, for example, Rankin & Becker, 2006; Stewart, 2006) in support of claims that SLA research has little to offer teachers. Freeman & Johnson (1998: 411) did write that 'much current knowledge in SLA may be of limited use and applicability to practicing teachers'; however, interpretations of this statement have, I feel, been exaggerated (and made out of context). Freeman & Johnson themselves have since explained that 'we do indeed value research in SLA and have always held that such knowledge needs to inform the work of language teachers' (Freeman & Johnson, 2005: 30). SLA research is clearly a foundational area of knowledge for language teaching professionals, and this is not a point I want to contest here. My specific concern is with the dissemination and use of this knowledge in language teaching.

There is clearly an awareness in our field of the complex relationship between research knowledge and teaching. Lightbown (2000: 454), for example, has noted that 'SLA research findings do not constitute the only or even the principal source of information to guide teachers in their daily practice', while more recently Ellis (2010: 197) suggests that 'SLA is best viewed as a body of technical knowledge that can illuminate pedagogically inspired questions'. There is no implication in the views expressed by these authoritative figures in SLA research that it should (or even can) be a major determinant of teachers' practice, and indeed there is even some degree of consensus with the view that 'simple prescriptions from researchers and theorists are not sufficient. Teachers need to evaluate such recommendations in the light of their own situations and to determine what exactly they will be able to use in their classrooms' (Clarke, 1994: 21). This is an important shift in attitude from one which assumes that published research should directly inform practice to one which reflects more sophisticated understandings of teacher knowledge. Such a shift, on its own, however, will have no impact on language teachers' willingness to engage with research. That is, if academics agree that teachers should critically engage with research knowledge, but then fail to take steps to facilitate this engagement, we will have not really moved away from the historically prevalent academic view that 'it is primarily the obligation of the recipients of our work … to understand the importance of, and to apply correctly, the findings we have so meticulously generated' (Barone, 1995: 109).

Teachers' practices in engaging with research

There has been limited empirical work on language teachers' practices in engaging with research and I discuss this here together with relevant work in education more generally in relation to a number of sub-themes. One study that merits comment at the outset here is the Teaching and Learning International Survey (TALIS) conducted by the Organisation for Economic Co-operation and Development (OECD, 2009). This project involved over 70,000 lower secondary school teachers in 23 countries and one question asked about the extent to which they read professional literature. Over 77% of the respondents said this was an activity they had engaged in during the previous 18 months. The corresponding figure for the subset of almost 9,000 teachers of modern and foreign languages in the sample was 79.3%. While these figures are positive, we must remember that teachers were not necessarily saying that they were reading research. Also, that there was no attempt here to distinguish between different levels of frequency in reading (i.e. teachers who read one article in 18 months and those who read several were treated similarly in the results). Nonetheless, TALIS is relevant here because it is based on systematic data about professional development activities, including about research engagement, from large samples of teachers internationally. It is an ongoing project and the latest information about it is available at www.oecd.org.

SOURCES OF RESEARCH INFORMATION

Outside language teaching, there have been some studies of teachers' sources of research information. Williams & Coles (2007), in a survey of 312 teachers in the UK, found that the three most common sources were informal discussions with colleagues, professional magazines (i.e. with a more practical orientation) and newspapers, and in-service teacher education. In Everton, Galton & Pell (2000), also in the UK, the three most popular sources of research for teachers were in-service courses, accredited courses, and official publications (e.g. produced by the Ministry of Education). Shkedi (1998), in a survey of 47 teachers in Israel, found that most teachers read 'practical' educational literature. Unsurprisingly, academic books and journals do not figure prominently in the results of these studies.

REASONS FOR NOT READING RESEARCH

A number of barriers to teachers' engagement with research have been identified. The review by Hemsley-Brown & Sharp (2003) highlighted problems of physical and conceptual accessibility (i.e. teachers could not obtain material and/or understand what they read), two barriers also noted in McDonough & McDonough's (1990) study of language teachers. In McNamara (2002), teachers also highlighted the need for published educational research to be both more accessible (i.e. easy to understand) as well as more applicable to their work, while Macaro's (2003) study of heads of modern foreign language departments in the UK also found that the inaccessibility of published language teaching research was a key barrier to engagement with it. He thus noted that 'if what little time they [teachers] can devote to reading about research is undermined by its inaccessibility, then aspirations about development towards research-informed practice are going to be quite unrealistic' (p. 5). Teachers' negative attitudes to research constitute another significant barrier. Williams & Coles (2007), for example, note that while a lack of access to research was a real problem for teachers, even where access existed, attitudinal factors limited the extent to which teachers engaged with research ('so access alone is not the whole story', p. 202). Shkedi (1998) also found that teachers were suspicious of and lacked trust in published research. A mismatch between teachers' narrative experience of classroom life and the portrayal of learning and teaching they encounter in research papers is another barrier to teachers' engagement with research (see Lo, 2005, which I discuss further below).

Case studies of teachers' engagement with research

A small number of studies shed light on teachers' practices in engaging with research. Zeuli (1994) examined how 13 teachers on a teacher education course read research articles and found that they were concerned mainly with what ideas they could find to take back to the classroom. As one teacher explained, 'I don't need to know about the research. I go for the steps that I need to know. What are the things that I can take back to the classroom that are going to work for me?' (p. 42). Zeuli's conclusion was that in reading research many teachers 'were more interested in products ... like consumers interested in making decisions about what goods to procure without understanding further why the decision is warranted' (for a related paper, see Tiezzi & Zeuli, 1994).

In language teaching, Bartels (2003) found differences in the ways teachers and researchers read academic articles and noted in particular that teachers, even when they had an academic background, showed 'little acceptance or understanding of the researcher Discourse' (p. 748). The converse was true of academics in relation to the Discourse of teacher research; an academic in this study who was asked to read and react to a teacher-oriented article concluded that 'this is a woefully way (sic) from doing an actual study ... I mean who cares? I mean it's just terrible. This kind of really, really reminds me of why I'd rather do research than teach. It's just not good enough' (Bartels, 2003: 745). While such a reaction to teacher research is, I would like to think, not representative of academics in our field, it does highlight the challenges we face in developing productive relationships between academics and teachers.

Another case study of a language teacher's experience of reading research is Lo (2005), which was conducted in the context of a Master's level SLA course. This study highlights tensions between the practical insights the teacher hoped to obtain through engaging with research and her view that 'most research-oriented papers were simply different experiments that had little to do with the real classroom situations' (p. 139). Clear tensions are also evident in this study between the teacher's expectations of reading SLA research and the goals the tutor had in assigning such reading (see also Busch, 2010; Kerekes, 2001; MacDonald, Badger, & White, 2001 for broader discussions of the impact of SLA courses on teachers).

In contrast to the negative conclusions of the above studies, Rankin & Becker's (2006) case study of a teacher of German's engagement with the SLA literature on corrective feedback found that such engagement supported the development of the teacher's pedagogical growth; in particular, it enriched his reflections on his teaching by providing new ways of describing and analyzing his own corrective feedback strategies in the classroom. The study suggests that connecting reading to the analysis of classroom events made the teacher's engagement with research more purposeful. Important insights into the way research knowledge becomes part of teachers' knowledge also emerged:

> ... the knowledge embedded in published research ... is not simply accumulated and then put into action. It is processed and filtered through layers of experience and belief, rendering the outcome far less predictable than a simple transmission model would suggest. Knowledge about teaching and the classroom becomes instantiated only after it has been integrated into the teacher's personal framework – contextualized, as it were, into a matrix of classroom experience and other sources of pedagogical input. (p. 366)

This conclusion illustrates the complex relationship between research knowledge and teaching discussed earlier. It also suggests that enhancing the impact of published research on teachers is not simply a matter of making it more accessible to them; teachers also need opportunities to reconcile and meld (to use terms from Thomas, 2004) research knowledge with their own practical knowledge.

4.3 Enhancing teachers' engagement with research

Engagement with research can be of value to teachers (keeping in mind the provisos noted so far in this chapter) in several ways. For example, it can help teachers

- make deeper sense of their work (new ways of seeing)
- identify ideas to experiment with in their classroom (new ways of doing)
- provide a discourse for talking about teaching (new ways of talking)
- validate with a theoretical rationale what they already do (new ways of knowing)
- examine their planning and decision-making processes (new ways of thinking).

These are substantial potential benefits and evidence of their value in practice does emerge from accounts of teachers who have been able to engage productively in teacher research projects. For example, in Rickinson et al. (2004: 216), teachers felt that using research 'can help you to become a more reflective and more confident teacher'. Our challenge, then, to give teachers a chance to experience such benefits, is to find ways of addressing the physical, practical, conceptual, linguistic, and attitudinal barriers to teacher engagement with research already noted. We also need to develop a deeper understanding of the ways in which practical knowledge and research knowledge can be productively integrated.

One response to this challenge, educating teachers to be consumers of research, was discussed earlier. A second strategy for making research more accessible to teachers is the 'implications' section commonly found at the end of research papers (see Chapelle, 2007; Han, 2007 for contrasting views on the value of such sections). This strategy, though, can only benefit those teachers who actually read research journals and the presence of 'implications' is not going to make a difference to those who do not. More substantial measures are thus needed to support teacher engagement with research. To consider the forms these might take, I will now first review research on the features of research reports which teachers seem to respond positively to, then comment on examples of initiatives whose goal has been to increase teacher engagement with research.

Positive teacher response to research reports

Considerable work has been undertaken in the UK to understand what features of published research facilitate teachers' access to and use of it. Hemsley-Brown & Sharp (2003) (a literature review) and Ratcliffe et al. (2004) (a study of science educators) are two relevant sources here. Collectively, they suggest that teacher engagement with research is enhanced when reports

- are relevant to teachers' contexts, concerns, interests and priorities
- provide detailed descriptions of classroom activities which teachers can relate to their own work
- build on what teachers already know
- are congruent with teachers' beliefs and values
- make clear and feasible recommended changes to practice.

In contrast, there is evidence that in reading research, teachers valued less its capacity to help them design their own research, or to enable them to interpret research data for their own benefit (Everton, Galton, & Pell, 2002: 387).

In a further study, Cordingley and the National Teacher Research Panel (2000) identified four key characteristics of research which teachers felt were important in facilitating their engagement with it: interest, credibility, usability, and accessibility. For example, teachers reported being interested in research which presented authentic teacher and learner perspectives. Teachers also found credible research which was conducted in real classroom settings. In terms of usability, 'research reports that suggest practical teaching and learning approaches to enable other teachers to try out or test new approaches in their own setting were welcomed' (p. 4). In relation to accessibility, this study found a preference among teachers 'for light referencing, bullet point summaries of arguments, lists of further reading and a brief summary of the literature, preferably in an appendix' (p. 3). What is described as a 'stepping stones' approach to reporting research outcomes was also preferred by the teachers in this study:

> Very brief (4 sides of A4) summaries with key findings, a short explanation of supporting evidence and of methods were thought to help teachers decide quickly whether they want to know more. Longer summaries which explain and illustrate approaches and evidence in a little more detail could help teachers to start to identify implications for their own practice, subject, classes or communities. Fuller reports were thought important in providing helpful reference for further study or to support interpretation and application. (p. 4)

In language teaching, the idea of producing tailored summaries of research of this kind to enhance its accessibility for teachers has been met with some caution. Ranta (2002), for example, (although she does argue for the need for more teacher friendly research) seems against the idea that research should be presented in '"pablum" form (i.e. easy to digest)' on the basis that 'research presented in this way does more harm than good because it makes it look all so simple' (see also the negative views of Jarvis, 2002: 2 on 'dumbing-down our research to make it more accessible to a less-informed audience'). Ellis (2010), though, argues for the use of summaries as a strategy for increasing language teachers' access to research (and suggests some principles which might govern the construction of such summaries). Arguably, many of the methodology handbooks written for language teachers do include summaries of research; however, their emphasis is often on the implications of research for classroom practice rather than on better enabling teachers to engage with research themselves.

Overall, particularly on the basis of the mainstream evidence from the UK, summaries of research written especially for teachers seem central to the goal of enabling them to become more research engaged. Similar points about the need for summaries of research are made, for example, in Bevan (2006) and McNamara (2002), while a major review of literature on models of research impact (Nutley, Percy-Smith, & Solesbury, 2003: 41) also concluded that 'research must be translated: to have an impact, research findings need to be adapted to, or reconstructed within, practice and policy contexts. This can involve tailoring findings to a target group.'

The need for research to be 'translated' – reported in forms that teachers can access quickly – has obvious implications for the manner in which reports are written and organized. In language teaching, Pachler (2003: 13) suggests that teacher research engagement can be supported where researchers 'write the findings up in a way that engages with the discourse conventions used by practitioners and disseminate them in forums practitioners readily access'. The need for researchers to consider alternatives to conventional expository modes of reporting research is also discussed by Ellis (2010), who, (echoing arguments put forward by, for example, Clarke, 1994) refers in particular to the use of narrative as a device for sharing research. 'Teachers' experience is storied, typified by detailed, dynamic, social interactions taking place in specific contexts' (Borg, 2003: 42) and research in the form, for example, of detailed case studies of aspects of classroom life, may represent language learning and teaching phenomena to teachers in ways which they can relate more immediately to their own experience. In addition to reporting research in different formats, researchers should also consider, as the second part of the Pachler quote above suggests, disseminating research in a wider range of outlets which teachers read. Academics, understandably, may not always feel they can do this because such publications are often not recognized by their institutions as legitimate research outputs.

Initiatives to facilitate engagement with research

In the UK, a number of initiatives have been set up in education generally to enhance teacher engagement with research (for a more detailed account of these and related resources see Bell et al., 2010; CERI/OECD, 2002). The National Teacher Research Panel (NTRP – www.ntrp.org. uk) seeks 'to ensure that all research in education takes account of the teacher perspective'; they thus provide 'a resource to researchers ... who require input from teachers with research expertise at all stages ... from identifying priorities to making published research accessible to teachers'. The notion of researchers seeking input from teachers on the focus, design, conduct, and dissemination of their studies may be worth exploring in language teaching.

Research for Teachers (now archived at www.tla.ac.uk/site/Pages/ RfT.aspx) provides downloadable summaries of research appearing in peer-reviewed journals. The summaries are produced by the Centre for the Use of Research and Evidence in Education (CUREE – www.curee-paccts.com), which selects articles felt to have potential for stimulating teacher engagement with research. One key feature of the summaries is a 'case studies' section where the issues dealt with in the research are illustrated with practical examples.

TLRP Practitioner Applications (www.tlrp.org/pa) provides materials which suggest ways in which research insights can be applied to the classroom, while *Research Bites* provides short PowerPoint presentations summarizing research findings. *Schools Research News* also provides summaries of newly published research. The latter two resources were at the time of writing available via the 'Schools Research Bulletins' pages on the UK Department for Education website (www.education.gov.uk).

The Evidence for Policy and Practice Information and Co-ordinating Centre (EPPI-Centre – http://eppi.ioe.ac.uk/cms) produces systematic reviews of research. The results of these reviews can be accessed either via the 'knowledge library', which provides a summary of key messages about specific subjects, or downloaded in more detailed summaries and reports (for example, in relation to modern foreign languages one report from 2004 is entitled 'A systematic review of the characteristics of effective foreign language teaching to pupils between the ages 7 and 11'). The scope of the EPPI-Centre's work is impressive; as a mechanism for providing practitioners and policy makers with accounts of 'what works' in education, though, it has been the subject of criticism. Similar criticisms have been directed at a comparable initiative in the USA, the What Works Clearinghouse (http://ies.ed.gov/ncee/wwc). Very briefly, the criticisms are based on the view that the criteria used in deciding which research to include in systematic reviews tend to favour 'scientific' research and to exclude research conducted by teachers, in addition to qualitative research generally. It has thus been argued that the criteria used imply that the '"research" deemed to be of value to practitioners in schools is of a specific kind, responds to certain questions – namely, causal questions of the formulation "x causes y", – and uses experimental methods' (Roulston et al., 2005: 173). For further perspectives on this debate, see Davies (2000), Feuer, Towne, & Shavelson (2002), Hammersley (2001; 2004) Maxwell (2004), and Morrison (2001).

   In language teaching I am not aware of initiatives comparable to those above, though some resources which may support teachers' engagement with research do exist. In the USA, the Center for Applied Linguistics (www.cal.org/resources/digest) provides evidence-based briefs on various issues in language learning while The International Research Foundation for English Language Education (TIRF – www.tirfonline.org) is developing 'a series of reports that addresses key, unanswered questions regarding policies and practices in English language education worldwide' (the first of these, entitled *The Impact of English and Plurilingualism in Global Corporations*, was published in 2009 and is available for download). In the UK, the National Research and Development Centre for adult literacy and numeracy (NRDC – www.nrdc.org.uk) supports practitioner research and makes its publications freely available, including some relevant to ESOL, while research reports are also available through the National Centre for Languages website (www.cilt.org.uk/secondary.aspx). At the European level, research reports can be accessed via the European Centre for Modern Languages in Graz (www.ecml.at/Resources/tabid/128/language/en-GB/Default.aspx). While the above initiatives all make research freely available to language teachers, the emphasis remains on disseminating research without any systematic approach to maximizing teachers' engagement with it. This is clearly a largely unexplored issue in our field, yet one which requires attention if using research is to become a more central part of language teachers' professional lives.

4.4 Insights into language teachers' engagement with research

The review of literature presented above illustrates very clearly that, empirically, our understandings of the nature of language teacher engagement with research are very limited. It is a field characterized more by rhetorical debate than by concrete investigation, and consequently, a sound basis for decision making in relation to promoting engagement with research in language teaching is lacking. The substantial work of relevance conducted in education generally is of course valuable here, but there is without doubt a need for specific studies of teacher engagement with research in language teaching contexts.

With these concerns in mind, I will now present data from all four studies in the programme of research described in Chapter 2 to provide insights into language teachers' engagement with research. Drawing on a range of questionnaire, interview and written responses, I will discuss the following questions:

1   How often do language teachers say they read research?
2   What sources of reading do they say they consult?
3   What influence do they say their reading has on their work?
4   What reasons do they give for not reading?

While such questions may seem overly descriptive, baseline data of this kind is in fact a valuable starting point in working towards more sophisticated analyses of teachers' engagement with research. In the same way that it is premature to analyze *why* teachers teach in particular ways without first understanding *what* it is they actually do, it is first necessary to obtain some general sense of the reported nature of language teachers' engagement with research as the basis for subsequent deeper study of this phenomenon.

Frequency of reading research

The teachers in Studies 1, 3 and 4 were asked via a questionnaire item to say how often they read published research. Table 4.1 summarizes the responses they provided.

We can conclude from these figures that almost 75% of the teachers said that they read research at least 'sometimes' (the corresponding figure for 375 managers in Studies 2, 3, and 4 who were asked about their reading was very similar – just over 75%). While this sounds positive, caution is required in interpreting such results, for at least two reasons. First, it is a well-known phenomenon on survey items

Table 4.1 Reported frequency of reading research

	N	%
Never	42	3.1
Rarely	301	22.3
Sometimes	679	50.3
Often	329	24.3
Total	1351	100.0

of this kind that respondents may 'boost' their self-assessment, consciously or otherwise. At least in some cases, then, 'sometimes' will have been a euphemism for 'rarely'. A second issue here is that teachers will assign a range of different meanings to the same frequency descriptors. I explored this issue with teachers during interviews and Figure 4.1 highlights some different interpretations of the meaning of 'sometimes'. A similar phenomenon is illustrated in Chapter 5, where teachers explain how often they do research. Returning to Table 4.1, the point here is that although just under 75% of the teachers in this study said they read research 'sometimes', this does not necessarily

'Honestly, I mean when I get my hands on something for example.' (Turkey)

'At the moment I'm reading a couple books of week but that's only because of what I'm doing with DELTA, otherwise I'd try and read an article a week I think.' (Spain)

'I don't know. I mean, I make an effort to always read the things that come into our staff room.' (Spain)

'... when I've got time to look up the internet maybe look at journals on the internet occasionally ... I'd say it's probably rarely and sometimes.' (Spain)

'Sometimes means I don't do it regularly so when I do it it's like a new experience, and it's not something I'm, it means I'm not in the habit of doing it, not accustomed to it, so when I do it it's something unusual.' (Spain)

'Actually, I think rarely would probably be more accurate. Over the summer ... sometimes means ... not often! [laughs] Summer! It means when time and coincidence sort of coincide. Or time and serendipity coincide and you find yourself – its not something that I, at the moment it's not something that I go out and look for.' (Turkey)

Figure 4.1   What teachers mean by reading research 'sometimes'

mean that they engaged with published research in any sustained and significant manner.

The questionnaires collected data about teachers' qualifications and years of experience in language teaching and these variables were analyzed (using Spearman's correlation) for associations with the levels of reading reported in Table 4.1. These analyses showed that more experienced and more qualified teachers reported reading research more frequently than those with fewer qualifications and less experience respectively. In both cases, though, although significant associations were found, these were very weak[1] (for qualifications, $N=1333$, $\rho=0.163$, $p<.001$, 1-tailed; for experience, $N=1333$, $\rho=0.171$, $p=.005$, 1-tailed). Teachers were also asked whether they worked in a school that was part of a university and this variable too was analyzed for an association with how often teachers said they read research. Contrary to what might be expected, higher levels of reported reading were associated with working in a school that was *not* attached to a university, though again the strength of the relationship was weak ($N=1327$, $\rho=-0.096$, $p<.001$, 1-tailed). Overall, then, we cannot conclude that there were any meaningful relationships here between how frequently teachers said they read research and their qualifications, experience, and whether or not they taught in a university.

Sources of reading

Teachers who said they read research at least sometimes were also asked (by selecting from a list of items presented in the questionnaire) to identify the sources they read. Figure 4.2 summarizes the responses of 1,008 teachers. Books were the most widely cited source, followed by academic journals. Also, over 600 teachers said they read professional magazines such as *English Teaching Professional* as a source of research, while 372 said they consulted newsletters, such as those produced by IATEFL's Special Interest Groups.

These figures are interesting given that professional magazines and newsletters are not typically research oriented and tend to contain material of a more immediately practical nature (for example, Borg & Ioannou-Georgiou, 2008 reviewed a range of IATEFL publications and found limited evidence of research outputs in these). This is not a criticism of such outlets – they are very popular with teachers and do, I am sure, make a positive contribution to teachers' pedagogies. These findings do raise further questions, though, about the manner in which teachers are interpreting 'research'. Many of the comments teachers made in interviews and written responses did in fact suggest that they may often assume that classroom-oriented material in practical

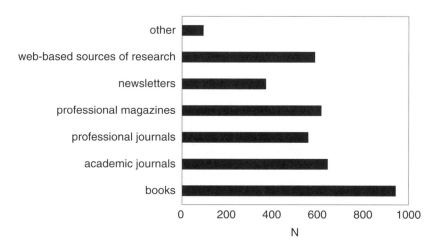

Figure 4.2   Sources of research (N=1008)

publications is based on research. (I am not suggesting that it should be, merely observing that teachers may assume it is). A teacher in Turkey, for example, talked enthusiastically about the impact on her of the research of a well-known language teaching practitioner and teacher trainer. However, when we explored the nature of this work further she concluded that it was 'not research, sure not research, but he has done lots of classroom research, hasn't he? Well, erm, maybe not. But practical ideas!' Another teacher from Switzerland, in explaining the influence of her reading on her teaching, explained that

> I'm interested in how people learn and what makes it easier for students to learn. I sometimes try out things I've read about but these are usually practical tips from teachers, some of which are 'research' based – depending, of course, on your definition of research!

One of the managers I interviewed also expressed his views on the kinds of material their teachers read:

> I think what most of our teachers read are not necessarily research. They read a lot of stuff about teaching ideas, you know, in publications like the MET [*Modern English Teacher*] or the ETP [*English Teaching Professional*], but they're looking for practical ideas that are not necessarily based on research, except in as much that it's something that a particular teacher had tried that worked for them. (UK)

It is very possible, then, and quite understandable, that teachers assume that practical material appearing in professional language teaching publications is research based. While this may often be the case, it will not always be, and this suggests that initiatives which focus on enhancing teachers' engagement with research could usefully address the extent to which different types of language teaching publications are research based. Such work would link in with the fundamental awareness-raising work on defining what research is, which Chapter 3 suggested would be beneficial as part of teachers' research education.

Almost 100 teachers said they read 'other' sources of research and explained their answer by giving examples. In many cases these reiterated categories already mentioned (e.g. websites) or provided specific illustrations of these categories (e.g. several teachers named specific academic journals they read). Some additional sources of research consulted by teachers were, however, noted. A few teachers mentioned newspaper articles – e.g. 'Any other articles summing up research in this field – as trickling down into newspapers and magazines' (Switzerland) while several mentioned material they obtain from conferences, particularly handouts. Thus one teacher noted that 'Handouts received from colleagues [are] the most frequent type of research that I read' (Australia). Both the newspapers and handouts suggest second-hand ways of engaging with research, i.e. not with the original research itself but via summaries. Given the comments made earlier in the chapter about enhancing the accessibility of research to teachers, good quality research summaries would seem to be one positive strategy for enhancing teacher engagement with research (newspapers, though, are often a questionable source of reliable information about research). Two further sources of research teachers said they consulted were publications in languages other than English (e.g. several Chinese teachers said they read language education journals in their mother tongue) and official reports produced by bodies such as The Council of Europe and Cambridge ESOL.

Amongst the open-ended comments provided by teachers on 'other' sources of research, two merit specific note. One teacher in Taiwan wrote, 'I used to occasionally read *ELT Journal* and *English Teaching Professional*, but I haven't seen it kicking around my current centre.' The notion of 'kicking about' here is interesting and suggests the importance for engagement with research not only of the availability of material but of its visibility (this theme recurs below where a teacher talks about journals being locked in a cupboard). In simple terms, teachers are more likely to read material they see as opposed to material they have to make a specific effort to seek out. The second comment, from a teacher in the USA, was 'I am currently reading books about the lexical method. I find that much of the "research" published in magazines is a bit trendy. I have read some pretty fluffy pieces in the *ELT Journal,* these frustrate me.' I will take up the theme of why teachers do not read research later in this chapter; the perceptions signalled here that published research may be 'trendy' and 'fluffy' (which I interpret to mean lacking in rigour) are ones that recur. Both the specific comments I have noted here also refer to professionally oriented types of reading, rather than that which is research oriented. Criticisms levelled at the material which appears in such journals do need to acknowledge, though, that presenting detailed accounts of rigorous research is not their primary purpose. It may be the case, then, that teachers are disappointed by the 'research' they engage with because there is a mismatch between what they expect and the predominantly professional or practical nature of the material they are reading.

By way of contrast with the sources of research teachers said they read, managers (in Studies 2 and 3) were asked how important they felt it was for teachers to read certain types of material. Figure 4.3 presents results based on 222 responses. This shows that on a scale of 1 = unimportant to 5 = highly important, greater value was, unsurprisingly, clearly attached to more practical types of reading than to research-oriented material. The thinking behind this position is discussed in Chapter 6, where I analyze managers' views about the relationship between research engagement and teaching quality.

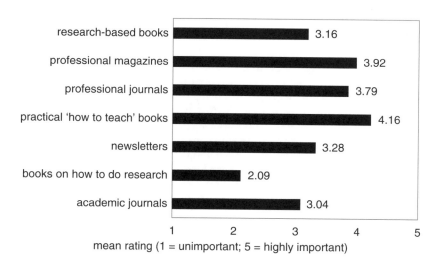

Figure 4.3   Importance of sources of reading for teachers, according to managers (N=222)

Impact of reading research

Teachers who said they read research sometimes or often were asked about the impact of this reading on their teaching. Out of 939 responses, almost 88% said it had at least a moderate influence, while fewer than 1% claimed it had none. Interviews with teachers (in Studies 1 and 3) provided insight into both the nature of this impact and the factors which shape its extent and I will now discuss these in turn.

NATURE OF IMPACT

Teachers talked about different ways in which reading research impacted on them. The most common of these was impact on their practices; teachers also noted, though, that reading research led to changes in their knowledge (e.g. of their thinking in relation to a particular area of language teaching), prompted them to reflect on and analyze their beliefs, and allowed them to stay up-to-date and fresh. In relation to this latter point, one teacher, for example, explained:

> I'm intensely interested in professional issues and I also have been involved in this field for a very long time so I'm very concerned that I keep on developing and keep abreast. The danger of turning into some kind of dinosaur is in front of me the whole time. Plus I'm actually very, very, very interested in these issues. So it's a pleasure to me to read. So I read everything I possibly can that comes in front of me. (Malaysia)

Another teacher outlined how reading encouraged reflection on her work as follows:

> Yes I think it [reading research] has had an impact but not in the sense that I've read this research and thought ooh, that's useful, I'm going to use it. But more making me aware of having to think about how I teach ... I think it's tempting sometimes in the ELT world to ... dare I say it ... flying by the seat of your pants. You know sort of running from one lesson to another and getting as many lessons done as you can in the day in a very restricted timetable without really having the time to sit back and think what am I doing? Am I doing it in the best way? Am I getting boring? Are there better methods that I can use that I'm simply not aware of? So I think it's affected me ... in that sort of way. (Italy)

This extract stresses the point that the impact of reading research on teachers is not limited to (and may not necessarily encompass) a direct influence on what they do in the classroom. And even where reading research does impact on the classroom, this impact may not necessarily be immediate; one teacher explained, 'I wouldn't read something and then go out straight away and try it out on a class. But it might stay in my head for a while' (Spain) while another expressed a similar point in more detail:

> I'm doing a Master's at the moment. I'm doing ... I'm doing a thesis. So a lot of it [my reading] is geared towards that ... and then from that I suppose comes some awareness which I will take into action in my practical work. But I think ... that awareness doesn't necessarily come immediately. It might sort of ... it might even take years to sort of drip down into ... into one's practice. (Italy)

In explaining the impact of reading research, therefore, teachers highlighted both practical and cognitive effects of a more and less immediate nature.

FACTORS MEDIATING IMPACT

Teachers also highlighted a range of factors which influence the impact reading research has on their teaching. Figure 4.4 lists the different factors teachers mentioned, with illustrative quotations for each. Clearly, the impact of research on teachers' work is mediated by a range of judgements they make about its applicability to their context, practicability, and testability. They also assess the relevance of the research to their current classroom needs, consider its congruence to their current practices, and weigh up the competing (and typically more powerful) influences which the curriculum exerts on their work. And in making all the above judgements teachers are drawing on their experience (the suggestion in one quotation in Figure 4.4 being that as experience increases, the impact of reading research decreases) and on what one teacher referred to here as her accumulated 'common sense' of what works in the classroom.

The overall picture which emerges here of the relationship between reading research and what teachers do in the classroom is thus characterized by dynamic interactions among various factors and further qualitative study of these is clearly warranted.

One factor from those mentioned above deserves separate discussion here – the congruence between the research teachers encounter and their existing practices. The relevant extract in Figure 4.4 comes from a teacher who was discussing the significant way that engagement with research on correcting writing had impacted on her teaching. In explaining this impact the main factor she stressed was that the new ideas validated existing practices for which she did not have a rationale and whose status she may have been uncertain about. After engaging with the research, she was able to implement these practices with more conviction, reassured by the knowledge that 'if

Factor	Illustrative quote
Teachers' experience	T: I've been teaching ten years plus ... by now I sort of feel I know the ropes in the class ... I know what to do, how to help the students, I mean there are always new ideas that are helpful but ... I: So you feel it's less likely that on a regular basis you're going to be reading things which change what you do in the classroom? T: Yes, exactly. (Spain)
Teachers' 'common sense'	'I have been teaching for 24 years and I got used to do a careful selection: some things are useful and some are not, some studies can be adapted to my students and some cannot. I have read a lot of studies which are a complete nonsense. The main guidance: (my) common sense.' (Slovenia)
Relevance of research to current needs	'I sort of tend to flick through magazines and look at things that I'm particularly interested in and I don't know, if I see an article on teaching reading, it depends on the relevance of what I'm teaching at the time ... So it [the impact of reading] changes from time to time depending on what I need.' (Kuwait)
Practicability of research	'Some of the research I read is purely for interest's sake, for example David Graddol's report on English as a Lingua Franca, obviously there is very little I can take into the classroom except for interesting facts about the future of world languages. However, I recently read some research into the usefulness of INSET training courses which I found enlightening ... The research has spurred me on to think about how I can provide and design workshops which teachers will find useful.' (Switzerland)
Curricular influences	'Well, what I do in the classroom I wasn't sure really – moderate or slight, I would think probably let's be honest, [the impact of reading is] slight [laughs]. Because what I do in the classroom is determined by so many other things – the curriculum, the objectives, the tests ... research partly yes, but there's so much more.' (Turkey)
Applicability of research	'The research that I read in the journals are applied on students outside of their cultures, different learning styles, their background is different ... I try to modify them according to our students' needs and try to implement them in my classroom. To the most possible extent, because some of the implications are not applicable to our students, especially the ones that I'm working with at the moment ... most of the implications do not fit into my situation here.' (Turkey)

(Continued)

Testability of research in practice	'If I can evaluate the results of research in the classroom I am definitely interested in it. As so it has much more influence on me.' (Slovenia)
Congruence with current practices	'I have changed the way I mark student essays. I wasn't doing the worst type of thing, sometimes I was actually doing the preferable one according to the research … [this research impacted on me] partly because it was actually easier – it actually reduced the workload, but also because intuitively I was actually doing that, I just didn't have the validation that it was actually right.' (Turkey)
Feasibility of research	T: [research I read will influence me] If I agree with it. So I look at it critically first, cause a lot of the things that are published I won't quite agree with it or I'll say yes, but … but if I agree with it I'll take it further and I'll try it and see if it works with my own students. I: What do you mean, if you agree with it? T: If I think yes that might work, well that's a good idea. (Spain)

Figure 4.4   Factors mediating the impact on teaching of reading research

they think you're a bad teacher [for teaching that way] you can justify it to them'. This resonates with findings from mainstream educational research highlighted earlier, which suggested that a perceived congruence with their existing practices influences the extent to which teachers engage productively with research. It also raises interesting questions about how teachers react to research which does not validate their existing practices in this way or which even questions them. Evidence relevant to this issue did not emerge in my work but it is clearly an important issue, given that tensions between what teachers do and what the research they read recommends will inevitably arise from time to time.

Reasons for not reading research

Teachers who said they read research rarely or never (N=343) were asked (in the questionnaire) to give reasons for this. Table 4.2 summarizes their responses, in descending order of frequency. A lack of time is the predominant reason cited here (by almost 70% of the teachers answering this question). A perceived lack of practical relevance was also cited as a common hindrance, as was the inaccessibility, both physical and conceptual, of published research. Just under 15% of the teachers said they were not interested in research; in this case the barrier to engagement with research seemed to be attitudinal, although one teacher in the UAE explained that they felt this way 'only because I rarely see research that is of interest to me; not because research per se is inherently uninteresting'.

Table 4.2   Reported reasons for not reading research (N=343)

Reasons	N
I do not have time	236
Published research does not give me practical advice for the classroom	130
I do not have access to books and journals	104
I find published research hard to understand	63
Other	52
I am not interested in research	50
I prefer to read practical teaching books and articles	15

Fifty-two teachers gave 'other' reasons for not reading research and the analysis of these responses extends in interesting ways the basic statistics reported above. A number of teachers said cost was a factor which limited their reading; for example, 'As a part-time ESL professor in a night ESL, adult education program, my financial resources for access to research journals and resources for obtaining such journals are limited' (USA). Working conditions, particularly a heavy workload, were also invoked a number of times, e.g. 'The work of two teachers is given to one' (Oman) and even where journals were available, access to them was sometimes difficult, as this teacher explained:

> We're subscribed to a couple of journals but they are not available to the teachers as such, they are in the teacher trainers' room. So you can borrow them, but it takes you a while to find out that they are there ... often the cabinets are locked and you have to go through some procedures if you want to gain access. (Spain)

In explaining their lack of reading, some teachers also expressed concerns about the actual quality of published language teaching research e.g. 'Research into ESL is not often done with a big enough sample or in stringent enough conditions to provide convincing results' (Australia), or 'I'm not sure people embark upon social science research without thinking that they have part of the answer already' (Turkey). For some teachers, too, reading research was an activity associated with formal study e.g. 'I suppose I connect research to doing some sort of qualification/teaching course' (Portugal). However, the dominant theme in the 'other' explanations teachers gave for their limited engagement with research was that research simply did not appeal. The sample of comments in Figure 4.5 illustrates this perspective.

As these comments indicate, the lack of appeal of published research is construed – by teachers in a range of international contexts – in terms of its lack of practical relevance to the classroom, its dryness, density, and linguistic inaccessibility. These themes illustrate in the context of language teaching some of the barriers to teachers' engagement with research discussed in the first part of this chapter. In particular, they highlight the attitudinal barriers created by the feeling among teachers that research lacks appeal and relevance. Whether published research does actually merit such characterization is of course a matter of opinion; it may be the case, though, that it is an opinion held by a substantial number of teachers, and therefore an issue that must be given careful consideration within any scheme whose goal is to enhance teacher engagement with research.

'The research/articles are often (usually?) completely unengaging and of no practical value in the classroom.' (Taiwan)

'Frequently, I do not find the research relevant to my teaching so I am not willing to invest the time.' (USA)

'I'm only interested in practical ways I can improve my teaching and have a low level of interest in reading about research.' (Spain)

'Have been in this field for a lo-o-o-nng time & am tired of reading dry research papers.' (USA)

'It is often dry, dense, statistical – lacking the 'human story' interest.' (Australia)

'The preponderance of jargon puts me off.' (Japan)

'My experience of doing the DELTA a few years ago was that some (but not all) of the course reading didn't bear much resemblance to reality.' (Czech Republic)

Figure 4.5   Teachers' lack of interest in reading research

4.5 Conclusion

The focus of this chapter has been language teachers' engagement with research. There is a growing awareness that the contribution of published (especially SLA) research to what teachers do is at best facilitative rather than determinative. However, there has been hardly any work aimed at better understanding language teachers' practices in engaging with research – if they read, what they read, why they read, how they read, what use they make of this reading, and, crucially, how their engagement with research can be facilitated.

The findings I have presented here provide insights into some of these issues which represent an important starting point for further in-depth study of these and related matters in specific educational and geographical contexts. While almost 75% of the teachers here said they read research at least 'sometimes', the variable and sometimes 'enhanced' interpretations assigned to this frequency word suggest that this does not point to a sustained and productive level of engagement with research. Further grounds for this conservative interpretation stem from the manner in which many teachers cited, as evidence of reading research, publications which are typically practical in nature. Teachers who said they read research generally felt it had some impact, practical and/or cognitive, on them; their comments also highlighted a range of factors – internal to teachers (e.g. their beliefs) as well as external (e.g. curricula) – which mediated such impact. The reasons teachers gave for not engaging with research were predictable in that a lack of time dominated; teachers' preference for practical advice, though, together with concerns about the physical, linguistic, and conceptual accessibility of published language teaching research were also influential barriers. Additionally, it is also clear that reading research is an activity that often has negative connotations for teachers; addressing this affective barrier, then, is at least as important in promoting teacher engagement with research as making relevant material available in a teacher friendly manner.

Continuing explorations of language teacher engagement with research can be informed by the findings presented in this chapter. The mechanisms through which, for example, the research teachers read influences, or fails to influence, their practice is not an issue we understand. More detailed case studies of the role that published research plays in the work of teachers – particularly outside the context of formal study – are also required. The findings here also suggest that teachers see as research practical publications which perhaps are not; qualitative investigations are thus required into how teachers make such judgements – i.e. how they decide (or indeed if they consider) whether the material they read is grounded in empirical evidence and/or practical experience.

Moreover, practical responses to these findings are required to facilitate language teacher engagement with research more widely and these can be informed by the literature discussed earlier in this chapter, in both language teaching and education more generally. This work suggests that teachers are more likely to be willing to engage with and use research to explore and inform their practice when it is accessible – physically, conceptually, linguistically, and practically – credible, useable, and interesting. In addition, teacher engagement with research is likely to impact more positively on teachers' work where they

- view published research as a source of enhanced understanding of their work, not as a direct solution to their problems
- are driven to seek out relevant research by an interest in exploring classroom issues of personal pedagogical relevance
- have assisted opportunities over time to integrate insights from reading with their existing pedagogical practices and theories.

In developing initiatives to create the kinds of conditions outlined here, academics too must assume some responsibility for considering how the results of their research can be made relevant to teachers. A concern for this kind of practical impact has in fact become a dominant theme in the context of higher education in the UK and in this context it is increasingly demanded of researchers that they demonstrate not only the academic value of their work but its value in real life (see, for example, the advice on impact provided by Research Councils UK at www.rcuk.ac.uk/kei/impacts). While this drive to demonstrate how research makes a difference to users has not been unproblematic (see, for example, Fielding, 2003), a desire to bridge traditional gaps between those who do educational research and teachers is clearly commendable; teacher research, of course, minimizes this dichotomy; nonetheless, it is important for us to develop mechanisms through which engagement with research generally can become a productive feature of teachers' professional activities. As Cordingley (2008) notes, though, the processes through which research knowledge is transformed for use in the classroom is a complex one which requires specialist brokers and mediators and the commitment of resources, not least funding. These are issues we have yet to engage with in the field of language teaching. There is also evidence that, 'primarily motivated by a desire to extract and apply what is immediately useful to their daily experience and the challenges of the classroom' (Bevan, 2004: 336), teachers' unconscious biases may distort their interpretations of the research they read. Again, we know nothing of how such processes might operate in language teaching contexts.

I will reflect in more practical terms on these issues in Chapter 9. Now I move on to examine the second dimension of research engagement – engagement *in* research, through actually doing it.

Notes

1   Following Salkind (2004: 88), here I treat correlations of less than 0.4 as weak and those between 0.4 and 0.6 as moderate.

References

Barone, T. (1995). Introduction. *International Journal of Educational Research,* 23(2), 109–112.

Bartels, N. (2003). How teachers and researchers read academic articles. *Teaching and Teacher Education, 19*(7), 737–753.

Bell, M., Cordingley, P., Isham, C., & Davis, R. (2010). Report of professional practitioner use of research review: Practitioner engagement in and/ or with research. Retrieved 9 February, 2012, from www.curee-paccts.com/ node/2303

Bevan, R. B. (2004). Filtering, fragmenting, and fiddling? Teachers' life cycles, and phases in their engagement with research. *Teacher Development, 8*(2/3), 325–339.

Bevan, R. B. (2006). *Teachers using research: What matters in transferring research knowledge into schools?* Paper presented at the Teacher Research Conference 2006, Birmingham, UK, 14 March 2006. Retrieved 9 February, 2012, from www.standards.dfes.gov.uk/ntrp/lib/pdf/bevan3.pdf

Borg, S. (2003). 'Research education' as an objective for teacher learning. In B. Beaven & S. Borg (Eds.), *The role of research in teacher education* (pp. 41–48). Whitstable, Kent: IATEFL.

Borg, S., & Ioannou-Georgiou, S. (2008). IATEFL research publications. *Language Teaching, 41*(3), 431–443.

Brown, J. D. (1988). *Understanding research in second language learning: A teacher's guide to statistics and research design.* Cambridge: Cambridge University Press.

Busch, D. (2010). Pre-service teacher beliefs about language learning: The second language acquisition course as an agent for change. *Language Teaching Research, 14*(3), 318–337.

CERI/OECD (2002). *Education research and development in England. Background report.* Paris: OECD.

Chapelle, C. (2007). Pedagogical implications in TESOL Quarterly? Yes, please! *TESOL Quarterly, 41*(2), 404–406.

Clarke, M. A. (1994). The dysfunctions of the theory/practice discourse. *TESOL Quarterly, 28*(1), 9–26.

Cordingley, P. (2004). Teachers using evidence: Using what we know about teaching and learning to reconceptualize evidence-based practice. In G. Thomas & R. Pring (Eds.), *Evidence-based practice in education* (pp. 77–87). Maidenhead: Open University Press.

Cordingley, P. (2008). Research and evidence-informed practice: Focusing on practice and practitioners. *Cambridge Journal of Education, 38*(1), 37–52.

Cordingley, P., & National Teacher Research Panel (2000). *Teacher perspectives on the accessibility and usability of research outputs.* Paper presented at the British Educational Research Association Conference, Cardiff University, 7–9 September 2000. Retrieved 15 July, 2011, from http://www.tda.gov.uk/upload/resources/doc/b/bera.doc

Davies, P. (2000). The relevance of systematic reviews to educational policy and practice. *Oxford Review of Education, 26*(3/4), 365–378.

Ellis, R. (2010). Second language acquisition, teacher education and language pedagogy. *Language Teaching, 43*(2), 182–201.

Everton, T., Galton, M., & Pell, T. (2000). Teachers' perspectives on educational research: Knowledge and context. *Journal of Education for Teaching, 26*(2), 167–182.

Everton, T., Galton, M., & Pell, T. (2002). Educational research and the teacher. *Research Papers in Education, 17*(4), 373–402.

Feuer, M. J., Towne, L., & Shavelson, R. J. (2002). Scientific culture and educational research. *Educational Researcher, 31*(8), 4–14.

Fielding, M. (2003). The impact of impact. *Cambridge Journal of Education, 33*(2), 289–295.

Freeman, D. (1996). Redefining the relationship between research and what teachers know. In K. M. Bailey & D. Nunan (Eds.), *Voices from the language classroom* (pp. 88–115). New York: Cambridge University Press.

Freeman, D., & Johnson, K. E. (1998). Reconceptualizing the knowledge-base of language teacher education. *TESOL Quarterly, 32*(3), 397–417.

Freeman, D., & Johnson, K. E. (2005). Response to Tarone and Allwright. In D. Tedick (Ed.), *Second language teacher education: International perspectives* (pp. 25–32). Mahwah, NJ: Lawrence Erlbaum.

Hammersley, M. (2001). On 'systematic' reviews of research literatures: A 'narrative' response to Evans & Benefield. *British Educational Research Journal, 27*(5), 543–554.

Hammersley, M. (2004). Some questions about evidence-based practice in education. In G. Thomas & R. Pring (Eds.), *Evidence-based practice in education* (pp. 133–149). Maidenhead: Open University Press.

Han, Z. (2007). Pedagogical implications: Genuine or pretentious? *TESOL Quarterly, 41*(2), 387–393.

Hemsley-Brown, J., & Sharp, C. (2003). The use of research to improve professional practice: A systematic review of the literature. *Oxford Review of Education, 29*(4), 449–470.

Jarvis, S. (2002). Research in TESOL: Part II. *TESOL Research Interest Section Newsletter, 9*(1), 1–11.

Kerekes, J. (2001). How can SLA theories and SLA researchers contribute to teachers' practices? In B. Johnston & S. Irujo (Eds.), *Research and practice in language teacher education: Voices from the field* (pp. 17–41). Minneapolis, MN: Center for Advanced Research on Language Acquisition.

Kiely, R., & Davis, M. (2010). From transmission to transformation: Teacher learning in English for speakers of other languages. *Language Teaching Research, 14*(3), 277–296.

Lightbown, P. M. (2000). Classroom SLA research and second language teaching. *Applied Linguistics, 21*(4), 431–462.

Lo, Y. H. G. (2005). Relevance of knowledge of second language acquisition: An in-depth case study of a non-native EFL teacher. In N. Bartels (Ed.), *Applied linguistics and language teacher education.* (pp. 135–157). New York: Kluwer Academic Publishers.

Macaro, E. (2003). *Teaching and learning a second language: A guide to recent research and its applications.* London: Continuum.

MacDonald, M., Badger, R., & White, G. (2001). Changing values: What use are theories of language learning and teaching? *Teaching and Teacher Education, 17*(8), 949–963.

Maxwell, J. A. (2004). Causal explanation, qualitative research, and scientific inquiry in education. *Educational Researcher, 33*(2), 3–11.

McDonough, J., & McDonough, S. (1990). What's the use of research? *ELT Journal, 44*(2), 102–109.

McMillan, J. H., & Wergin, J. F. (2010). *Understanding and evaluating educational research* 4th ed. Upper Saddle River, NJ: Pearson Education.

McNamara, O. (2002). Evidence-based practice through practice-based evidence. In O. McNamara (Ed.), *Becoming an evidence-based practitioner* (pp. 15–26). London: Routledge Falmer.

Morrison, K. (2001). Randomised controlled trials for evidence-based education: Some problems in judging 'what works'. *Evaluation and Research in Education, 15*(2), 69–83.

Nutley, S., Percy-Smith, J., & Solesbury, W. (2003). *Models of research impact: A cross-sector review of literature and practice.* London: Learning and Skills Research Centre.

OECD (2009). Creating effective teaching and learning environments: First results from TALIS. Retrieved 9 February, 2012, from www.oecd.org/dataoecd/17/51/43023606.pdf

Pachler, N. (2003). Foreign language teaching as an evidence-based profession? *Language Learning Journal, 27*(1), 4–14.

Perry, F. L., Jr. (2005). *Research in applied linguistics. Becoming a discerning consumer.* Mahwah, NJ: Lawrence Erlbaum.

Porte, G. K. (2002). *Appraising research in second language learning: A practical approach to critical analysis of quantitative research.* Amsterdam: John Benjamins.

Rankin, J., & Becker, F. (2006). Does reading the research make a difference? A case study of teacher growth in FL German. *Modern Language Journal, 90*(3), 353–372.

Ranta, L. (2002). 'Academic' doesn't have to be a dirty word! *TESOL Research Interest Section Newsletter, 9*(1), 7.

Ratcliffe, M., Bartholomew, H., Hames, V., Hind, A., Leach, J., & Millar, R. (2004). *Science education practitioners' views of research and its influence on their practice.* York: Department of Educational Studies, University of York.

Rickinson, M., Clark, A., McLeod, S., Poulton, P., & Sargent, J. (2004). What on earth has research got to do with me? *Teacher Development, 8*(2/3), 201–220.

Roulston, K., Legette, R., DeLoach, M., & Pittman, C. B. (2005). What is 'research' for teacher-researchers? *Educational Action Research, 13*(2), 169–190.

Salkind, N. J. (2004). *Statistics for people who (think they) hate statistics* 2nd ed. Thousand Oaks: Sage.

Shank, G. D., & Brown, L. (2007). *Exploring educational research literacy.* New York and London: Routledge.

Shkedi, A. (1998). Teachers' attitudes towards research: A challenge for qualitative researchers. *International Journal of Qualitative Studies in Education, 11*(4), 559–578.

Stewart, T. (2006). Teacher-researcher collaboration or teachers' research? *TESOL Quarterly, 40*(2), 421–429.

Thomas, G. (2004). Introduction: Evidence and practice. In G. Thomas & R. Pring (Eds.), *Evidence-based practice in education* (pp. 1–18). Maidenhead: Open University Press.

Tiezzi, L. J., & Zeuli, J. S. (1994). *Supporting teachers' understanding of educational research in a master's level research course.* Paper presented at the American Educational Research Association Conference, New Orleans, Louisiana, April 1994.

Williams, D., & Coles, L. (2007). Teachers' approaches to finding and using research evidence: An information literacy perspective. *Educational Research, 49*(2), 185–206.

Zeuli, J. S. (1994). How do teachers understand research when they read it? *Teaching and Teacher Education, 10*(1), 39–55.

5 Teacher engagement in research

5.1 Introduction

Empirical evidence of how often teachers do research is limited, and due to the nature of the phenomenon under study, such evidence typically takes the form of teacher self-reports. (It would not be particularly feasible to observe teachers over time to document their involvement in research.) In education generally, large-scale research with over 70,000 secondary school teachers in 23 countries (OECD, 2009) reports that 35.4% of them said they had participated in individual or collaborative research in the previous 18 months. The corresponding figure for the subset of almost 9,000 modern and foreign language teachers in the sample was 31.2%. In contrast to these modest reported levels of engagement in research, doing research was overall felt by teachers to be the most effective strategy (among nine options) for promoting their professional development. These findings suggest a tension, then, between the perceived value by teachers of engagement in research and the extent to which they engage in it. On a much smaller scale, McNamara (2002: 18), based on a sample of 100 respondents, found that only 4 per cent of teachers who responded felt that being involved in educational research would be 'very manageable', but otherwise, despite extensive interest in teacher research, quantitative data about how frequently teachers engage in research is lacking. Of course, it can be inferred from the number of teacher research projects discussed in the international literature (e.g. Davies, Hamilton, & James, 2007; Meyers & Rust, 2003; Sharp et al., 2005) that considerable numbers of teachers have been periodically engaged in teacher research over the years.

In the field of language teaching, as noted in Chapter 1, a number of publications exist which provide evidence of teachers doing research, though one of my general claims in this book is that, for most language teachers, engagement in research is not part of their professional lives. In terms of empirical evidence, Rainey (2000) asked teachers about their engagement in action research and found that over 75% of her 226 respondents said they had never heard the term; of the 55 teachers who said they had, almost 58% were described as 'not very active researchers' (p. 75). Thus, over 70% of the total sample in this study did not engage in action research in any active way. In Brown et al. (1992), just over 51% of the 667 respondents said they did their own research, though, as noted in Chapter 3, it is not clear in this study what percentage of the responses were teachers – researchers, teacher educators and administrators also participated. In recent work with Chinese TEFL academics (both teachers of English and lecturers in linguistics, literature, translation, and culture studies), Bai & Hudson (2011) reported that 18% of 182 respondents had not produced any research outputs in the period 2004–8 (research outputs here were defined in fairly formal terms, e.g. journal articles, books, and conference papers). The paper concluded that the research productivity of the participating academics was relatively low, although respondents were positive about the benefits of doing research.

In this chapter I am also interested in teachers' reasons for doing research. Noffke (1997) suggests three possibilities: a desire to understand and improve one's teaching; a motivation to produce knowledge that will be of use to other professionals; and a democratic drive to contribute more generally to a more equitable society. In a recent study by Gao, Barkhuizen, & Chow (2011), teachers' primary reasons for doing research reflected Noffke's first option – to solve problems in their classes. Another key finding in this study was that, especially in elite schools led by ambitious school principals, teachers, despite significant obstacles, often felt 'obliged to do research for their personal honour as well as for their schools' collective honour' (p. 74).

Drawing on issues highlighted above, this chapter contributes to our understanding of language teachers' engagement in research by examining these specific questions:

1 To what extent do language teachers say they do research?
2 Where teachers say they do research:
    a   what reasons do they give for doing so?
    b   what kinds of research do they say they do?
    c   what impact do they say this work has on their teaching?
3 Where teachers say they do not do research, what reasons do they give?

In addressing these issues, I draw mainly on questionnaire and interview data collected from the teachers in Studies 1, 3 and 4 (see Chapter 2).

Table 5.1   Reported frequency of doing research

	N	%
Never	198	14.7
Rarely	498	36.9
Sometimes	479	35.5
Often	174	12.9
Total	1349	100.0

5.2 Prevalence of doing research

Table 5.1 presents the responses teachers in my studies gave when they were asked (on a scale of 'often' to 'never') how frequently they do research. As these figures show, just over 48% of the 1,349 teachers responding said they did research at least sometimes; 363 managers (in Studies 2, 3 and 4) answered the same question and the corresponding figure was lower, at 37.5%. The extent to which teachers said they did research was not associated with their experience and was only weakly (though significantly) associated with their qualifications (N=1334, ρ=0.063, p<.001, 1-tailed).

As noted in Chapter 4, teachers will interpret descriptors such as 'sometimes' in various ways, and in interviews and written questions I therefore asked teachers who said they did research 'sometimes' to explain what they meant. Figure 5.1 presents illustrative responses which highlight a range of more and less frequent degrees of engagement in research. In some cases, 'sometimes' refers to an activity teachers engaged with in the past rather than at present; in others it refers to an annual event or one completed when teachers are 'away from teaching'. Clearly, given these variations, we need to be conservative in interpreting the finding that almost half the teachers in this study said they do research sometimes. Further evidence for such caution emerges as this chapter unfolds.

'Not often.' (Australia)

'Sometimes I am so fully occupied with teaching and correcting that I cannot afford the time. Sometimes when I am away from teaching, I have the time to reflect upon what I have practised routinely.' (China)

'It means once or twice a year. But I am often thinking about doing research.' (Japan)

'Every end of the school year.' (Slovenia)

'I did research in my last year in my Bachelor Degree ... Before that, I did a preliminary research before staring this one. So, I might consider this as sometimes.' (UAE)

'No time now – in the past at University.' (Switzerland)

'In the course of my work as a DOS, I am often asked to evaluate course books and ideas for new courses etc. I create questionnaires and involve teachers in the evaluation process. With regards to my personal teaching I have carried out action research projects ... I will continue to do such projects throughout my career as a teacher on an irregular basis.' (Switzerland)

Figure 5.1   What teachers mean by doing research 'sometimes'

5.3 Reasons for doing research

Teachers who said they did research at least sometimes were asked to give reasons for their engagement. Table 5.2 summarizes their responses, in descending order of frequency.

The three most common answers share a professional-pedagogical focus, suggesting that language teachers' primary reasons for doing research relate to the improvement of themselves as professionals and of their classroom practices. Over 45% also said they do research as part of their studies; formal courses which include a compulsory research project are of course an effective way of engaging teachers in research, although as I discuss in Chapter 8, in the context of higher academic studies the need to obtain a qualification can overshadow

Table 5.2   Reasons for doing research (N=653)

	N	%
To find better ways of teaching	564	86.4
Because it is good for my professional development	496	76.0
To solve problems in my professional work	444	68.0
Because I enjoy it	336	51.5
As part of a course I am studying	296	45.3
To contribute to the improvement of my institution	253	38.7
Because other professionals can learn from the findings of my work	206	31.5
To contribute knowledge to the field of TESOL generally	124	19.0
Because it will help me get a promotion	79	12.1
Because my employer expects me to	76	11.6
Other	57	8.7

teachers' genuine interest in the research they are doing. At the same time, though, I would argue that structured opportunities for teacher engagement can be more productive than those which are not part of a formal initiative of some kind. Table 5.2 also suggests that more instrumental factors such as promotion and employer pressure were not felt by teachers in my studies to exert a significant influence on their decisions to do research (but see Borg & Liu, forthcoming, for insights into the influence that such instrumental factors can have on language teachers' engagement in research).

Fifty-seven teachers suggested 'other' reasons for doing research. The most common theme among these (mentioned by 13 teachers) was improving teaching and learning (a point which echoes the most popular reason given in Table 5.2). Thus teachers explained that they do research 'to find the most effective way of helping my students personally' (Spain) or 'to help my students learn better and faster' (USA); they also wrote about doing research 'to teach in a way which will be of greater benefit to the learners in my classes' (Spain) or to 'help me in reading about new ways or techniques of teaching and learning' (Oman). The latter comment – with its specific reference to reading about teaching techniques – again raises questions about teachers' interpretations of what doing research involves. Teachers also talked about doing research as part of lesson planning; one, for example, said they do research to 'prepare for giving a class' (USA) and this too raises questions about the precise nature of the activity implied here. Other reasons for doing research noted by several teachers were keeping up-to-date, curiosity, being involved in PhD research, self-improvement, and as part of educational reforms. Regarding the latter, for example, a teacher from China wrote:

> China is carrying out Education Reform, and teachers are supposed to do research on teaching and learning skills. I have taken part in it, and have been studying how to be a good teacher to help my students to become better learners. My colleagues and I form a team, we try our best to do research work. We can be given suggestions and help straight by our provincial education bureau. We attend training courses and make progress bit by bit. We enjoy the process.

Further reasons for doing research noted by individual teachers were guilt (i.e. teachers do research because they feel guilty if they do not) and a deep commitment to the profession. Overall, what emerges here is a wide range of motivations for engaging in research, though predominant amongst these were an interest in professional development and more effective language teaching and learning.

5.4 The research teachers do

Teachers who said they did research at least sometimes were asked to give examples of the kind of work they do. Figure 5.2 summarizes the orientations to research reflected in the examples they provided and I will now discuss these. The orientations are not exclusive and are not meant to represent a typology of approaches to research; they simply reflect the dimensions emphasized by teachers when they described the research they do.

Orientation	Description
Evaluating learning and teaching strategies, activities and materials	Pedagogically oriented inquiry which involves evaluating the effectiveness of, or reactions of learners and teachers to, new approaches to teaching and learning, new activities or new instructional materials.
Surveying learners and teachers	Using questionnaires and/or interviews with learners and/or teachers to examine their views, attitudes or preferences in relation to a specific aspect of language learning and teaching, and using the findings as the basis for practical action.
Analyzing literary texts	Inquiry conducted by language teachers whose primary interests and expertise are literary.
Needs analysis	Inquiry which aims to learn about language learners' needs and to use that information as the basis of planning a course.
Research conducted for Master's or doctoral studies	Formal investigations completed to obtain a higher degree.
Informal research with colleagues	Inquiry which involves informal conversations among teachers about aspects of their work.
Teacher education research	For teachers who also work as teacher trainers, inquiry which examines aspects of the teacher education process.
Acting as a research participant or facilitator	Teachers are not themselves doing research but are participants in or facilitators for someone else's research.
No engagement in research	Teachers who say they have done research but who subsequently characterize their inquiries as not 'real' research.

Figure 5.2   The research teachers do

The dominant form of research in teachers' accounts was the first category of evaluative studies. Figure 5.3 lists some examples in this group and, given the dominance of this type of work in teachers' accounts of their research, I will comment on each in turn. Example 1 captures concisely the basic thinking behind all examples in this category – that the evaluation of teaching and learning is a kind of research. This connects with some of the examples highlighted in Chapter 3, where research and forms of 'good practice' involving reflective teaching were seen to be synonymous. Example 2 involves a teacher evaluating the effectiveness of the vocabulary learning strategies their students use, while example 3 similarly has a focus on seeking feedback on the success of teaching and on 'what worked' in class. Example 4 refers specifically to action research, though on the basis of the description provided here, there was no evidence of the cyclical processes that this form of research involves; rather, the focus here was on trying out in class ideas obtained through reading. I will also comment on two longer responses that teachers provided and which further illustrate this predominant notion of research as pedagogical evaluation. Here is the first:

> I'll give you a concrete example of what I did. I've got a B2 class and one of the students in that class really wants to improve his listening, and the

---

1 'Classroom research I think I'm doing it all the time. I just check whether my materials work or not and I'm just constantly re-evaluating.' (Turkey)

2 'I have done certain things which you could describe as research with my students. Testing on how they best remember vocabulary, testing on their understanding of the meanings of words in their own language in order to know whether it's a good translation for words in English.' (Spain)

3 '... when I've done something very different, a project on organising a social function which turned into a fashion show and things like that, I really wanted to know after this had continued for two weeks, to get feedback and also to look at how it could have been organised better and things. So it's more what I do is looking at the practical, what I've done in class, what worked, and what I could use with other classes.' (Spain)

4 '... a new academic manager came in and suggested that we all try and do some action research, so she gave us a couple of articles and we were more or less given free range in our two hours administration time to go and do whatever we wanted. So I just read a book and tried out some ideas.' (Hungary)

Figure 5.3   Examples of evaluative research

others agree ... so I try to do different activities with listening, some of them I've learned from my MAs, some of them I've come up with myself, so I did something different the last day and then I ask for their own view about how did that make you feel? would you like to do the same thing again? if you did it again, what would you change? On the basis of what they told me, and having asked them would they like to do the same thing again, if I put into practice what they suggested, and would you like to do it again and they say yes, so I'm gonna try it again now, incorporating their suggestions. (Spain)

This description illustrates a teacher's attempt to support student learning by trying out, over various cycles, different activities and eliciting learners' reactions to them. In this case the basic elements of action research are present, such as implementing a change and monitoring its effects, though as implemented here the inquiry is better characterized not as research (see Chapter 1 for a definition of teacher research) but as a systematic process of seeking and responding to student evaluations of learning activities. Another example of a teacher describing the evaluative research they did is the following:

I can tell you about something that I was connected with which was looking at the use of L1 and L2 in young learner classes where ... well to try and simplify it there was basically a public sphere where learners were in the presence of a teacher and they would use L2, and then there was a private sphere where students would just use L1 and we were looking at ways of making it easier for students to cross over from L1 to L2 and trying to permeate the public sphere and the private sphere, and so of course looking at techniques like that ... looking at problems like that forces you to come up with different ways of trying ... you know different things to try out in class, different techniques, uses of different groups, uses of different materials or different timing, or you know different ... even different questions or where the questions come from you know, or looking at different ways of doing penalties in class for example, you know you like lose two counters if you speak you know Cantonese here for example. (Hong Kong)

This example also embodies some elements of action research (see Chapter 1 for comments on the defining features of this form of teacher research); it describes how a teacher experimented with different classroom options in order to promote more L2 use by learners and assessed the effectiveness of these options through observing how learners reacted.

Overall, then, when teachers were asked to give examples of the research they did, the dominant orientation to research to emerge was one that involved pedagogically oriented evaluations of teaching and learning strategies and materials. These evaluations involved implementing changes to classroom practice and reflecting, mainly through observation, on their impact. From the evidence teachers provided, the research they did did not include formal 'data' and data analysis, nor was the work made public (in the broad sense defined in Chapter 1). In essence, then, these inquiries were individual, private, and reflective exercises in evaluating teaching and learning processes. This is in no way a criticism of such activities or of their value for teachers' professional development. One of my goals in this book is to deepen our understandings of what research means to teachers, and these kinds of examples make an important contribution to this goal. As I have already argued, though, I do feel that reflective practice and research should not be used synonymously, and this is a point I will take up again later in this chapter.

The other orientations to research listed in Figure 5.2 were, relative to that just discussed, minor. A number of examples involved teachers surveying students to understand their attitudes, views, or preferences in relation to a particular issue. For example:

> We asked students what they wanted and they said they didn't want tapes or CDs anymore. They wanted easy access to listening materials so we converted those and put them up on the G drive [i.e. on a computer network]. (Colombia)

In some cases such surveys also involved teachers, as in this example:

> Another bit of research done is focus groups with students about our conversation courses and well with students initially and then also with the teachers for conversation courses ... and using the findings really, why they do them and what people are expecting from them, drawing up some learning aids and trying to structure the courses so that they're a better product, also they're achieving what people want, which they weren't. (Egypt)

In a sense such surveys, particularly those involving learners, were a form of market research – an attempt to understand what learners wanted (this was particularly a concern in private fee-paying language schools). Teachers who talked about needs analysis as a form of research were also primarily concerned with gathering information to improve course design, teaching, and learning. Another orientation to research cited by many teachers was that their inquiries were conducted for the purposes of an academic qualification (just over 50% of the 1,363 teachers in my combined studies said they had an MA while just under 6% reported having a doctorate). I have already expressed concerns about the impact which formal study can have on teachers' purposes in being research engaged and I will develop this point in Chapter 8.

To conclude, this section, we can also note some additional and interesting, though minor, items from Figure 5.2. First, there was the notion of 'informal research', which one teacher described as follows:

> What I find very interesting is ... in talking about informal research is teachers getting together informally and just chatting about observations. Observations they have had on their practice and I always find so much interesting stuff comes out of that. (Italy)

'Informal' was a term repeatedly used by teachers to distinguish their research from what they saw as more formal academic inquiry. In this case, the investigative activity being described involved teachers engaging in collaborative oral reflections on their teaching.

There were also cases here where teachers who originally said in their questionnaire that they did research at least sometimes consequently implied through interviews and further written comments that the extent of their engagement in language teaching research was actually minimal. Three orientations to research in Figure 5.2 fall into this category. First, there are those teachers with backgrounds in literature rather than language teaching and who described their research as focusing on the analysis of literary texts, rather than language teaching (I discuss such teachers in more detail later in this chapter). Second, there were teachers who described their engagement in research as a facilitative one – they either provided data as participants or supported others doing research (e.g. by providing access to research settings and participants). Finally, some teachers admitted that the activities they engaged in were not really research. For example, one teacher from Slovenia explained:

> I can't say that this was research, more an evaluation of my work with the course books that I have been using. The parents of my students were given the questionnaires and they had completed some forms. The results were useful for my further planning and organisation.

A teacher from Australia similarly noted that 'I haven't done 'real' research as it involves an incredible amount of work and presentation at the end etc.' Such findings lend further weight to my earlier point about the need to interpret with caution the degree of engagement in research that teachers report.

5.5 Impact of doing research

So far we have examined teachers' reported levels of doing research and their reasons for doing so. In one of my studies (Study 3) teachers who said they did research were asked whether it had an impact on their work or that of their colleagues. Of 47 teachers, 43 (over 91%) said that it had. These teachers were also asked to explain the nature of this impact and Table 5.3 summarizes the forms of impact they mentioned and the frequency of each. Illustrative quotes for each theme are also provided.

These teachers identified a range of ways in which doing research had impacted on their work. The most commonly cited benefit of research was learning about new techniques and methods to apply in the classroom, though sharing ideas with colleagues and improved teaching were also commonly cited. Teachers also felt that doing research made them more aware of their work and of their students, as well as enhancing their confidence in the classroom by providing confirmation for existing beliefs and practices. Several other benefits which implied better-quality teaching – such as improved materials writing and lesson planning – were also noted. The strong and often immediate practical orientation of the benefits typically cited by teachers once again suggests a notion of doing research which falls

Table 5.3   Impact of doing research (N=47)

Impact	N	Illustrative quote
Learning new teaching techniques	10	'... it has opened my eyes to new methodologies (which I now experiment with).' (Malaysia)
Sharing ideas with colleagues	7	'I've recently completed my Diploma. All work has been informally made available to the teachers.' (Thailand)
Improved teaching	7	'Have been able to benefit from research by improving my teaching.' (Kuwait)
Greater awareness of teaching and students	6	'Increased my level of awareness and hence affected the classroom decisions I make.' (Bahrain)
Greater confidence in the classroom by confirming beliefs and practices	5	'It also has confirmed some of my own philosophies on teaching, and this gives me added confidence in the classroom.' (Malaysia)

(Continued)

Table 5.3   (Continued)

Impact	N	Illustrative quote
Improved course design	3	'Allowed me to develop better programmes/courses that fulfil the needs of the learners.' (Malaysia)
Deeper knowledge of ELT	2	'I feel my depth of knowledge has improved.' (Kuwait)
Enhanced reflection	2	'I am more reflective and more willing to experiment with new techniques.' (Czech Republic)
Improved lesson planning		'It enables me to deliver well planned lessons, therefore the students benefit.' (Kuwait)
Improved materials writing	2	'Informed my teaching, and my production of teaching materials.' (Colombia)
Greater cultural sensitivity	1	'Improved methodology, cultural sensitivity.' (Egypt)
Deeper understanding of rationale for teaching	1	'I also have a sounder understanding of why existing practices are appropriate.' (Czech Republic)

short of the way I have defined it here; it is quite likely that in several of these cases, teachers saw research as reading to find out about new methods and activities or to deepen their knowledge of particular areas of language. This interpretation of research would explain, for example, the close links teachers implied between doing research and planning lessons, or between research and becoming aware of new language teaching methodologies.

5.6 Reasons for not doing research

In my programme of research, 696 teachers said they did research never or rarely, and I will now focus on the reasons they gave for their limited engagement. These reasons are summarized in Table 5.4, in descending order of frequency.

Once again (see the reasons for not reading research discussed in Chapter 4), time is cited here as the dominant barrier. Considerable numbers of teachers also felt that research was not part of their job, that they lacked the knowledge of research methods that doing

Table 5.4   Reasons for not doing research (N=696)

	N	%
I do not have time to do research	529	76.0
My job is to teach, not to do research	275	39.5
I do not know enough about research methods	227	32.6
Most of my colleagues do not do research	212	30.5
I need someone to advise me but no one is available	137	19.7
Other	119	17.1
I am not interested in doing research	101	14.5
Doing research is not part of my job description	101	14.5
I do not have access to the books and journals I need	82	11.8
Other teachers would not cooperate if I asked for their help	53	7.6
The learners would not cooperate if I did research in class	39	5.6
My employer discourages it	33	4.7

research calls for, and that their colleagues were also not typically involved in doing research. In a subsequent interview one teacher explained the effect that colleagues' lack of engagement in research had on her as follows: 'if they [colleagues] don't do it [research] then I don't need to bother, I don't need to worry about the fact that I don't do it' (Italy). There was almost a sense of relief here at the way that colleagues' inactivity freed her from the obligation to be engaged in research. At the other end of the scale in Table 5.4, discouragement from employers, lack of co-operation from teachers and learners, and limited access to relevant literature did not emerge here as major factors which teachers felt limited their engagement in research.

I explored some of these issues further with teachers in interviews. One issue raised by a subset of teachers – those working for private EFL schools on hourly paid contracts – was that research was not an attractive option for them because it would represent time spent on unpaid work. One teacher noted that 'you know, English language teachers … we only get paid the actual hours of it in the class' (Spain), while another teacher, also in Spain, explained:

> Well I suppose a lot of it is a question of time and money. Teaching English is not well paid, but it leaves free time. If that free time is taken up with something else that's not well paid, or even not paid at all, then it's not the kind of thing that attracts my interest. There are other things that if I'm

going to fill my free time with, something which may or may not be paid, I like writing. I'd rather sit at my table and do some writing.

Even in contexts, however, where teachers enjoyed more favourable employment conditions (e.g. longer full-time contracts), there was still often a feeling that, outside periods of leave for formal study, no time was available for teachers to do research:

> I think one of the main obstacles … is that the culture in our organization doesn't allow people time to do this kind of thing. So people who are involved in any kind of research are people who are doing MAs and they're quite often doing that in their own time. They're granted study leave and things sometimes to get involved with things like that. But generally on a day to day basis there is no time provision for this kind of thing. (Italy)

It was not just the time to do research that teachers felt was lacking, but also the time required – where teachers were positively disposed – to learn about doing research. As one teacher explained:

> When I read the [research] papers that we referred to earlier I actually find it quite interesting and inspiring, if you will, and quite encouraging and I do have a genuine interest in the material. Perhaps I don't know enough about research methods because I haven't had time to look into them. (Italy)

As Table 5.4 above shows, 119 teachers suggested 'other' reasons for not doing research more often, and Figure 5.4. summarizes the main themes in teachers' comments, in descending order of frequency.

Thus, in explaining their lack of engagement in research, the most common 'other' response provided by teachers was to say that they *did* do research, but not of the formal kind. Rather, they characterized their work as reflective inquiry based on informal classroom observation and evaluation. Figure 5.5 provides further examples of how teachers described this kind of activity and these consolidate the picture that is emerging here of teachers' strong pedagogically oriented notions of research.

I will comment on these examples of 'informal research' (an expression I find oxymoronic) before returning to the broader discussion of the 'other' reasons teachers gave for not doing research. Many of the examples in Figure 5.5 emphasize the classroom-based, ongoing, pedagogically oriented, and informal nature of the inquiry teachers see themselves engaging in. This often involves observation of what works in the classroom and making subsequent adjustments to practice (examples 1, 6, 8 & 9), sometimes informed by input from professional reading (example 4). There are also references here to action research (example 3) and to in-house surveys and focus groups

Reasons	Illustrative quotes
A preference for less formal classroom-based reflections	'I don't engage in formal research as defined by the scientific method. I do engage in informal research which can be defined as reflective teaching.' (USA)
The lack of any motivating reason	'There is no incentive for me to do research in my current job: no prestige, no tenure possibilities, no salary increase.' (South Korea)
Respondents' professional and personal identity or identities	'I am trained in American studies, a content field, so I feel misplaced in ESL.' (Japan)
The costs of doing research and the lack of pay for this activity	'Doing research would be entirely unpaid and on my own time.' (USA)
Lack of a mentor or supportive colleagues	'I need someone to advise me but teachers I work with do it very unwillingly, justifying it with their lack of time.' (Poland)
Lack of ideas or of ideas felt to merit studying or of wider interest	'I don't seem to have good ideas. I mean everything I think of seems to already have been done.' (Japan)
Lack of support	'I get no support in terms of time, money (or pat on the back) for research.' (Spain)
Lack of access to research participants	'I do not have access to a large enough sample.' (USA)
Not being associated with a university	'I pretty much need to be affiliated with a university to do "real" research.' (Brazil)
Respondents being at an early stage of their career	'I am a new teacher. Although I am not doing formal research at the present time, I want to do research in the future.' (USA)
Respondents being at the end of their career	'I am about to retire from paid work and have no impetus to do research at present.' (Australia)
Difficulties in getting research published	'It seems that doing research at school is useless. It won't be published anyway.' (Hong Kong)
The need to deliver the curriculum	'I am evaluated on delivering curriculum. Research in the classroom might fall outside the prescribed curriculum.' (USA)
Doubts about the value of doing research	'Some of the people I know who do "research" seem much more focused on going through the motions than on actually learning anything.' (USA)
Low levels of interest in and motivation to do research	'My general level of interest in research is too low.' (Spain)

Figure 5.4   Other reasons for not doing research (N=113)

1 'I believe in teacher observation. That's my research. What works for my students, I keep doing; what doesn't work, goes out the window. I believe in trying everything. My kids need variety, as well as routine.' (Puerto Rico)

2 'Teaching IS DOING RESEARCH!' (USA)

3 'I do action research in my classroom and encourage other teachers to do the same.' (USA)

4 'I don't do formal research. Finding information on line or in professional literature helps broaden my perspectives. Informally, I can compare what I read with what I see in real life and develop teaching ideas as it appears possible.' (USA)

5 'We occasionally do things like student surveys and focus groups but they are mostly related to our specific institution and our students' needs.' (USA)

6 'I have done plenty of observation adjustments in my teaching, and find that a teacher adjusts methods according to class.' (USA)

7 'It [doing research] should be rarely! I do research for practical use in the classroom on the internet.' (Netherlands)

8 'Teacher classroom research is something I do – if students indicate that X activity isn't working for them, I then try other things. This is not controlled generalizable research, perhaps assessment only, but it is an attempt to understand objectively, worthwhile, I think.' (USA)

9 'The research I do all the time is constant assessment of student achievement, for the purpose of improving my teaching in the future. But this is not the kind of research we publish – nothing so formal as a control group and an experimental group and a research instrument, for example.' (USA)

10 'When I go online to look at the collocations of a word, should I consider that research?' (USA)

11 'I think that unless research is backed up by practical application, it is an academic exercise and not useful for classroom teachers.' (USA)

Figure 5.5   Reflective practice and informal classroom research

(example 5). Additionally, some of these responses provide specific insight into teachers' understandings of research. Example 2 (capitals in the original) argues that teaching is doing research, a point I find arguable, given the inevitable tensions between the automatized nature of skilled teaching and the deliberate nature of research (but see Duckworth, 1986 for a more supportive position). In example 7, perhaps feeling I was somehow seeking to criticize teachers for not doing research, the teacher argues that research should be a rare activity for teachers; using the Internet to find practical material was also cited here as an example of research (example 7). Example 10 also captures the dilemmas many teachers seem to experience in distinguishing research in the sense of looking for information (much as I would research flight prices before purchasing a ticket) from research as a form of systematic, empirical, and public activity. The final example in Figure 5.5 reflects a view that has come across strongly in this chapter – that for teachers, research needs to have a practical dimension. All of the above examples reinforce further the message emerging here that for many teachers doing research is a practical activity through which they search for information to support their practice or observe and reflect on their teaching with a view to improving it.

Returning to Figure 5.4, several of the additional reasons for not doing research noted there by teachers are ones we would expect to be cited: lack of incentives, lack of support, and curricular pressures. Three further points, though, do merit particular discussion. The first of these is that several teachers felt they did not have any ideas that merited researching. The relevant example quoted in Figure 5.4 implies the teacher was concerned about originality and was therefore deterred from doing research by their inability to find an unstudied issue. This, of course, is not a realistic perspective to adopt as wholly original and innovative research is rare. Another teacher said 'I'm not sure who else would gain from the research I'm interested in doing' (USA). The concerns this time relate not to the originality of the research but to its broader value. This position contrasts with many of the examples of research teachers have described in this chapter and where the primary focus has been on resolving local problems without any reference to the broader implications of the work.

A second point from Figure 5.4 to note here is the issue of money. A number of teachers noted that because they were not affiliated to a university, accessing literature to support their research was costly. Others, as noted above, stressed the fact that they were only paid for teaching hours; this was especially true of EFL teachers working in private language schools. Additionally, a number of teachers noted that they worked part-time (or as adjunct faculty) in one or more institutions and this not only left no time for research but also meant that their status within those institutions was not particularly high. It is clear then that – particularly, but not only, in the commercial language teaching sector – teachers' employment conditions and the status these afford teachers are often not at all conducive to their engagement in research. This is an issue I discuss further in Chapter 7.

The third point from Figure 5.4 I want to comment on here is that of identity (see also the further examples in Figure 5.6). One university-based language teacher noted that 'Reading and doing research is

1 '... perhaps I think that it's the people at the top of the game who are involved in research, you know. We've got XXX around in our city and you know, he's like, he's the kind of person who does research, not me. Perhaps it's that kind of attitude going on somewhere.' (Spain)

2 'I do not know what I would do with the research. I feel marginalized as an ESL teacher in my school, and marginalized as (only) a high school teacher in TESOL (not a professor, not affiliated with a university).' (USA)

3 'I teach English and American literature mainly and teaching English as a second language is additional – within the full time job.' (Poland)

4 '... my time as a mother of two young children is limited to 'must do' tasks these days.' (USA)

5 'My major is not ELT, but linguistics. I have to write papers on linguistics.' (Japan)

6 'Well, I try to avoid making statements such as "I do not have time for ..." because we always have time for what we want to do in life; it's rather a question of priorities! In my case, my work includes many other roles in and out of the classroom, and I have many obligations outside of work.' (USA)

7 'My speciality is literature, therefore I write a paper by reading written texts from a literary and philosophical point of view, though occasionally I write a paper on how to teach literature in Japanese education.' (Japan)

8 'I started with BA Law in France, Philosophy in South Africa, then I went to France and studied French and Linguistics at Master's and then I did another Master's in literature in translation and then went into Modern Literature ... modern languages, more sort of learning language and research based ... I mean the research I do myself is more sort of literature based, reading texts.' (Turkey)

Figure 5.6   Teacher identity and engagement in research

part of my identity as a university professor. Without these activities, I would merely be a fake' (Japan), but identity was more commonly invoked in the context of teachers explaining their lack of engagement in research. For example, a number of language teachers around the world – often those working in university language centres – were originally trained as specialists in fields such as literary studies, translation studies, linguistics, media studies, and cultural studies. (In a study I completed recently with college English teachers in China – Borg & Liu, forthcoming – only 26% of 611 respondents said they specialized in foreign language education, compared to, for example, 36% in applied linguistics, 19.3% in linguistics and 15.2% in literature.) Feedback from teachers not specialized in language teaching suggests that they may experience tensions between their job as a language teacher and their primary interests outside this field (in Figure 5.4, for example, the teacher in the identity example talks about feeling 'misplaced in ESL'). And this tension may be particularly felt in relation to research, where these teachers have low motivation to examine language teaching matters and are more disposed to focus on their specialist areas of expertise, such as analyzing literary texts or doing linguistic research.

This was not the only dimension of identity that is relevant here to understanding teachers' lack of engagement in research. The teacher in example 1 in Figure 5.6 sees research as an exclusive activity engaged in by those 'at the top of the game'. He thus associates doing research with a particular higher-status identity that he feels does not apply to him – and by definition to most language teachers (though as we have seen in this chapter, many teachers do not necessarily share these views about the exclusivity of engagement in research). Example 2 reflects a similar stance, by associating engagement in research with university professors, who are also portrayed here as having higher status; in contrast, this teacher feels marginalized by her identity as 'only' a high school teacher. Finally, we also see here references to identities outside of work; in example 4, the respondent sees her identity as a mother of young children as a powerful shaping force on the professional activities she can engage in, and this means that doing research is not an option; example 6 similarly refers to roles and obligations outside the classroom and which limit engagement in research. These latter two examples should not be interpreted as teachers making excuses for not doing research; they reflect the priorities which individuals set for themselves in life, priorities which in turn are determined by the professional and personal identities which language teachers assume (or are bestowed with). Language teacher identity – which is an increasingly important focus of research in our field (Miller, 2009; Tsui, 2011) – is thus a concept which can help us understand the different ways in which teachers respond to the idea of doing research; for those whose current or prospective identity sees them contributing to knowledge of the field and publishing, for example, or for those who see language teaching as a deep professional commitment, the response will be very different to those who see language teaching as a transient job or a travel opportunity. Of course, identities are themselves socially, culturally, and politically constructed (Varghese at al., 2005); thus teachers' attitudes to research – e.g. the extent to which they see it as a desirable and feasible activity – will be shaped by the broader social, cultural, political, and often economic structures which characterize both the current environments teachers work in and those which have defined their experiences as teachers over the course of their career. I will focus on teachers' perceptions of their working environments in Chapter 7, but it is clear that examining teacher identity in relation to language teachers' attitudes to research has exciting research potential. For example, from an identity perspective one might argue that by claiming to do research teachers are striving for legitimacy – i.e. to be recognized as professionals. Marginalization is also an important theme in teacher identity research (e.g. Pennington, 1992) and is relevant to exploring how language teachers feel about research; for example, might collaborative teacher research be seen as a way of countering language teachers' feelings of marginalization, where these exist? The teacher researchers in Davies, Hamilton & James (2007), for example, talked positively about how engagement in research raised their profile within their own organizations and externally, giving them an authoritative voice and boosting their sense of status. The case of language teachers who see their expertise and interests as lying in fields such as literature and linguistics also presents interesting research possibilities from a teacher identity perspective. The tension between established teacher identities and emergent teacher-researcher identities is also another area for further research. In their account of a teacher research project, for example, Gewirtz et al. (2009) describe the significant efforts made by teachers to develop identities as researchers 'in a context where nearly everything else presents obstacles to their emergence' (p. 576). They conclude that 'the time pressures faced by the teacher researchers mean that it is hard for them to carve out a researcher identity as part of their teacher identity without very substantial interventions and supports' (p. 580). Rethinking what it means to be a teacher and extending established notions of teacher role to create space for a teacher-researcher identity was seen in this study to be a basic condition for productive engagement by teachers in research.

5.7 Conclusion

This chapter has examined a range of issues relevant to language teachers' engagement in research. Just under 50% of over 1,300 teachers from around the world said they did research at least sometimes, though further analysis suggested that caution is required in interpreting this finding, given the variable meanings teachers assign both to 'sometimes' and to 'research'. In relation to the latter, a key finding to emerge here is the predominantly private, reflective, pedagogical, evaluative, informal, and internal focus of the kinds of research teachers said they do. This contrasts with the more formal and scientific notions of research which were predominant when teachers' conceptions of research were examined in Chapter 3. Here, too, teachers' reasons for doing research were defined primarily by professional and pedagogical concerns rather than (consciously at least) instrumental drivers such as status. The impacts of their research that teachers cited were additionally also strongly pedagogical in nature. In terms of reasons for not doing research, a lack of time was (predictably) the main explanation teachers cited; what many teachers saw as unsupportive working conditions were also influential in limiting their engagement in research (particularly in cases where teachers worked part-time and/or on hourly paid contracts). Identity-related issues were also a particularly interesting perspective to emerge here and one which, as discussed above, provides a valuable theoretical perspective (or set of perspectives, given the different ways that teacher identity can be conceptualized) for a continued and deeper understanding of the extent that teachers see engagement in research as a legitimate and feasible part of their professional role. On the basis of the findings reported in this chapter, my general conclusion would be that many language teachers do not recognize the legitimacy of such a role; others do, but do not find the notion a feasible one; while many who see their role as teacher researchers as both legitimate and feasible, limit their inquiries to reflective practices that lack the systematicity and public dimension which are core characteristics of research. I will explore the practical implications of this conclusion in Chapter 9.

References

Bai, L., & Hudson, P. (2011). Understanding Chinese TEFL academics' capacity for research. *Journal of Further and Higher Education, 35*(3), 391–407.

Borg, S., & Liu, Y. (forthcoming) Chinese College English teachers' research engagement. *TESOL Quarterly.*

Brown, J. D., Knowles, M., Murray, D., Neu, J., & Violand-Sanchez, E. (1992). *The place of research within the TESOL organization*. Alexandria, VA: TESOL.

Davies, P., Hamilton, M., & James, K. (2007). *Practitioners leading research*. London: NRDC.

Duckworth, E. (1986). Teaching as research. *Harvard Educational Review, 56*(4), 481–495.

Gao, X., Barkhuizen, G., & Chow, A. W. K. (2011). 'Nowadays teachers are relatively obedient': Understanding primary school English teachers' conceptions of and drives for research in China. *Language Teaching Research, 15*(1), 61–81.

Gewirtz, S., Shapiro, J., Maguire, M., Mahony, P., & Cribb, A. (2009). Doing teacher research: A qualitative analysis of purposes, processes and experiences. *Educational Action Research, 17*(4), 567–583.

McNamara, O. (2002). Evidence-based practice through practice-based evidence. In O. McNamara (Ed.), *Becoming an evidence-based practitioner* (pp. 15–26). London: Routledge Falmer.

Meyers, E., & Rust, F. (Eds.). (2003). *Taking action with teacher research*. Portsmouth, NH: Heinemann.

Miller, J. (2009). Teacher identity. In A. Burns & J. C. Richards (Eds.), *The Cambridge guide to second language teacher education* (pp. 172–181). Cambridge: Cambridge University Press.

Noffke, S. E. (1997). Professional, personal, and political dimensions of action research. *Review of Research in Education, 22*, 305–343.

OECD (2009). Creating effective teaching and learning environments: First results from TALIS. Retrieved 9 February, 2012, from www.oecd.org/dataoecd/17/51/43023606.pdf

Pennington, M. C. (1992). Second class or economy? The status of the English language teaching profession in tertiary education. *Prospect, 7*(3), 7–19.

Rainey, I. (2000). Action research and the English as a foreign language practitioner: Time to take stock. *Educational Action Research, 8*(1), 65–91.

Sharp, C., Eames, A., Sanders, D., & Tomlinson, K. (2005). *Postcards from research-engaged schools*. Slough: NFER.

Tsui, A. B. M. (2011). Teacher education and development. In E. Hinkel (Ed.), *Handbook of research in second language teaching and learning* (pp. 21–39). London: Routledge.

Varghese, M., Morgan, B., Johnston, B., & Johnson, K. A. (2005). Theorizing language teacher identity: Three perspectives and beyond. *Journal of Language, Identity & Education, 4*(1), 21–44.

6 Research engagement and teaching quality

6.1 Introduction

The previous two chapters focused on teacher engagement in reading and doing research respectively. This chapter looks more holistically at the relationship between these forms of research engagement and the quality of teachers' classroom practices. In examining this relationship I draw on data from the language teaching managers in my programme of research (Studies 2 and 3) as well as the perspectives of teachers (in Study 3). The previous two chapters have, of course, already provided numerous insights into the benefits which teachers feel research engagement does or can have, and before proceeding here I will provide a summary of the key points already made in this respect.

In relation to reading research, it was noted earlier that claims about any direct and immediate impact on what teachers do were likely to be simplistic and exaggerated. Published research may provide ideas and guidelines for teachers to explore, but the very nature of such externally generated research knowledge means that its impact will necessarily be mediated by the teacher. A range of factors which shaped this process of mediation (i.e. issues teachers attended to in making decisions about whether to base practice on research) were highlighted in Chapter 4. I also reported earlier that almost 88% of the 939 teachers who said they read research reported that it had at least a moderate influence on their teaching. What this means in practice is likely to vary significantly across individual teachers; and because many teachers see reading practical teaching articles as reading research, these figures do need to be interpreted very conservatively. In terms of available empirical evidence of the impact of reading research on teachers, little exists. Some of this (Zeuli, 1994) suggests that teachers do not really engage critically with the research they read (thus limiting any productive impact it might have); there is also evidence of ways in which teachers' personal dispositions can lead to biased interpretations of what they read (Bevan, 2004). In contrast, one study (Rankin & Becker, 2006) does illustrate how, with appropriate support and space for reflection, engagement with research can support the development of teachers' understandings and practices.

In terms of doing research, Chapter 5 reported that just under half of 1,349 teachers said they did research at least sometimes and that the primary reasons they gave for doing so were professional and pedagogical – they saw it as a strategy for enhancing the quality of their work and of their students' learning. In one of my studies (Study 3), over 91% of the teachers who said they did research believed it had impacted on their work or that of their colleagues, and a range of benefits associated with doing research were reported (see Table 5.3); these included learning new teaching techniques, sharing ideas with colleagues, improved teaching, and a greater awareness of teaching and students. Overall, these findings lend support to claims in the literature (see Chapter 1) about the potential benefits to teachers of doing research. Caution, as previously stressed, is required, however, in interpreting the claims teachers make about the positive impact of doing research, given the varying ways in which they define research and the manner in which it is often equated with private reflection.

6.2 Teacher perspectives on research engagement and teaching quality

I will now move on to consider further sets of data which shed light on the relationship between research engagement and classroom practice. Here research engagement is considered broadly rather than with specific reference to reading and doing research as in previous chapters. In Study 3, 100 teachers were asked to express their views on the following questionnaire statement: 'Teachers who read and do research also teach more effectively in the classroom.' Their responses are summarized in Figure 6.1 and this shows that a clear majority (72%) agreed or agreed strongly with the statement. The percentage of 'unsure' answers here (22%) suggests that the relationship between research engagement and teaching quality is an issue on which teachers may often have undefined views. This is not surprising if we accept that explicit discussions of what research is and of its relevance to teaching are rarely part of pre- and in-service language teacher education.

Respondents were also asked to explain their answer; 89% of them did this in writing and 16 of these teachers were also interviewed. I will now discuss in turn teachers' positive, uncertain, and negative views on how research engagement relates to teaching quality.

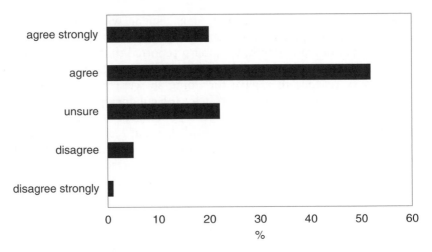

Figure 6.1   Teachers' views on whether research engagement enhances teaching effectiveness (N=100)

Positive teacher perspectives

As noted above, 72% of the 100 teachers who were asked about the impact of research engagement on teaching quality agreed that it was positive. Figure 6.2 lists the arguments teachers made in explaining this position and provides illustrative quotes for each. By far the dominant argument teachers presented in favour of research engagement was that listed first here: it allowed teachers to learn about new pedagogical strategies. The general logic behind this argument was that 'research and reading will hopefully introduce teachers to new ideas that they will try out in the classroom and contribute to their effectiveness' (Malaysia). Clearly, then, teachers conceived of the value of research engagement in immediate practical terms: reading and doing research were ways of learning about new ideas and activities which could be applied in the classroom to support more effective learning.

The remaining arguments teachers cited in explaining the positive impact of research engagement on teaching were, relative to the main theme discussed above, mentioned infrequently. Collectively, though, they do highlight a range of ways in which the processes of doing and reading research are seen to impact positively on the quality of teachers' work. In particular, research engagement was seen to promote reflection, particularly through countering the tendency for teachers to be 'running from one lesson to another and getting as many lessons done as you can in the day in a very restricted timetable

Impact	Illustrative quote
Awareness of new ideas, activities, methods and technologies	'I feel that teachers who read and do research also teach more effectively in the classroom, because they are up to date on current practice and are able to apply this in their own lessons.' (Hong Kong)
Reflective practice	'Research informs practice. It also encourages reflection, which is essential if a teacher is to develop as an effective practitioner.' (Czech Republic)
Deeper understanding of learners and context	'Teacher-researchers understand better the teaching context and the learners they teach.' (Colombia)
More informed decision making	'You are more aware of possibilities and their results and can make better decisions in a particular situation.' (Hong Kong)
Testing of intuitive understandings	'Research allows teachers to ... test approaches/ understanding that may be intuitive in a systematic way.' (Hong Kong)
More confidence	'They feel more confident about trying new techniques.' (Bahrain)
Enhanced knowledge	'The more you know the more efficient you become as a teacher.' (Egypt)
Reduces complacency	'I think reading and doing research mean that people are not complacent – they are interested in new ideas and challenges.' (Colombia)
Sustained teacher and learner interest	'Development and change is essential to challenge students and keep the teacher interested in what they are doing.' (Kuwait)
Awareness of and confidence in rationale	'They tend to have a deeper awareness of the rationale behind what they are doing and more confidence in it.' (Hong Kong)

Figure 6.2   Positive teacher perspectives on the impact of research engagement on teaching quality

without really having the time to sit back and think what am I doing?' (Italy). The point was also made, though, that reflection stimulated by research engagement might not always translate directly into observable changes in the classroom; as one teacher put it, research

... helps me to think about things and be reflective in a way that I wouldn't otherwise, but whether that translates directly into what I do particularly on a day to day basis in the classroom, I'm not really that sure about it. (Singapore)

The potential of research engagement to energize teachers and to push them to examine their beliefs were also themes highlighted by teachers. In relation to the latter, a teacher explained their position as follows:

> ... you know teachers who've been 10–15 years teaching, I think you know you can get in a bit of a rut and I think reading is a great way to kick start things and get you thinking and try things out and it definitely keeps life interesting ... it challenges maybe your accepted beliefs about things to a certain extent and because you go into the classroom and you've read these things connections appear immediately. (Hungary)

Uncertain teacher perspectives

The teachers who said they were unsure about whether research engagement had a positive impact on teaching raised a number of issues to explain their position. One recurrent argument was that being an effective teacher requires much more than research knowledge. One teacher argued, for example, that 'research is only one aspect of being an effective teacher and I doubt it's one of the most important' (Thailand). Teachers repeatedly noted that a knowledge of theory (which respondents saw as a product of reading or doing research) did not necessarily translate into improved practice. Thus a teacher noted that 'some teachers might be very involved in theory but find it difficult to put into practice' (Jordan), while another explained that 'teachers may receive knowledge ... but it doesn't necessarily increase awareness of practice in the classroom' (Bahrain). Teachers also cited personal experience of colleagues to support the view that research knowledge did not correlate with good quality teaching:

> I know a teacher ... and this person is not qualified to teach English as a foreign language yet she has done lots and lots of reading ... she's done lots of reading and she's actually very articulate about theories, but I was in a position to observe her teaching and she just doesn't have basic skills of our field. I think in my opinion, no matter how many theories you can spout, if you don't have some basic skills for one thing then you're not going to be a particularly good teacher. (Taiwan)

Without dismissing the relevance of research to teachers, other respondents argued that, to benefit from research knowledge, teachers require the skills to connect such knowledge to the classroom:

> An awareness of research is definitely enriching for developing teachers, but whether this makes them more effective in the classroom also depends on the ability to think critically about the issues involved and to

supplement this reflection with the 'lessons' learned from practical class-room experience. (Singapore)

The extent to which research engagement could impact positively on teachers' work thus was seen to depend on whether teachers 'are sufficiently skilled/insightful to put theory into practice' (Czech Republic). Such arguments about the application to practice of research knowledge see research engagement as an activity which is wholly external to teaching rather than at least partly integrated with it. This is a fundamental misconception which underlies many of the adverse arguments presented in this chapter about the value of teacher engagement with and in research.

In explaining their uncertainty about the value of research engage-ment to teachers, some respondents also claimed that 'many teachers are very effective despite a lack of research credentials' (Bahrain). Research engagement, or at least 'research credentials' (conceivably higher-level academic qualifications) – it was often suggested here, may not even be necessary for good quality teaching. These are legitimate arguments and it was not my intention in asking about the relationship between research engagement and teaching quality to imply that such engagement was an essential or primary criterion for effective classroom practice. Teachers' responses to my prompts, though, with their focus on research generated outside the classroom, do reveal conceptions of research which are not conducive to the goal of making research engagement a more central part of teachers' pro-fessional activity.

Several other points were raised by teachers in explaining why they were unsure of whether teaching quality might be enhanced through research engagement. Some were concerned that research would consume too much of the teachers' time and consequently hinder effective practice, while others felt that research might, at least in the short-term, involve experimentation in class which might result in less effective practice. There were also comments which equated research with developing a detailed understanding of the target language for a lesson. One teacher noted that 'such research is usually of such depth that it becomes irrelevant in any-thing other than a very high level class' (Kuwait), while another felt that

With the amount of detail in the teacher's notes nowadays I find that read-ing those carefully beforehand and researching (there – I've used it!) the grammar (reading the grammar reference in the book and/or elsewhere) and anticipating problems makes you 'sufficiently' effective without having to do further research. (Italy)

Such perspectives remind us once again of the variable ways in which teachers interpret the term 'research' and emphasize what is emerging here as one key theme in this book – the need for teacher education programmes to dedicate some time to the task of clarifying the characteristics of those activities that can justifiably be called 'research' and distinguishing these from other forms of professional activity such as reflection and reading for lesson planning. As I have stressed already, I am not seeking to elevate research to a status superior to such activities, but to argue that it is not productive for 'research' to be used to describe every activity that involves an element of searching for information and/or reflection on practice. Such definitional looseness is at the heart of much of the confusion that exists about teacher research engagement.

Negative teacher perspectives

The handful of teachers who disagreed that research engagement enhances teaching typically justified their position with reference to the distinction between theory and practice; one teacher argued that 'research has little or nothing to do with classroom practice' (Taiwan) while others explained that teaching is a practical activity and that, while research can enhance its effectiveness, it cannot compensate for deficiencies in teachers' practical (and interpersonal) skills. Thus one teacher explained that research

> ... certainly helps a teacher know more about the choices out there and why we do certain things, but if they are not already strong in the classroom I'm not sure it can give them that. (country unspecified)

Elaborating on this argument, another teacher explained that research-engaged teachers

> ... may be better able to explain their rationale, or are more informed regarding classroom practices/tasks/skills development, etc. but to teach effectively a teacher must be able to gauge the students, interest them, motivate them, monitor their learning/progress, form relationships with them, help them form relationships with each other, generally foster an atmosphere in which the learners feel confident enough to take risks with their language use, and, which is most important, to do this, and show the learners that they are learning, it takes more than background reading and classroom research, it takes humanistic qualities such as leadership skills, empathy, social skills, group awareness, sensitivity, and the ability to build trust in the classroom. (Singapore)

The basic point being made here is, once again, that there is much more to being a teacher than theoretical knowledge. I agree. What is problematic in these arguments, though, is the way in which research engagement is equated with formal knowledge disassociated from the classroom. This is clearly not the concept of teacher research engagement I wish to advance here.

Overall, then, the 100 teachers in the study I have discussed here saw productive links between research engagement and teachers' classroom practices. In particular, the value of research engagement was seen to reside primarily in the way it allowed teachers to expand their pedagogical repertoires. In this sense, teachers posited a fairly direct link between research and teaching, though in such arguments research was equated largely with reading practical teaching material. In others cases, though, the relationship between research engagement and teaching implied in teachers' comments was a more indirect one, with research stimulating new ideas, knowledge, awareness, and understandings which in turn shaped the development of practices seen to be more effective in supporting language learning. This notion of an indirect and not necessarily immediate relationship between research engagement and classroom practice is a feasible one to entertain; in contrast, the view that teaching and learning can experience sudden and significant leaps in quality as a result of research engagement by teachers reflects a simplistic understanding both of the dynamics of the language classroom and of the process of teacher learning more generally.

Finally, before I move on to discuss further perspectives on the value of research engagement, it is important to acknowledge the points raised by teachers about the limits of the contribution of research engagement to teaching quality; clearly, the latter needs to be underpinned by a range of personal attributes, pedagogical skills, and practical and propositional knowledge, and deficiencies in the personal and practical dimensions of teachers' work cannot be simply compensated for by knowledge developed through research engagement. The role of such engagement in teachers' work, then, must be seen as facilitative, rather than a determinant of good practice. I am certainly not seeking to argue here that research engagement on its own holds the key to effective teaching. At the same time, it must be noted that teachers who were critical of the relevance of research to teaching conceived of research engagement in academic terms and displayed limited awareness of its potential to be part of teachers' ongoing professional activity.

6.3 Managers' perspectives on research engagement and teaching quality

I will now examine the perspectives held by managers on the relationship between research engagement and teaching quality. As noted in Chapter 3, there has been little international research into the roles of school leaders in promoting research engagement and none I am aware of in the field of language teaching. Managers, though, can exert a significant influence on the extent to which teachers engage in research, and an understanding of their perspectives on teacher research engagement has been an important dimension of my programme of research.

Language teaching managers' perspectives on the value of research engagement emerged through two of the studies described in Chapter 2. The first (Study 2) involved 209 directors of EFL schools in the UK, while the second (Study 3) involved a further 33 managers working for a language teaching organization with schools around the world. All managers in these studies completed a questionnaire, and a smaller subset (43 in the first study and 16 in the second) were also interviewed. The relationship between teacher research engagement and teaching was one of the themes covered in both the questionnaires and the interviews.

The 242 managers were first asked how important they felt it was for their teachers to do research. Opinions were mixed here, with 49.6% saying it was 'unimportant' or 'slightly important' and 38.2% saying it was 'important' or 'highly important'. Just over 12% had 'no opinion'. Clearly, though, the largest percentage of responses represented less positive views about the importance for teachers of engagement in research.

Managers were also asked to express their views on the same statement teachers responded to regarding whether research engagement enhanced teaching quality. As Figure 6.3 indicates, just under 54% of the managers 'agreed' or 'agreed strongly' with this statement while almost 10% 'disagreed' or 'disagreed strongly'. A significant proportion – over 34% – said they were unsure. In comparison to the way teachers responded to this same statement (see Figure 6.1), managers were significantly less positive (statistically) about the potential benefits to teaching effectiveness of research engagement by teachers (using Mann-Whitney, managers' mean for the statement = 3.56, teachers' mean=3.85, U=9516, p=.002).

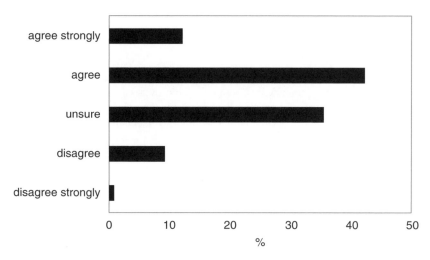

Figure 6.3   Managers' views about whether research engagement enhances teaching effectiveness (N=237)

In the questionnaire, and at more length in the interviews, managers were also asked to explain their views on the relationship between teacher research engagement and teaching quality. I will now present an analysis of these explanations, dealing in turn with arguments that were positive, uncertain, and negative.

Positive manager perspectives

In the questionnaires, managers who agreed that research engagement by teachers enhanced teaching quality cited a wide range of arguments in support of their position. Table 6.1 lists the 10 positive impacts most commonly cited by the managers, in descending order of frequency. An illustrative quote is also provided for each form of impact.

Table 6.1   Positive manager perspectives on the impact of research engagement on teaching quality (N=129)

Impacts of research engagement	N	Illustrative quote
Keeps teachers fresh	21	'In order to keep one's teaching fresh and innovative, reading about different approaches and conducting research within the class or school can radically improve one's teaching.' (UK)

(Continued)

Table 6.1   (Continued)

Impacts of research engagement	N	Illustrative quote
Promotes reflective practice	16	'Classroom research provides an additional level of self reflection which can only be positive in enhancing teaching skills.' (Thailand)
Enhances awareness of teaching and learning	13	'Based on my experience I feel it is usually likely that any practical investigation of teaching practice/methodology will result in an increased awareness and better application of teaching skills in the classroom.' (UK)
Provides new ideas and practical techniques	12	'I feel that researching new methods enhances the effectiveness in the classroom. It demonstrates new ways of doing things and allows the teacher to develop.' (UK)
Motivates teachers	7	'In my experience teachers who have some involvement (however limited) in research are likely to be more motivated and committed to CPD.' (UK)
Sustains teacher interest in their work	6	'It's very important to do your own research as a) you learn, and b) it keeps the job interesting.' (UK)
Deepens teachers' knowledge	5	'Better Knowledge = better expertise. Knowledge is power inside and outside the ELT classroom.' (UK)
Promotes more informed teaching	5	'They [research-engaged teachers] are more likely to teach more effectively because they are better informed, more reflective and more inquiring.' (UK)
Promotes self-evaluation of teaching	5	'Research provides teachers with an opportunity to reflect and evaluate their practice and question some of the received wisdom in language teaching.' (UK)
Encourages experimentation in the classroom	4	'This [research engagement] encourages an experimental approach which rejuvenates their planning / decision making and presence in the classroom.' (Bahrain)

While not direct evidence of good quality classroom practice, the issues highlighted here were considered by managers to be significant in improving the quality of teachers' work. Thus, for example, there was a common view that keeping up-to-date with current ideas in the field would improve teaching effectiveness; similarly, being a reflective practitioner, or maintaining motivation and interest in teaching, were also seen to contribute to the improvement of teachers' work. There is further evidence in the list of issues highlighted that managers' notions of research engagement were typically associated with reflective, practically oriented, classroom-based explorations of teaching and learning. In many cases the managers cited a series of interacting factors in explaining the positive impact of research engagement (i.e. they did not see the relationship between teaching and reading and/or doing research in simple linear terms). For example, one manager explained their beliefs in the value of research engagement as follows:

> I feel strongly about the value of research because I feel that too many EFL teachers ... rely on their initial training (CELTA) and then DELTA to inform their decision making and do not question any of the assumptions about language learning/teaching that they were exposed to during those teacher training courses. This leads to a rather tired delivery of 'the tricks of the trade'. However when they do hear about / read about / get involved in some research they get into the critical and analytical thinking it requires and find it motivating. This then encourages an experimental approach which rejuvenates their planning / decision making and presence in the classroom. (Bahrain)

Teacher research engagement is thus seen here to counter the tendency to accept received wisdom and to promote a more critical perspective on language teaching. This in turn stimulates motivation in teachers, which encourages them to experiment in the classroom and thus to 'rejuvenate' their teaching and indeed their 'presence' in the classroom. It is easy – but also facile – to argue for teacher research engagement by linking it directly to singular benefits for teachers; it is important, though, to recognize the more complex array of interactions which teacher research engagement can stimulate in teachers and which can dynamically combine to support growth in their professional development and their practices.

Returning to Table 6.1, keeping teachers fresh was the benefit of research engagement most commonly noted by managers; references to avoiding 'ruts' were particularly salient:

> ... there's that idea of sort of wide research and I think you know, without being encouraged to do that, it's easy to sort of get into ruts ... to know what type of things work with certain groups and just to get into a routine. (Jordan)

> ... it's very easy to trot along ... you know to get sort of almost in a rut ... you know doing the same thing day in day out ... secure ... you know not pushing your boundaries at all ... just staying in your comfort zone ...

And it's very easy to get into that way when you're teaching and I think if you're doing any research then that constantly keeps you thinking about what you're doing in class. (UK)

... the teachers who are excited and engaged with these questions just are more excited as teachers than those who aren't asking questions, and who aren't engaging with the profession more broadly ... they're looking for change, they don't get into ruts ... they think about new ideas more, they're the ones that are more open to what's happening in the field, and the ones who don't do that are just ... just often play safe and do what they're familiar with. (UK)

Also recurrent in managers' comments on the value of research engagement was its contribution to promoting reflective practice and classroom experimentation:

... the teacher is actually thinking about what they're doing ... or reflecting on what they're doing, looking at outcomes, and then changing their behaviour as a result of whatever they've discovered as a result of the process. (UK)

... from observation, the teachers which seem to be more effective, more self-aware and more aware of what's actually happening in terms of the dynamics with the students, it's those teachers who are trying and testing things in the classroom and doing it more systematically. (Taiwan)

In some cases the potential of research engagement for promoting reflection of this kind was seen to be more important than the actual findings of any research the teachers did:

... obviously there's the practical side of it ... sometimes it comes up with some good ideas, some good theories and you know some new practical applications but it's really the keeping people reflective I think more than anything that's so valuable. (UK)

It is clear from managers' comments on the value of teacher research engagement that they saw it as a powerful professional development strategy, at individual and group levels, rather than an exercise focused primarily on generating robust findings. In fact, most references to 'new ideas' in the data cited so far refer to ideas derived from engagement with research (or, more commonly perhaps, with practical teaching literature) than to the findings of teachers' own investigations.

Enhanced teacher motivation, as noted above and in Table 6.1, was also seen by managers to be a benefit of research engagement. In addition to the benefits for individual teachers, though, managers also talked about the positive impact on staff motivation generally which an interest in research by a small number of teachers can have:

> ... the motivation that it generates, certainly ... the change in the staffroom atmosphere when projects are ... are going on, which involve research ... for example, a couple of teachers have just trialled an online platform to support students, so their students ... had an online access to things like their homework and course plans and things like that. A few teachers worked on it as research to see what the effect was on learning and student motivation, but all the other teachers in the school wanted to get on board, there was a lot of discussion about it, general interest in how the project was going ... so it kind of drives ... drives the teaching centre forwards. (Thailand)

> I suppose it's the motivation of the teachers to continue learning, therefore it's they're continuing to learn and they're likely, in my opinion, I think they're likely to be a more inspiring teacher, you know, inspiring their students as well and also in the staffroom with their colleagues if the interest is still there, hopefully they're generating enthusiasm around them. (UK)

> I've got a couple of members of staff who are doing Master's Degrees and again it's really a tool to keeping them fresh ... keeping them open to new ideas and then by extension showing ideas and talking to other members of staff. Maybe not actually doing it themselves but you know still it kind of like generates a positive feel about it. (UK)

Overall, then, what emerges from the perspectives of the managers who see positive connections between teacher research engagement and teaching quality is a process-oriented, practical, and professional development focused conception of research engagement. This group of managers assigns value to activities through which teachers become familiar and experiment with new practical ideas in the classroom, and through which teachers are encouraged to examine, question, and become more aware of their own practices; such activities, which some managers described as having a level of formality and systematicity that goes beyond routine practice, are seen to have a positive impact on teaching quality because they motivate teachers, individually and collectively, and sustain their interest and enthusiasm.

Uncertain manager perspectives

As noted earlier, a significant proportion (over 34%) of the managers who completed the questionnaire said they were not sure whether teacher research engagement enhanced teaching quality. In this section

I will examine the reasons for their position, drawing also on a set of 20 interviews.

Table 6.2 summarizes the most common issues raised by this group of managers in their questionnaire responses. In some cases, managers were uncertain simply because they had never worked with teachers who were research engaged (see the quote in the table). In several other cases, managers' comments seemed to be a response to the implication – wholly unintended – that research engagement could on its own lead to high-quality teaching. Thus we see the most common argument here being that individuals in possession of good research skills are not necessarily skilled teachers. In questionnaire responses, several managers went so far as to suggest that, in their experience, teachers interested in research were *less* effective as practitioners:

> Sometimes the theorists who enjoy the research aspect are not the greatest practitioners and can be more interested in their research than in their relations with the students. (Hungary)

Table 6.2   Managers' uncertainties about the effect of research engagement on teaching quality

Reasons for uncertainty	N	Illustrative quote
Being a good researcher does not imply being a good teacher	11	'Lots of people I know who read and research are completely out of touch with students' needs, interests.' (UK)
Teaching effectiveness is due to various factors and skills which cannot be obtained through research	10	'There's no substitute for experience. Personality is an important factor too – this can't be gained from research.' (Poland)
Limited evidence of working with teachers who do research	5	'I have known few teachers who do research, certainly very few indeed who would admit to having the time to do any.' (Qatar)
It is possible to be an excellent teacher without being research engaged	4	'Researching and teaching are very different skills and some excellent teachers may not be inclined towards research.' (UK)
Other ways of improving teaching quality exist which are more powerful than research engagement	4	'Most productive learning comes from sharing experiences with other colleagues.' (UK)

... there are also those teachers who are interested in research but do not have the presence/charisma to teach effectively in a classroom or those who are unable to translate what is written on a page into practice. (UK)

Those teachers who carry out research are sometimes more interested in the academic rather than the practical side of teaching. (UK)

Such views were evident in interview comments as well:

... my experience here and for a lot of years in other schools like this has been that I don't think there is necessarily any connection. I've sat and done an MA myself and some of the people who were very good at doing research, or did very well on it, didn't necessarily make or wouldn't sort of have necessarily made good teachers. And certainly the best teachers here in terms of the feedback we get are not necessarily the most highly qualified. (UK)

This latter point – that effective teachers were often not research engaged – was reiterated, sometimes with frustration, by other managers:

We have a couple of teachers here who are fantastically good teachers, very inspirational, really get the students onside. The students come out having learnt something and also very happy with their experience. Now, these teachers I know are the last, last, last people who would ever open a journal or a book ... Because I think it's their own belief that actually they don't need this kind of research, this is not valuable for them to be able to teach well and I think they're kind of proving it day to day because they are, I mean, you know, they might not be able to tell me who wrote this about that or, you know, what the latest kind of pronunciation theory is but they can go in and they can, you know, in a classroom situation, they can deliver a really, really good lesson. (UK)

Even where managers disagreed with the above arguments, they found it difficult to argue with the fact that successful teachers were often ones who showed no interest in reading and/or doing research:

They're often teachers who even without being necessarily aware of it have developed a particular teaching style that really works. They're confident in what they know, the students trust them, they give the students lots and lots of practice and lots and lots of examples and it works fine, and they don't see any need to read and that attitude annoys me, but it's hard to argue against it. (UK)

In explaining their uncertainties about the value of research engagement, managers were also concerned that teachers' interest in research could distract them from a focus on providing quality teaching. Thus one manager felt that 'teachers could become more theoretically minded and teach for research rather than to their students' needs' (UK) while another added that 'teachers can become so involved in their own research project that they may try to tailor their teaching to the project rather than to the need of the students or of the course' (UK). In one case, a manager explained how his own involvement in research had had negative consequences for his teaching:

> ... it increases general awareness and perhaps knowledge and understanding of classroom problems and learning styles but I felt that some people got so wrapped up in it that it was, I wouldn't say a waste of time 'cause it never is a waste of time but the students were a bit like guinea pigs and I found myself getting all wrapped up in the theory of it and perhaps not the practicalities. (UK)

As Table 6.2 also shows, a common argument raised by managers uncertain about the impact of research engagement on teaching quality was one that teachers also raised – namely that being a good teacher depended on a range of attitudes, traits, and skills which cannot be developed through reading or doing research. Again, this argument seems to respond to the perceived implication that research engagement is the sole requirement for effective teaching. That was in no way suggested to the managers; rather, what I wanted to elicit were their views on whether research engagement could enhance the quality of teachers' work. Managers thus argued that teaching and research are different skills, and that traits such as commitment, personality, experience, rapport, sensitivity, awareness, and an interest in students cannot be obtained through research. As one manager pithily noted, 'rapport with students cannot be learned from books' (UK). The argument that effective teaching needs to be informed by practical knowledge derived experientially also resurfaced in the interviews:

> ... good teachers will adapt what they do in any case to the needs of the learners they've got in front of them and to the resources that they've got available because of course not all ESOL teachers teach in a nice, neat classroom with desks and lots of resources. They may be out in a community centre or sitting at the back of an Indian restaurant or whatever and they adapt what they have to do to the circumstances and I don't think they need research to tell them that. That comes through experience. (UK)

In themselves, these are not arguments against research engagement when this is viewed as an additional facet of teachers' ongoing professional learning. They are, however, strong arguments against conceptualizations of effective teaching which inflate the importance of propositional knowledge whilse downplaying the value for teachers of personal and interpersonal skills and of experiential learning.

Several interviewees also reiterated the view that research engagement was just one form – and not necessarily an especially effective one – of teacher development:

> I don't think it's the reading that's the issue, I think reflection and learning is the issue and these are all internal processes that we can promote in a number of different ways, one of which is reading. It could be chatting with colleagues. It could be peer observation ... I think there are lots of things that we need to think about that contribute towards learning which is not reading or attending formal sessions. (Hong Kong)

I fully agree that in professional learning contexts where research engagement is being promoted this should not occur at the expense of alternative strategies for teacher growth. In their responses, managers suggested a number of these, such as peer observation, reflective practice, sharing experience and exchanging ideas, and I would join them in advocating the value of such strategies in supporting teacher development.

There were several other arguments raised by managers who were unsure about whether research engagement could support teaching quality. One was that the value of research engagement depended on the teacher, specifically on their years of experience:

> Most of my teachers are relatively inexperienced and are more in need of basic teaching ideas than starting research of their own. I can see value in classroom research for very experienced teachers. (Egypt)

Others argued that the value of research engagement for teachers depended on the type of research. In this case a manager is contrasting the relative value of 'academic' and action research:

> Reading and 'doing research' as academic activities do not link directly with more effective teaching, but an effective teacher is someone who seeks to evaluate and develop their practice in relation to different learning groups and is an active action researcher. (UK)

The focus of the teachers' research activities was also seen to be a relevant consideration here:

> If the subject is related to what they are doing in class and has been a study of learner problems, cultural perspectives, error analysis, ways of looking how to develop the skills then there can be positive research done but if a teacher is researching in an unrelated area the academic side of their study can dominate their work time and teaching can suffer. (UK)

In many cases, managers' concerns about the relevance of research to teachers were based on unstated assumptions about the academic nature of research; in some cases these misconceptions were articulated very explicitly:

> I am quite unsure about that. I know that what I was thinking of at the time was the next academic level of my studies, which would be the MA, I know there's a lot of statistical research involved and I think you study statistics a little bit and I doubt the value of that to be honest. (UK)

Understandably, if managers see research as being about statistics, it is not an activity they will feel is of much practical value to their teachers.

Overall, the arguments raised by managers who were unsure about the relationship of research engagement to teaching quality highlight a concern for ensuring that the focus of teachers' work and their development remains on the core skills and attributes required for effective classroom practice. Among this group of respondents, there was no hostility to research engagement, rather doubts, often based on experience and on misconceptions, about the feasibility of enabling teachers to be research engaged and of the connections of reading and doing research to teachers' everyday practices. Managers were often torn between, on the one hand, a belief in the theoretical value of research engagement for teachers, and, on the other, leadership experience which suggests that teachers (often successful ones) are frequently ambivalent about reading and doing research.

Negative manager perspectives

A small proportion (under 10%) of the 242 managers under discussion here disagreed that teacher research engagement enhanced teaching quality. I will now examine the arguments presented by these respondents, also drawing on interviews with eight managers (see Figure 6.4). Most of these arguments were highlighted in the previous section; here they are made more forcefully and, often, with an additional dose of cynicism in relation to research engagement by teachers.

Thus we note here, once again, claims by managers that in their experience more qualified or academic practitioners are often also those who are less effective in the classroom; also recurring here is the argument that the qualities that make teachers effective are personal, interpersonal, and experiential rather than based on theoretical knowledge derived from reading or doing research. Additionally,

Reason for disagreeing	Illustrative quote
A focus on research can impair the quality of teaching	'I have seen a number of instances where teachers fired up with a bit of classroom research (particularly post DELTA level) lose the plot with regard to the learners' needs and why they have enrolled for a particular course.' (Colombia)
Teaching quality is not defined by research engagement	'I feel there are many more factors, to do with the student, the course, the environment and the teacher, which influence teaching/learning success, much more than knowledge/insight gained from research.' (UK)
Many research-oriented individuals are not effective teachers	'In my experience over 28 years, I have met many teachers. The best ones are seldom the ones with the greatest number of qualifications and the most research. I have met MAs who have been useless in the classroom, and people with 'A' levels who have been fantastic.' (UK)
Theoretical knowledge does not necessarily transfer into effective practice	'Acquiring more knowledge does not necessarily translate into "more effective" teaching. It simply means that teachers have more knowledge.' (UK)
The quality of much research in ELT makes it an unreliable basis for classroom practice	'Much of the research I come across, although thought provoking, seems to be based on some fairly poor science and could be described as quasi-scientific at best, yet people in this field seem happier to draw strong conclusions from subjective experience than in other fields of study.' (UK)

Figure 6.4   Managers' reasons for disagreeing that research engagement enhances teaching quality

some managers explained that a focus on research could actually lead to a *loss* in teaching quality, as teachers may lose sight of the learners and their learning.

Interviews with this group of managers confirmed these kinds of views; many had experience which had led them to see a negative correlation between research engagement and teaching quality:

I have at least two experiences in my career where actually a teacher, particularly one involved in doing an MA ... ended up having terrible classroom problems because the research was actually taking over the syllabus. (Colombia)

I've been recruiting teachers for 20 years ... and I think the only correlation, one might say, between sort of people who love research and practical teachers in the classroom it's sometimes the people who love research in good faith sometimes don't make the best teachers. (UK)

... in my experience, people who are heavily into reading research material, and have, well, higher qualifications like doctorates, they ... they often don't ... don't do terribly well with ... with the students. (UK)

It is important to stress, though, that the notion research managers were basing these views on was a formal one associated with academic postgraduate qualifications. It was in fact such a conception of research that underpinned many of the negative comments about the value of research engagement that managers made.

6.4 Conclusion

This chapter has examined the relationship between research engagement and teaching quality as conceptualized by teachers and managers in the field of language teaching. It has presented a range of positive, hesitant, and negative perspectives on the extent to which research engagement by teachers can enhance the quality of their classroom practice. While the levels of antagonism regarding research engagement were low in both teachers and managers, the former were more forthright about its potential value in improving teaching quality; managers, in contrast, displayed a more significant degree of uncertainty – and in some cases cynicism – about the benefits of research engagement to teachers' work.

A number of key themes can be distilled from the analysis presented in this chapter and which take forward the narrative unfolding in this book. First, the conceptions of research, tacit or explicit, in teachers' and managers' comments fell into two categories; the more practically oriented responses saw as research a wide range of activities including reading practical teaching magazines, experimenting with new teaching activities, thinking about teaching, self-evaluation, reading language reference books, and studying the teachers' notes that came with coursebooks; the more formally oriented responses saw research as academic, statistical, theoretical, associated with study for higher qualifications, and detached from the core concerns of the classroom. Neither of these positions is satisfactory in promoting a view of research engagement which both supports teacher development and has value which goes beyond its relevance to individual teachers. The formal notions of research are restrictive and lacking in relevance to the practice of teaching; the practical notions are very relevant to teachers' work but – given that they are typically not examples of 'systematic inquiry made public' (Stenhouse, 1975: 142) – are better described as professional (development) activities. Typically, no evidence is made available of the procedures that teachers follow in activities such as personal reading, lesson planning, and private reflection and thus it is not possible to assess the confidence with which any findings derived from such activities provide the basis for action. A concern with the quality of the evidence generated by the activities teachers and managers saw as research was in fact not at all evident here. As noted by some managers, the value of research engagement for teachers may thus be seen largely in its ability to keep teachers fresh and motivated than for the value of any results which teachers generate.

This chapter also provides further evidence that reactions to the notion of research engagement are rooted in the conceptions of – and misconceptions about – research held by professionals in our field. Arguments for the value of research engagement in enhancing teaching quality were typically linked to notions of classroom-based and pedagogically oriented inquiry having goals which were predominantly practical (e.g. extending one's repertoire of teaching techniques). In contrast, less positive views about the value of research engagement often invoked more academic and formal notions of research and stressed the gap between theory and practice in language teaching; this was particularly the case in the views of managers, who, as a group, may have had more first-hand experience of higher academic study (e.g. via MA degrees) than many of their teachers. It was clear that in some cases it was actually managers' own negative experiences of academic research which had shaped their views about the value of research engagement for their staff. One implication here, then, is that managers – given that they can often influence the extent to which teachers are encouraged to be research engaged – can benefit from opportunities to analyze and review their own beliefs about research and its contribution to professional practice and development.

A further theme here concerns understandings of the mechanisms through which research engagement impacts on teachers' work. There were suggestions that, particularly through reading, teachers can enhance their pedagogical repertoire and subject matter knowledge, thus allowing for a direct relationship between research engagement and classroom practice. However, as noted above, many respondents interpreted research very broadly to include the reading teachers do in planning lessons (e.g. reading about the present perfect) as well as the reading of practical teaching material. In the data examined here, there was very limited reference to teachers reading material which reports empirical research. Additionally, in comments implying this kind of direct and immediate relationship between reading research and classroom practice there was limited awareness of the manner in which teachers mediate external knowledge in the process of integrating it into their pedagogies. Worryingly, this position might reflect a tendency to accept and import, without critical analysis, practical teaching ideas encountered through reading.

In contrast, it was also clear that respondents recognized a less direct potential relationship between research engagement and teaching quality. Thus, research engagement was seen to stimulate processes – such as reflection or enhanced motivation and interest – which in turn were believed to lead to improvements in teachers' work. There was a sense here of a longer-term process, including periods of experimentation and potential temporary regression in teaching quality, driven by teachers' commitment to develop. Key to this notion of research engagement was the process of reflecting on one's practice – evaluating, reviewing, and learning from practical classroom experience. These are of course notions which sit comfortably with contemporary understandings of teacher learning and professional development (Darling-Hammond, 2006; Farrell, 2007; Johnson, 2009).

Claims made here about the positive collective impact on staff of research engagement by small groups of teachers are also worth highlighting once again. This suggests that initiatives that seek to foster research engagement may feasibly begin with a smaller group of committed and motivated teachers who, through their enthusiasm and example, can generate the positive atmosphere that is conducive to teacher research engagement on a wider scale. Of course, this is likely to be a more effective strategy when research engagement focuses on issues that are of general interest and relevance; if this is not the case, the motivation of a group of enthusiasts is less likely to spread to colleagues.

The final theme I will comment on here relates to the necessity or otherwise of research engagement for good quality teaching. It has not been my intention to argue that good teaching is not possible without research engagement; as many respondents pointed out, effective teaching calls for a range of personal traits, interpersonal skills and pedagogical and practical knowledge that are acquired intuitively, collegially, and experientially rather than formally, through reading and doing research. Support for the importance of the many dimensions of teaching is evident in research into the 'good' language teacher (e.g. Brosh, 1996; Brown, 2009; Mullock, 2003; Walls et al., 2002). However, the argument that teachers who have demonstrated their effectiveness in the classroom do not need to be research engaged is, I believe, suspect. First, it reflects a restricted view of what it means to be a professional (i.e. it dismisses the possibility of change or the need for improvement in favour of the unquestioned repetition of the same practices over time); second, it places excessive emphasis on the role of intuition, collegiality, and experience in teacher learning – as important as these are, their impact on teacher learning can be enriched through engagement with reading and classroom inquiry; and third, this position limits teachers' potential for growth by dismissing a valuable and accessible professional development strategy. It is by no means the only strategy available to teachers, and as respondents in this chapter argued, collegial activities such as peer observation and informal sharing of ideas are very valuable for teachers. Research engagement, though, provides teachers with an additional powerful option.

Numerous benefits of research engagement for teachers were outlined in earlier chapters of this book; teachers and managers who seem to dismiss these do not do so, I believe, largely on theoretical grounds; rather, their position is shaped first by misconceptions about what research engagement involves, and thus they may find it informative to read real examples of teacher researchers at work – e.g. Allwright & Hanks, 2009; Davies, Hamilton, & James, 2007; de Silva Joyce 2000; Meyers & Rust, 2003; Mohr, 1994; Rickinson et al., 2004; Sharp et al., 2005. Second, their negative views are influenced by their perceptions of the extent to which the environments they work in are conducive to teacher research engagement. An analysis of these perceptions provides the basis of the next chapter.

References

Allwright, D., & Hanks, J. (2009). *The developing language learner: An introduction to exploratory practice*. Basingstoke: Palgrave Macmillan.

Bevan, R. M. (2004). Filtering, fragmenting, and fiddling? Teachers' life cycles, and phases in their engagement with research. *Teacher Development*, 8(2/3), 325–339.

Brosh, H. (1996). Perceived characteristics of the effective language teacher. *Foreign Language Annals*, 29(2), 125–138.

Brown, A. V. (2009). Students' and teachers' perceptions of effective foreign language teaching: A comparison of ideals. *Modern Language Journal*, 93(1), 46–60.

Darling-Hammond, L. (2006). *Creating powerful teacher education: Lessons from excellent teacher education programs*. San Francisco: Jossey Bass.

Davies, P., Hamilton, M., & James, K. (2007). *Practitioners leading research*. London: NRDC.

de Silva Joyce , H. (Ed.). (2000). *Teachers' Voices 6: Teaching casual conversation.* Sydney, Australia: NCELTR.

Farrell, T. S. C. (2007). *Reflective language teaching: From research to practice.* London: Continuum.

Johnson, K. E. (2009). *Second language teacher education: A sociocultural perspective.* London: Routledge.

Meyers, E., & Rust, F. (Eds.). (2003). *Taking action with teacher research.* Portsmouth, NH: Heinemann.

Mohr, M. M. (1994). Teacher-researchers at work. *The English Journal, 83*(6), 19–21.

Mullock, B. (2003). What makes a good teacher? The perceptions of postgraduate TESOL students. *Prospect, 18*(3), 3–24.

Rankin, J., & Becker, F. (2006). Does reading the research make a difference? A case study of teacher growth in FL German. *Modern Language Journal, 90*(3), 353–372.

Rickinson, M., Clark, A., McLeod, S., Poulton, P., & Sargent, J. (2004). What on earth has research got to do with me? *Teacher Development, 8*(2/3), 201–220.

Sharp, C., Eames, A., Sanders, D., & Tomlinson, K. (2005). *Postcards from research-engaged schools.* Slough: NFER.

Stenhouse, L. (1975). *An introduction to curriculum research and development.* London: Heinemann.

Walls, R. T., Nardi, A. H., von Minden, A. M., & Hoffman, N. (2002). The characteristics of effective and ineffective teachers. *Teacher Education Quarterly, 29*(1), 39–48.

Zeuli, J. S. (1994). How do teachers understand research when they read it? *Teaching and Teacher Education, 10*(1), 39–55.

7 Research cultures in language teaching

7.1 Introduction

A number of issues highlighted in the previous chapters suggest that teachers' and managers' attitudes towards and practices in relation to research engagement need to be understood in the context of the environments these individuals work in. Of course, these immediate institutional environments themselves are shaped by the broader disciplinary culture of language teaching (or more specifically in this chapter, of teaching English as a foreign language). However, a detailed analysis on that scale is beyond the scope of the empirical data I will examine in this chapter and the focus here will thus be on the extent to which language teachers and managers feel that the institutions they work in are conducive to teacher research engagement. Before presenting findings relevant to this issue, below I provide a brief discussion of the notion of research cultures in educational settings.

In higher education, where research engagement is a primary activity for academics, and where research performance often has significant financial implications, (e.g. in the context of the RAE/REF exercises in the UK, see www.hefce.ac.uk/research/ref) institutions invest (admittedly to significantly differing degrees worldwide) in creating the conditions which are believed to support research excellence. Mechanisms such as study leave, a workload allocation for research time, investment in books and journals, and the provision of pump-priming research funding are examples of strategies that higher education institutions adopt to enable their staff to be research active. Additionally, career progression as an academic remains heavily influenced by one's performance as a researcher.

Schools, however, typically constitute a very different environment. As we have seen in previous chapters, teachers' and managers' concerns will be more practical in nature and effective performance is defined primarily in relation to the quality of teaching; such quality is additionally attributed to a range of personal and skill-related qualities acquired through experience and practical training rather than to theoretical knowledge derived from research. In such contexts, even where research engagement is promoted, it is likely to have a strong pedagogical orientation and to be valued, as we have seen, more for its potential to keep staff fresh and motivated, than for any broader contribution to knowledge that results from the process. These points are likely to be largely true even in language centres which are attached to universities. In fact, the situation for practitioners in such contexts may be particularly difficult because although they are officially part of a higher education institution, their status is often clearly distinct from that of academic staff (e.g. in many contexts university language teachers are called 'instructors' and not 'lecturers' and language centres are seen as 'service' departments, in the same way that, for example, IT support services are).

These differences can be explained with reference to the notion of research cultures. Culture can be defined in many ways, but from an organizational perspective a commonly cited definition is that by Schein (1985: 6): 'the deeper level of basic assumptions and beliefs that are shared by members of an organisation, that operate unconsciously, and that define in a basic "taken-for-granted" fashion, an organisation's view of itself and its environment'. In the context of schools, Halsall (1998: 29) echoes elements of the above definition by writing that culture is a 'set of assumptions, beliefs and values that predominate in an organization, and which operate in an unconscious or semi-unconscious way'.

With specific reference to educational research cultures, Ebbutt (2002: 124) has argued that 'a viable research culture in schools is fundamental to the production of useful professional knowledge' and suggests that research cultures can be described 'as a series of developmental stages along an evolutionary path' (p. 138). The stages he defines along this path are that a research culture in a school is non-existent, emergent, established and, at its most advanced stage, established-embedded. In an established research culture, for example, research is widely recognized as an unquestioned and important element in school improvement. In contrast, in schools with an emergent research culture there is a recently developed awareness of the positive contribution to teacher and school improvement that research can make, but there are also a range of constraints which limit the extent of productive teacher research engagement. One key question in this chapter, then, concerns the manner in which research cultures in language teaching contexts might be characterized, based on the perceptions of such cultures held by teachers and managers.

In education generally in the UK, much has been written about the research-engaged school (e.g. Handscomb & Macbeath, 2003; Sharp et al., 2005). Sharp et al. (2006: 3), reviewing a project involving 15 schools, define such a school as one that

- investigates key issues in teaching and learning
- uses inquiry for staff development
- turns data and experience into knowledge
- uses evidence for decision making
- promotes learning communities.

Other analyses have focused on the conditions which support schools in becoming research engaged. For example, McLaughlin, Black-Hawkins, & McIntyre (2004: 10), drawing on their experience of the Schools–University Partnership for Educational Research (SUPER) project, hypothesize that research cultures in schools are more likely if

- teacher research engagement is one element of a larger integrated strategy for school improvement
- senior management are committed to the initiative
- projects are voluntarily undertaken by individuals or groups of teachers and are effectively co-ordinated
- teachers' research activities are supported by a university
- there is a concern for the rigour and quality of the research that teachers engage in
- resources, especially time, are provided by the management to facilitate both teacher research and its effective use
- there is a long-term commitment to teacher research by the school.

Carter & Halsall (1998: 84) also suggest the following questions to highlight the conditions required in a school seeking to promote a research culture:

- Is there a practice of teachers working with and for each other, and is there a co-operative set of relationships?
- Is there a belief that teacher research is a meaningful activity, that it can make a difference to student progress?
- Do teachers believe that they are, or should be, (continuing) learners, and that learning comes about from self and peer assessments of how well their judgements are working?
- Is there openness and trust, a willingness and ability to speak one's mind and to listen to others?
- Is there a willingness to take risks, to try something different?

I will now proceed to explore the extent to which the kinds of facilitative conditions listed above are seen to exist in language teaching contexts.

7.2 Language teachers' perspectives on research cultures

In my programme of research, insights into teachers' perspectives on their working contexts as research cultures were obtained via questionnaires and interviews. For the questionnaire (N=1,363), teachers in Studies 1, 3 and 4 (see Chapter 2) were presented with a total of eleven statements about research cultures (nine of which, see Table 7.1 on page 156, were core across the three studies) and asked to indicate, on a five-point scale of agreement, their views about each in relation to their own context. The statements were derived from an analysis of the literature on promoting teacher research engagement and were also informed by my experience of and reflections on promoting research engagement with teachers (see, for example, Borg, 2006). These items were also devised on the assumption that they addressed a common underlying concept, which we may refer to as institutional research culture. A measure of the extent to which this assumption is justified is provided by Cronbach's alpha; an alpha level for the nine core statements (N =1089) of 0.82[1] suggests that the items in this question were in fact conceptually related[2]. It is reasonable to suggest then, that the teachers' degree of agreement with these statements reflects their views about the extent to which their workplaces constitute productive research cultures.

Figure 7.1 summarizes teachers' responses to these statements. The five original response categories (from 'strongly agree' to 'strongly disagree') are here collapsed into three ('agree', 'don't know', and 'disagree') to highlight trends in these data. It is thus clear that teachers generally agreed that they have opportunities to learn about current research (66.7% agreement) and that research books and journals were available (66.4% agreement); smaller proportions, though still a majority for these items, agreed that they receive support to attend conferences (54.5% agreement) and that teachers do research (52.5% agreement). In contrast, three items where disagreement was the predominant response were: time for doing research is built into teachers' workloads (71.4% disagreement), teachers feel that doing research is an important part of their job (45% disagreement) and the management encourages teachers to do research (43.8% disagreement). Bai & Hudson (2011), using a set of questionnaire statements derived from my own, found that 75% of 182 Chinese TEFL academics agreed that the management does encourage them to do research; participants in that study, though, were both language teachers and lecturers in subjects such as linguistics and it is therefore difficult to make direct comparisons with my results.

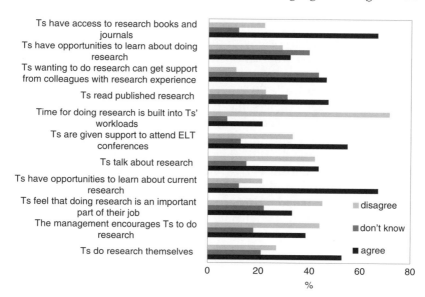

Figure 7.1 Teachers' assessments of the research cultures of their schools (N=1363)

These findings support points emerging from previous chapters. For example, teachers' views here about the lack of official allocation of time for research are consistent with their earlier views that a lack of time is a primary factor in explaining their lack of research engagement. As already noted, this is particularly the case in commercial contexts where teachers work on hourly contracts and are paid only for the time they spend teaching. Under such conditions, it is not at all surprising that teachers do not see research as an important part of their work. A comparison of the workload responses according to private (i.e. typically commercial EFL schools) and state schools did show that private school teachers disagreed significantly more that official research time was provided (t=2.65, df=1237, p=.008). Teachers are also likely to see research as substantially time consuming (and hence to be more aware of the lack of time available for it) when they associate it with the large-scale and formal type of inquiry highlighted in Chapter 3. If we add into this mix the perceived absence of explicit support by managers for research engagement, then it is easy to understand why this activity may often not be particularly prevalent. Nonetheless, the evidence here also points to the availability of resources which support research engagement, such as books and journals, as well as opportunities to learn about current research (e.g. through seminars and in-service training).

It is feasible to surmise that teachers' assessments of their research cultures might vary according to the type of institution in which they worked, in particular whether this was attached to a university or not. Of the 1,335 teachers who provided this data, 434 (32.5%) worked in a university setting while 901 (67.5%) did not. Table 7.1 shows that university language teachers' mean ratings (out of 5) of their research cultures were in fact higher than those of non-university teachers on all nine of the statements on which comparable data were available, and on eight of these the differences between the mean ratings of the two groups were statistically significant (as indicated by a t-test for independent samples and with a confidence level of 95%).

Teachers' summated scores on the research culture items in Table 7.1 were correlated (using Pearson's coefficient) with their

Table 7.1   Mean ratings of research cultures by university and non-university language teachers

	University		Non-university		Sig.
	N	Mean	N	Mean	
Teachers have opportunities to learn about current research	426	3.69	773	3.46	.000*
Teachers have access to research books and journals	425	3.74	775	3.45	.000*
Teachers do research themselves	428	3.41	870	3.23	.006*
Teachers read published research	381	3.36	817	3.23	.021*
Teachers are given funding to attend ELT conferences	425	3.36	869	3.20	.040*
Teachers talk about research	427	3.03	867	2.95	.264
The management encourages teachers to do research	423	3.06	871	2.87	.007*
Teachers feel that doing research is an important part of their job	426	3.00	870	2.78	.001*
Time for doing research is built into teachers' workloads	427	2.28	870	2.08	.006*

* indicates that the differences between the two means are statistically significant

reported frequencies of reading and doing research (as reported in previous chapters). A weak but significant positive relationship was found in both cases (for reading, N=1320, r=0.109, p<0.001, 2-tailed; for doing, N=1322, r=0.273, p<0.001, 2-tailed). Teachers reporting more favourable perceptions of their institutional research culture, then, also said they read and did research more often.

Interviews conducted with teachers working for three organizations provided further insight into the perceived lack of research cultures in their workplaces. The first group of teachers interviewed (N=5, Study 1) worked in a language centre in a university in Turkey. A key theme to arise from my discussions with these teachers was a perceived tension between explicit and implicit messages about the value of research communicated by the management. As one teacher explained:

> ... there is sort of a sense from high management that research is very important. But in terms of our teaching load, it's impossible. So it's one of those contradictions ... we don't think that they actually want us to do research ... At best it's a contradiction. The sense is, and it's quite a strong sense, is that research is important and publishing is important – not so much the publishing, but research is important to improve. There's a heavy emphasis on improving our things ... but they do not want to give us a reduced course load in order to make this possible. So time spent researching is still not worth the time lost from the classroom. (Turkey)

The same perspective was articulated more concisely by another teacher in the same institution who said that 'any research we do is great and they'll [the management] encourage it, but we don't get any compensation' (Turkey). This comment connects with one of the recurrent themes in this book – the common feeling among teachers that productive engagement in research was not feasible unless time was officially allocated to this task. The lack of an official workload allocation for research was thus for many teachers evidence of a lack of a strong research culture in their institutions. Teachers working at this university language centre were often very aware that the lack of formally allocated time for research was what distinguished them from academic staff working in the faculties. One teacher talked about this distinction as follows:

> ... of course in the faculties, the teachers teach so little – I know, I have friends. Like something like four hours some of them – would you believe that? And so, I mean teaching four hours?! There is a huge amount of time for research. If I taught four hours, oh I would be a pro [= a professional researcher]! I mean definitely. Time is a big factor. (Turkey)

The second context where teachers were interviewed was a private language school in Spain (N=7, Study 1). Here the key theme in teachers' comments on the research culture in their schools was that their professional activities had a very strong practical focus. Thus, for example, in reflecting on the extent to which teachers talked about research, one teacher explained that

> We do have a staff room upstairs and we coincide frequently there. And we do talk about teaching and we do give each other ideas and the younger teachers or the newer teachers do ask for advice. But we don't often talk about research. (Spain)

Similarly in this context, while the management were seen to be supportive in encouraging teachers to do research, this activity focused on pedagogical experimentation in class, particularly on the practical testing out of materials and activities. Thus one teacher, in explaining how her manager encouraged teachers to do research, said that 'if teachers want to try out new ideas, we're not stopped' (Spain).

Further insight into research cultures in language teaching comes from a set of interviews with 16 teachers working for an international organization (Study 3). In some cases, these teachers felt that the research culture in their school was fairly positive, and they related this to four factors: a commitment to teacher development, regular training opportunities, links between career progression and research engagement, and access to resources. The first two of these factors focus on opportunities for professional development, either individually (e.g. through personal development plans) or collegially (e.g. by attending training courses). In both cases, though, the underlying conception of research was not explicitly one that required teachers to engage in systematic classroom inquiry. The second two features of positive research cultures mentioned here, though, were more clearly research oriented. In terms of career progression, one teacher explained that (T: Teacher I: Interviewer)

> T: We've also just introduced a co-ordinator position as well which gives teachers another reason to do research, to go on and you know to develop themselves professionally and places to go within the ... the organization.
>
> I: Right so there's ... there's opportunities for ... for progression. In a sense for promotion?
>
> T: Yeah, yeah and those tend to be very much linked to, covertly anyway, very much linked to ... to professional development in terms of reading, research and so on. (Hong Kong)

The admission here that career progression was linked only 'covertly' to research engagement suggests, though, that this may not have been an issue that was openly discussed in the organization. The final feature mentioned above that was seen to promote a research culture was access to resources. In relation to this issue, though, it is worth stressing once again that what teachers perceived as research materials were often practically oriented professional publications. Thus in explaining the positive features of the research culture she worked in, one teacher noted that 'we have a lot of the publications we get, the *ELT Journal, Modern English Teacher*, we get a lot of those' (Hong Kong). As I have already stressed, I am not dismissing the value of such reading to teachers – these are the kinds of sources which will always be of primary interest to classroom practitioners. My concerns throughout have been, though, about the manner in which such materials are often seen by teachers to constitute research publications.

The majority of the 16 teachers in this final interview sample, however, had much more to say about the *lack* of strong research cultures in their schools. Some of the factors they mentioned (e.g. lack of incentive, encouragement and guidance) have surfaced in earlier discussions of the reasons why teachers do not read and do research more often. The lack of reference to research in teachers' job descriptions was an additional factor seen by some to imply that research was an 'extra' job:

> ... when you actually read our contract and you look at how the percentages are broken down, there isn't really anything there for research. So if someone did want to do research, it'd be almost above and beyond the call of duty. You know, I think we've got a lot of hardworking teachers here but again, I don't want to speak for my colleagues but my personal feeling is you know, I work hard Monday to Friday doing the teaching and the planning and you know, marking homework but I don't really want to be doing research, you know maybe, analysing statistics over the weekend. (Czech Republic)

The over-riding concern for practical activity noted above in the interviews from Spain also recurred here and was seen by some teachers to constitute a barrier to deeper levels of research engagement:

> I feel it's very, very pragmatic. I mean people want ... you know the place that we work in people want good quality, effective, practical projects. You know they want things that work on the ground, very sort of chalk under the fingernails type thing that are based on sound pedagogical principles. But really that doesn't really push the envelope into research and real inquiry. (Hong Kong)

The greater value attached to practical work by teachers was also explained in terms of its greater immediate relevance to the classroom, compared to research:

> I think maybe they see that [research] as something theoretical and their job is to do the practical, get them through three units of *Cutting Edge*, hit the five language areas and make sure they can use them competently. I think what they think of, their expectations, are much more immediate and that research might be too sort of background which doesn't apply to what they're going to do that afternoon. (Egypt)

Limitations in research cultures in language schools were, additionally, related to more general characteristics of the private EFL sector:

> Well, I think it's obviously something in the industry has been a kind of tradition that we get groups of teachers who come through, do a CELTA, maybe work in two or three centres for a few years and then decide to move on to some other kind of career that fits, being back in UK or something like that. So there's still a group of teachers who haven't really made a very strong commitment to the career. They tend to still see it as okay, something I'm doing now but not in the long term. (Malaysia)

From this perspective, limitations in research cultures were not simply a product of the characteristics of individual schools but related to trends in the field more generally. Of course, the above observations about the short-term commitment of language teachers do not normally apply to the state sector, where teaching is often valued as a secure and long-term career.

Enhancing research cultures

In one study (Study 3), teachers who said they did research rarely or never (N=52) were also asked to make suggestions about what their schools could do to make research a more central part of teachers' work. Figure 7.2 lists the key themes highlighted by the 39 teachers who responded to this question. This constitutes an interesting set of practical measures teachers feel would strengthen the research cultures in their workplaces. The issues highlighted point to the role in promoting teacher research engagement that can be played by support (especially time), access to information, opportunities to join projects, and training. Importantly, too, teachers felt that to promote stronger research cultures it is important that research be made relevant to teachers' professional goals (as we saw earlier, a common complaint by teachers is that research is not relevant to their work). Such suggestions will inform my discussion of ways of promoting research cultures in Chapter 9.

- Build (paid) time for research into teachers' timetables
- Include research in teachers' job descriptions
- Create opportunities for teachers to be part of a research team
- Create an awareness of the value of research to teachers
- Create a journal to allow teachers to get professional credit for their research
- Set up research projects and encourage teachers to participate
- Reward teachers' commitment to research through career opportunities
- Make doing research relevant to teachers' professional goals
- Provide training/workshops on how to do research
- Provide information about research projects teachers can participate in on a website
- Make sure all teachers have access to ELT research journals
- Allocate resources and financial support
- Provide study leave
- Make results of teachers' research projects available to other teachers
- Encourage academic managers to find out which teachers are interested in research and what support they need

Figure 7.2   Ways of enhancing research cultures, according to teachers

7.3 Managers' perspectives on research cultures

Perspectives on research cultures in language teaching were also obtained (in Studies 2, 3 and 4) through questionnaire responses from 357 individuals in managerial positions (primarily in the USA and the UK) and interviews (in Studies 2 and 3) with 59 of these (working primarily in the UK private EFL sector).

Questionnaire responses

Table 7.2 provides a global summary of managers' assessments of the research cultures in their institutions. There were three areas here which managers rated very positively – the availability of research books, research journals, and funding to attend conferences. At the opposite end of the scale, over 82% of the managers disagreed that teachers are allocated time for research, just over 68% disagreed that most teachers do research themselves, and almost 63% disagreed that teachers feel that doing research is an important part of their job. In response to the statement 'the management encourages teachers to do research', opinions here were evenly split – 45% agreed while 46.4% disagreed.

Table 7.2   Managers' assessments of research cultures

	N	Agree	Don't know	Disagree
Teachers have access to research books	346	82.0%	3.4%	14.6%
Funding to attend ELT conferences is available to teachers	347	75.5%	4.0%	20.5%
Teachers have access to research journals	346	72.5%	8.2%	19.3%
Teachers wanting to do research can get support from colleagues with research experience	93	57.4%	18.5%	24.2%
Teachers have opportunities to learn about doing research	94	54.7%	13.4%	31.9%
The management encourages teachers to do research	347	45.0%	8.6%	46.4%
Teachers like to talk about research	346	34.6%	14.2%	51.2%
Teachers read published ELT research	350	32.0%	13.4%	54.5%
Teachers do research themselves	349	22.6%	9.2%	68.2%
Teachers feel that doing research is an important part of their job	347	14.7%	22.8%	62.6%
Time for doing research is built into teachers' workloads	347	13.5%	4.0%	82.4%

Figure 7.3 compares teacher and manager assessments of research cultures. The figures being compared here are the percentages of teachers and managers who agreed that a factor was present in their institutions. While on certain issues teachers and managers held comparable views (e.g. on the fact that research time was not officially allocated or on the availability of books and journals), on several issues there are notable differences of opinion.

Thus while almost 50% of the teachers agree that teachers do research, less than 23% of the managers felt this was the case; and although the percentage of teachers who agreed that teachers see

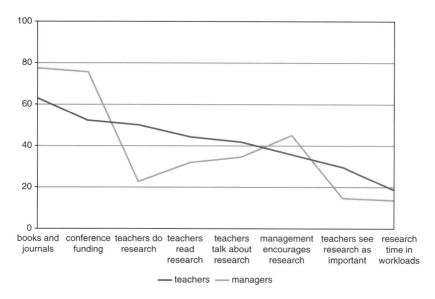

Figure 7.3   Percentages of teachers and managers agreeing that features of research cultures were present

research as an important part of their job was low (29.5%), the corresponding figure for managers was only half that (14.7%). Another difference was that the percentage of teachers who felt the management support research (35.4%) was lower than the comparative figure for managers (45%). Overall, managers tended to be more positive than teachers about the availability of support and resources, while teachers were more positive than managers in assessing teachers' attitudes to and engagement in and with research. A statistical comparison of the mean ratings teachers and managers assigned (on a scale of 1 = disagree strongly to 5 = agree strongly) to the various aspects of research cultures they were asked about does actually show that on practically every measure the opinions of the two groups differed in a significant manner (see Table 7.3).

Of course, in interpreting these results we need to remember that the teachers and managers whose views are being compared here did not necessarily work in the same institutions (but see below for a comparison within the same organization); also, as noted earlier, none of the managers worked in state schools. Further investigations of research cultures involving more specific localized comparisons of teachers and their managers are thus desirable, with greater attention also to the nature of how research cultures are perceived in state sector secondary and high schools around the world. Nonetheless,

Table 7.3   Mean ratings of research cultures by teachers and managers

	Teachers		Managers		Sig.
	N	Mean	N	Mean	
Teachers have access to research books and journals	1226	3.52	346	3.84	.001*
Teachers do research themselves	1324	3.28	349	2.36	.000*
Teachers read published research	1222	3.27	350	2.69	.000*
Teachers are given funding to attend ELT conferences	1319	3.26	347	3.72	.000*
Teachers talk about research	1319	2.98	346	2.76	.001*
The management encourages teachers to do research	1319	2.94	347	2.98	.547
Teachers feel that doing research is an important part of their job	1321	2.85	347	2.41	.000*
Time for doing research is built into teachers' workloads	1322	2.16	347	1.97	.005*

* indicates that the differences between the two means are statistically significant

the findings reported here do suggest that the lack of official time for teachers to be research engaged is recognized by managers and teachers; these findings also highlight ways in which teachers and managers have diverging perceptions of various aspects of research culture. Such differing views, I would argue, are themselves a barrier to the development of productive research cultures; i.e. promoting an environment conducive to research engagement is difficult when the management and teachers have very different views about the extent to which various elements of such an environment actually exist. This suggests that a useful starting point for institutions wishing to foster a stronger research culture would be an exercise through which the perceptions of teachers and managers of the current situation are elicited and discussed at institutional level.

Above I noted that the teachers and managers being compared here came from a range of schools and contexts worldwide. In one study (Study 3) I was able to obtain comparable data from teachers (N=100) and managers (N=33) working for different schools within the same organization. Comparisons at this level reflected the more global findings reported above. Thus, for example, while less than 12% of the teachers felt research was an important part of their job, only 6.3% of the managers expressed the same opinion; and while 34.1% of the teachers agreed that teachers do research themselves, only 6.3% of the managers felt this was the case.

In one of the studies involving managers, they were asked not only to assess the research culture of their institutions but additionally to indicate how influential certain factors were in determining the extent to which teachers were research engaged. Figure 7.4 summarizes their responses.

Here, the nine factors the managers were asked to comment on are listed according to the mean rating each received (the higher the mean rating, the more influential a factor was seen to be in influencing the degree of research engagement). Overall, we can note that all of the factors were seen to be at least moderately influential in shaping research engagement, with the least influential factor receiving a mean rating of 3.1 out of 5. It is also interesting that the factor seen to be least influential was the management's own attitude to research; I would suggest, though, that the managers who provided these ratings are underestimating the impact their own attitudes to research can have on teachers' engagement in and with research.

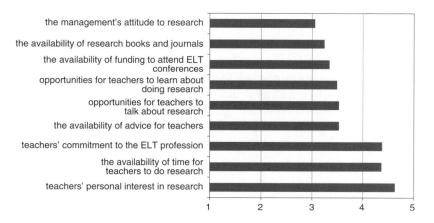

Figure 7.4   Managers' ratings of the impact (1=low to 5=high) of aspects of research cultures on teacher research engagement (N=32)

If we look at the top three factors considered by managers to be most influential here, the first is teachers' own personal interests in research while the third is their more general commitment to language teaching as a profession (the second, the availability of time, has been noted so often here that it needs no further comment). As we saw earlier, in their interviews some teachers did refer to the lack of commitment to the profession as a factor which hinders research engagement and the views expressed by managers here corroborate this position and will be supported further by data I report later in this chapter.

I have only been able to provide brief insights here into the relative impact of the many factors which can influence teacher research engagement, but this is clearly an area of research that merits further attention as it can allow us to move beyond identifying those factors which are influential to a deeper understanding of the weight that each factor carries. Such insights can be valuable when decisions are being made about creating opportunities for teachers to be research engaged – i.e. an understanding of the relative weight of various influential factors means that priority can be awarded to those which are seen to be most influential. On the basis of the findings here, it would seem important not only to create time for teachers to be research engaged but also to foster more positive attitudes to research among teachers. This finding also suggests that creating time, on its own, and without the development of positive dispositions among teachers, may not result in a significant increase in teacher research engagement.

Interview responses

Substantial additional insights regarding research cultures in language teaching contexts were obtained via extensive interviews with 59 managers (Studies 2 and 3). The bulk of these (43) worked in private EFL schools in the UK; the remainder worked in different schools around the world which were part of the same organization. The material relevant to research cultures derived from these interviews is presented below under three headings: (a) factors contributing to positive research cultures; (b) factors contributing to negative research cultures; and (c) the desirability and feasibility of improving research cultures.

FACTORS CONTRIBUTING TO POSITIVE RESEARCH CULTURES

Although, as shown above, the overall view among the managers who contributed to my programme of research was that strong research cultures did not exist in their institutions, there were nonetheless

Feature	Description
Conducive teacher attributes	Teacher characteristics which make them more positively disposed to reading and doing research.
Availability of mentoring	The presence of individuals within or external to the institution who can advise teachers on research matters.
Supportive management	Managers who are either proactive in creating opportunities for teacher research engagement or who respond supportively when teachers express an interest in being research engaged.
Incentives	Paid time off, financial support and similar incentives to encourage teachers to be research engaged.
Availability of time	Formally allocated and paid time for the purposes of research.
Regular development opportunities	Regular opportunities provided by institutions (e.g. INSET sessions) for teachers to develop professionally.
Opportunities for sharing findings	Mechanisms which allow teachers to share the findings of the research they read or do with others, including through written publications.

Figure 7.5   Managers' views on the features of positive research cultures

individuals whose perspectives were more positive. These individuals were invited to comment on the factors which they felt supported the positive research culture which they perceived in their workplace and Figure 7.5 lists the issues they highlighted. The importance of some of these (e.g. the availability of time) has already been stressed and we need not dwell on them further here. Others merit more specific consideration, particularly because they provide further insights into how research engagement is often conceptualized by language school managers.

The first item in Figure 7.5 is 'conducive teacher attributes'. In the interviews, several managers explained that positive research cultures were defined to a certain extent by the characteristics of the teachers themselves; as discussed earlier, this is in contrast to a view of research cultures as being externally defined, independent of the teachers. A number of teacher attributes were seen to be conducive to positive research cultures: more advanced qualifications, previous experience of doing research, an interest in professional development, professional curiosity, and an interest in research. One manager described how teachers' interest in development contributed to a positive research culture in their institution:

> Most of the teachers are interested in developing their knowledge and they both read and they do ... I mean we sit around a table and discuss what are you trying out? Is it worth it? We've got practical experiments going on all the time. (UK)

And in relation to teachers' interest in research, another manager added that 'I don't think you can do research if you're not really interested' (UK). Managers' comments on how they provided time and/or funding to support research engagement provided further insights into their understandings of what such engagement involved. One manager, who said that time for research was part of his teachers' workload, explained the situation as follows:

> Okay, the only thing that I was referring to then I suppose is that people are expected to give [i.e. attend] one hour of in-service training, I mean to allow one hour of in-service training per week and within that, it could be that we decide, you know, we want to spend that on research. Teachers and me together, we decide on what we're going to do every week ... And we usually build in a publications one as I say, you know, where we all read a publication, come back with an article that interested us and feedback to the group, or it might be material development that we spend our hour doing, but in that sense it's built in. It's built in to, you know, they are required to do an hour of training. (UK)

In this case, then, teachers were required to undertake one hour of professional development each week and research, particularly through reading, was one of the activities they could engage in. Another manager explained the provision of time and funding for research as follows (I = Interviewer, M = Manager):

> I: Just here in the questionnaire you said that time for doing research is built into teachers' workloads and you said you agree with that. That's interesting because you know most people I've spoken to so far you know time seems to be a major obstacle to getting teachers into sort of a sort of a research sort of mode.

M: Yeah right.

I: So how do you achieve that?

M: I've got another little pot of money for administration and that kind
      of thing and I'll dip into that and get people to design materials that
      they ask, you know, if we've got a lack of materials I might get some-
      one to do that. So, for example, I got a teacher to design a sort of
      what's the word ... a guide to the self access centre ... So the teacher
      went off and spoke to students and found out how best they liked
      to learn and then introduced this, basically compiled a list of activi-
      ties ... now when we have a new student we will induct them based
      upon this sort of list. So it's locating materials, working with others,
      looking at multimedia, looking at textbooks, that kind of thing. So I
      actually paid the teacher administration money to basically do that
      and then trial the materials and then tweak them accordingly. (UK)

As we saw in Chapter 5, many managers associated research with
materials development and that notion is evident again here; a number of managers did in fact explain that they were able to relieve
teachers of classes and/or pay them to develop materials for the
school. Support of this kind was not available though, especially in
the private sector schools, for teachers who wanted to undertake their
own research projects. Another use to which institutional funds were
put was to support teachers in obtaining further qualifications, such
as DELTAs and MAs. This use of funds was cited by a number of
managers as evidence of the ways in which their schools fostered a
positive research culture. Overall, then, these interview findings suggest that in several cases, managers from private EFL schools who
replied in their questionnaires that research was supported through
time and funding interpreted research as either materials development and evaluation or further formal studies. Managers in university language centres and further education colleges did also refer to
such matters; additionally, though, they referred to action research
projects which teachers were supported in doing. One manager, for
example, recalled such a project:

    I think it's 2001 to 2004, something like that. We had a three-year period
    where I would say everybody was doing a little bit of action research
    because there was time given over to it, there was a formal structure to
    it, each person had a mentor and so if you'd asked me then [about our
    research culture], that would've been different. (UK)

No examples of such initiatives in private EFL contexts, though, were
cited in the interviews.

Barrier	Description
Teacher attitudes	Negative attitudes which hinder teachers from being research engaged
Lack of knowledge and skills	The lack of the theoretical knowledge and practical skills required to do research
Lack of time	The absence of formally allocated time for research
Funding issues	The lack of funding to support research
Contractual issues	Part-time or hourly contracts which pay only for in-class contact time
Lack of support from management	Research is not seen as important and supported by the management
Lack of professionalism in TEFL	EFL is not seen as a profession and many teachers teach English as a short-term job

Figure 7.6   Managers' views on the barriers to positive research cultures

FACTORS CONTRIBUTING TO NEGATIVE RESEARCH
CULTURES

The majority of the managers interviewed, in line with the overall findings to emerge here, did not feel that the research cultures in their schools were strong. One focus of our discussions, therefore, was the factors which contributed to this situation. Figure 7.6 summarizes the barriers to positive research cultures highlighted by managers. Again, several of these have been noted in this and previous chapters and I will limit my comments here to those which merit particular attention.

Supporting the point made in Figure 7.4, managers again stressed the point here that adverse teacher attitudes can significantly hinder the development of a positive research culture. For example, managers felt that many teachers lacked the motivation to be research engaged. As one manager explained:

> Well partly here it's changing now but partly here it [the main problem] was the motivation. I had a team that had been here for a long time and they were a bit stale and they've got sort of baggage and history from before I came along and things are now much more organised but yeah, they're very resentful of doing anything extra. (UK)

Some managers felt this lack of motivation to read and do research was manifest in the way that many teachers 'just want to get in, get their lesson plans done and out' (UK). As another respondent put it:

> ... quite a number of our staff very much come ... I come, I do my six hours teaching, I prep what I need to do for the next six hours and I go home and that's it ... They're sort of come, do it, go home type of people. (UK)

Although such attitudes can be interpreted in relation to teachers' employment conditions (e.g. hourly contracts), some managers felt that even if conditions were more favourable teachers would not be interested in being research engaged; as one explained, 'I think if it was we'll pay you to just sit down and read journals I don't think people ... even for the pay I don't think people would be interested. I think they just want their time away from work' (UK).

Apart from a general lack of motivation and interest, managers also felt that teachers, particularly those with more experience, were often complacent and did not recognize (especially when their teaching was seen to be effective) any need to seek new ideas through reading and doing research. Thus one manager referred to 'older teachers who feel, you know, I have nothing new to learn' (UK) while another noted that teachers resist research because 'they feel that they're teaching okay. They perhaps don't feel the need for it' (UK). Another added, 'To a certain extent, some of the teachers will say well I've been teaching for ten years, I know what I'm doing, I'm not going to go and learn a new way to skin that cat' (Taiwan).

Another teacher attitude that managers felt hindered the development of stronger research cultures was that research was a theoretical or academic pursuit with little direct practical relevance to the classroom. Many teachers, according to one manager, 'see research as something that happens in a laboratory in front of a computer' (UK), while another noted that during weekly INSET sessions, teachers' attitude was 'I don't want to know all the theory. I just want more ideas to help my preparation be quicker' (UK). Managers felt that such attitudes to research were often the result of the inaccessibility of much published language teaching research ('... even some of the articles in *ELT Journal* were maybe you know not that easy to understand' UK). This perceived divide between the classroom and research was seen to be a powerful influence on teachers' lack of interest in being research engaged:

> ... if I sort of said, no more research ever, no more INSET, I don't think there'd be any tears, okay, I think these people are, you know, most of

them are teachers, they're happiest in the classroom, that's the context they know, they're not academics, they don't have Master's. They have first degrees, they have DELTAs most of them but you know, they're not interested in sort of sitting and reading endlessly for its own sake. I think if they can see some practical application of what they're reading, that's good for them. If this can help their students, if this can help them in the classroom but they're not writing dissertations. (UK)

These kinds of perceptions suggest very strongly that an important element in creating research cultures in language teaching contexts is to create an awareness of the ways in which teacher-led, classroom-oriented inquiry can be eminently practical in its focus and can both draw on and feed back into teachers' classroom practices. If for teachers, as discussed in Chapter 3, research is associated with academic, theoretical pursuits bearing no connection to teaching, then of course teachers' motivation to be research engaged will understandably not be high. Here, and in Chapter 5, there was also evidence that managers too, and not just teachers, may hold such unhelpful conceptions of research.

As Figure 7.6 shows, managers felt there were several other factors apart from teacher attitudes which hindered the development of research cultures. The issues of time, funding and teacher contracts are interconnected and have a direct bearing on the problems with teacher motivation and interest in relation to research engagement discussed above. As already noted, private EFL sector teachers are very often employed on part-time or hourly contracts which may pay them only for the time they actually spend in class; one manager explained that 'we don't pay for breaks, we don't pay for preparation time and they're just far too busy getting through the lessons, getting things prepared, queuing up at the photocopier. It would be completely impractical to ask them to do that [be research engaged]' (UK). Teachers working on such contracts, understandably, are less likely to be interested in additional unpaid research-related work:

> And it tends to be the hourly paid staff in general like in many institutions [who] feel they're not paid well enough for what they do per hour and that's it they don't want to do anything more ... they'll just come in, do their prep, do their teaching, do what ever admin they've got to do and that's it, interest ends. (UK)

And of course, as managers noted, language schools are often businesses and this influences the extent to which research engagement by teachers can be supported: 'If there is no funding available, then certainly, for myself as a manager, my job is to make sure that teachers' hours are maximised in the classroom cause that's how we bring the money in, so that doesn't enable us to free up any time for teachers to do research work' (Thailand).

Echoing comments made earlier by some teachers, managers also related these barriers to teacher research engagement to broader issues in the culture of EFL, particularly the manner in which it was not seen to be a profession or a long-term career choice for many teachers; in the words of one manager, 'we've got quite ... they're very good teachers but the ... you know they're doing it while they write their great British novel or study or ... it's not their priority' (UK); another explained that 'most of the teachers here are newly qualified with a year or two's experience and I don't think most of them have very much intention of staying in the business' (UK). Consequently, teacher commitment to language teaching was often seen to be low, with little resultant interest in professional development generally and certainly not in reading and doing research:

> I think most teachers themselves unfortunately don't necessarily view ELT as a long-term career, and therefore the ... the investment that perhaps research suggests, you know, someone who is undertaking research is more than probably a committed ELT professional, and I think if we're talking globally, there are not many of them. (UK)

In a similar vein:

> I mean, you see the thing that I find very sad is the whole perception of TEFL and it's largely from the outside and from the inside perceived as not being a proper job and I think it's related to all these factors, like lack of security, lack of training, lack of opportunities for promotion. I mean I find it sad, I hear teachers in TEFL sort of talking about real teachers and they're talking about state school teachers and I think that's very, very sad. I mean I'd like to see the whole nature of TEFL sort of go up a gear and become more professional but ... (UK)

Managers working in university settings were also aware of the low status that language teaching was seen to have, compared to academic subjects; this, they felt, had implications for the extent that teachers wanted to be research engaged. One manager explained that 'the attitude in this university is that EFL teaching is not an academic subject and therefore it's not worthwhile pursuing a research agenda' (UK), while another added that 'one issue about ELT in higher education is that it ... it doesn't have a firm, established position there, and it tends to be marginalised and treated ... as a business'. (UK)

Managers' commentaries on the factors which hinder the development of research cultures thus highlight a range of interacting factors – personal, institutional, commercial, and more broadly relevant to the culture of EFL. Thus while teachers do seem to hold certain attitudes which limit their ability to be research engaged, it is clearly the case too that such attitudes are often responsive to the working environment that characterizes many language teaching contexts, particularly in terms of heavy teaching loads and limited space or support for professional development. More generally, the rather bleak picture that emerges here is that many teachers who become EFL teachers do not see this as a career option and often leave after a few years, while many of those who stay in EFL become complacent; in both cases, research engagement holds no appeal (though, it must be noted, this is at least partly due to misconceptions about what this activity entails). Of course, this picture reflects the comments of the managers who contributed to my programme of research, and although support for many of their views is reflected in teacher responses in my various studies, it is important to stress that I am not seeking to paint a negative picture of the EFL industry generally. As I have noted too, while teachers from secondary state schools did contribute to the questionnaire responses, the more detailed interview commentaries come from managers working in the private sector. What is clear, though, based on the evidence discussed here, is that many language teaching schools do not constitute environments where productive teacher research engagement is a feasible proposition. Teachers do in many contexts receive support to further their studies through Diploma and Master's programmes, but these activities do not seem to contribute to research cultures in schools; the qualifications are seen primarily as a route to promotion and, from the school's perspective, assurance that their staff are suitably qualified.

DESIRABILITY AND FEASIBILITY OF CREATING RESEARCH CULTURES

Practically all of the managers who felt that the research cultures in their schools were not strong also agreed that it would, in theory, be desirable to create strong research cultures. In explaining their views, they highlighted a number of perceived benefits of greater teacher research engagement and these are summarized, with illustrative quote, in Figure 7.7.

Benefit	Illustrative quote
Improve teacher development and teaching	'Yes, for the sake of individual teachers' development and perhaps at the end of the day for the people that we're actually selling the product to. I guess, yes, yes [a stronger research culture would be beneficial].' (UK)
Improve academic self-esteem	'Well, I think I'd like to see a stronger research culture ... it would be good for our academic self-esteem.' (UK)
Contribute to long-term business development	'... for me, a business is only going to flourish in the long term if it has the people ready to do so. So if we're not doing the training now, in five years' time we're going to be completely outdated and people will not be coming to us. So I don't find there's a conflict at all [between promoting research and growing the business]. I think it's actually a requirement.' (Italy)
Maintain freshness in staff	'I think it would just sort of keep a freshness to the job, the main business and I think without it, you know you just worry if people are getting a bit stale or not being that interested in it.' (Jordan)
Improve staff retention	'We have a big issue about retention of happy and interested teachers. So if we're moving towards ways we can think of, of enriching jobs, then I think this [research] is possibly a very lucrative line to follow. We want people who are interested and keen ... we have quite a lot of more highly qualified teachers who are not, I feel, that motivated about what they're doing any more ... So if an outcome of this is that we can make things a bit more interesting for everyone, then that would be fine.' (Hungary)

Figure 7.7   Benefits of promoting stronger research cultures, according to managers

Extending points about the impact of research engagement on teaching quality made in Chapter 6, these benefits affect individual teachers (i.e. by enhanced self-esteem), students (who receive an improved 'product'), and organizations more generally (i.e. improved staff retention). Managers were also asked about the extent to which creating stronger research cultures in their institutions was feasible. Here, their responses were more varied, falling into two camps – those who felt that, under certain conditions, change would be feasible, and those who were not optimistic about the feasibility of such change. I will comment on each position in turn now.

Several managers felt that it would be feasible to create stronger research cultures in their schools, under certain conditions. A summary of the conditions they mentioned appears in Figure 7.8. Some of these relate to adjustments required in teachers' attitudes, such as a greater willingness to work collaboratively and a better understanding of the value of research engagement; another set of changes listed here highlights the role that managers need to play in fostering a research culture; managers themselves may need development opportunities to prepare them for this role. The point about research guidelines which provide teachers with direction about how to do research is also important, particularly as we have seen that many teachers see a lack of knowledge about doing research as a factor which limits their research engagement. The need for structured guidance was also emphasized by the manager who said, 'If we are looking to get a wide range of people involved in research, even if it's not a very high-level research, having a methodology, a framework and some guidance would be a good thing' (Singapore). Also important here are suggestions about the need for clear-shared understandings within organizations of what research means; one of the central themes to emerge from this book is that the term is conceptualized in a range of ways – both overly narrow and too broadly inclusive – that are often unproductive for the purposes of supporting teacher research engagement. The comment in Figure 7.8 that research needs to be defined in an inclusive manner is one I am sympathetic to and I agree that unreasonably stringent conceptions of what counts as research will only deter teachers from being research engaged; at the same time, though, I want to continue to argue that caution is required to avoid a situation where any form of professional development starts to be called research.

In a number of cases managers' views that change was feasible were further qualified; for some, teachers could only be research engaged outside the peak teaching seasons (in the private EFL sector, for example, summer is typically much busier than winter). As one manager put it:

> Certain times of the year, yes. During the winter months, sort of November to March really there's not really a problem although we reduce our staff and just tend to keep the permanent people ... If someone were studying or doing research of some sort that we thought was useful then yeah, no problem. They would be given more time. (UK)

Change	Illustrative quote
Adjustments to teacher attitudes and working practices	'I would want to see more flexibility, more understanding of the need, the essential need for this sort of activity and more collaboration. There's a lack of team, what's the word, teammanship. There's a lack of sense of team that people are sharing and doing things together and actually benefiting from each other. They're a bunch of individuals who come and do a reasonably good job and then go home but I want more than that.' (UK)
Greater awareness of value of research	'And so I think that we need to work harder to try and make it clearer for teachers why research is valuable for them.' (Taiwan)
A shared understanding of what research is	'I think there needs to be very clear definitions of what we mean by a research culture. I mean, we're very different from academia where, as teachers or trainers, we're not assessed by number of publications or number of times we speak at the conference. It's not reflected in our job careers in some ways.' (Malaysia)
An inclusive and practical view of research	'I think it is because the more inclusive we are the more it celebrates and legitimises what people are doing and that has a big part to play in motivating our teachers to do more of it. If we start saying to people "oh that thing you thought you were doing isn't actually research" they'll start saying "oh why should I bother".' (Hong Kong)
More proactive staff	'I think a little nudge here and there and people being perhaps a little bit more proactive instead of just sitting back and letting things not happen, make things happen.' (UK)
Research relevant to the school's work	'If there was a research project going on that was, you know, of obvious interest to us, because it gelled well with the sorts of things we do and I felt that it would enable us to move forward as a centre, then I'd be very interested in it. If it was a more esoteric, shall we say, research project, which would have no obvious benefits to us as a centre, I would be less interested in it.' (UK)
Research guidelines	'I think it would be feasible if we had the structure in place you know this is what you need to do ... this is how we suggest you do it ... this is the benefit ... potential benefit to you ... this is how little effort it would take ... that kind of thing. I think it would be feasible yeah and it would be beneficial definitely for students and teachers ... Somebody would need to produce the ... I don't know what you would call it really ... the not syllabus but somebody would have to ... say this is what would need to be done and this is how I see it fitting in and this is how often you'd need to do it and this is an example of what you need to.' (UK)

(Continued)

A network of researchers	'I think the answer really is just to have ... not to have the time but to belong to a network perhaps where people who face similar kinds of problems were trying out different things, which need to be almost done on a daily basis.' (UK)
Managers' own research under-standings and skills	'... if I had the experience myself, 'cause I'm not an expe-rienced classroom research practitioner by any stretch of the imagination, and if I had the tools myself with which to assist people, then I reckon I'd get a fair amount of take up.' (Portugal)
Research leaders	'It would require somebody to lead it and to, an enthu-siastic approach so somebody who wanted to try and encourage that sort of culture.' (UK)
Balance between business and profes-sional development concerns	'Yes I think again you know it goes back to the sort of busi-ness versus the professionalism really I mean obviously centres make a lot more money or meet targets more easily if they use their teacher's time effectively but I have also experienced being in places where teachers were given time off to do various things and the centre really benefited from that in the long-term I think there needs to be a sort of change of emphasis really from the sort of management point of view that work done on research is well worth doing.' (Bahrain)
Reference to research in job descriptions	'... it needs to be built into job descriptions, it needs to be built into the evaluation, it needs to be built into hours.' (Malaysia)

Figure 7.8   Managers' views on the changes needed for stronger research cultures

And returning to the commercial themes discussed earlier, for others change was feasible 'as long as it's not costing huge pots of money ... that's the bottom line to be honest with you' (UK).

A second group of managers were not positive about the feasibil-ity of creating research cultures in their organizations. The obstacles they cited are ones which were highlighted in the earlier discus-sion of the factors which hinder research cultures: heavy teaching workloads and contracts which often pay for teaching time only; commercial priorities and a consequent lack of funds to create time for staff to be research engaged – 'Money, in further education in particular is the single biggest issue that stops everything' (UK); a general perception that if students are happy and the teaching is good then there is no need for research engagement, or at least no need to invest in it:

> I think just the, you know, the business side of the equation, you know, from a head office point of view I would imagine that, you know, the feedback is good, the teaching is generally seen as being good, so why should we pay to change it? You know, it's kind of, if it ain't broke don't fix it. (UK)

Continuing this theme, research engagement is viewed in the next comment as a luxury:

> I think in the current financial climate, [change is] probably not as likely as I would like it to be, for the simple reason that we are sort of you know, in a period of consolidation and growth, where sort of bums on seats have to come first, and therefore to have the ... I was going to say to have the luxury to allow research to take place, that's badly worded, but at this stage, in economic times, it is a luxury. (UK)

One additional point that was raised and which managers felt hinders the development of research cultures was the fact that the nature of the market (again, in the private sector) meant that the number of staff at a school might fluctuate significantly over the course of a year; this lack of stability made it difficult to create a research culture:

> ... if we were certain of ... the student base, and consequently staff numbers, you know ... because of the sort of continuous enrolment aspect, whilst we're choc-a-bloc in July, the numbers fluctuate wildly the rest of the year ... if we had you know, a fully employed staff, 10 say, that [research] is one area that I would be looking into. It tends to be fairly, at the moment, fire-fighting, simply because ... we're constantly unsure ... you know, the last year or so, it's ... it's really been sort of thinking on our feet time, and ... and not ... not planning ahead ... If we had more solid, you know, guarantees of ... of employment, and sort of permanence, then that's you know, research is one area that would move with the school. (UK)

Again, such conditions will be not be typical of language teaching contexts everywhere; in state school contexts, for example, managers are able to plan on the basis of predictable and stable student and staff numbers, thus avoiding some of the uncertainty caused by the issues described in the comment above.

7.4 Conclusion

The purpose of this chapter has been to examine the extent to which, according to teachers and managers, language teaching contexts are seen to provide an environment conductive to teacher research engagement. Overall, the conclusion that emerges here is not a positive one. While both teachers and managers felt that some elements of productive research cultures (such as access to books and journals) were present in their institutions, other important facilitative conditions were generally not (this applies to the sample overall, although attitudes in state sector contexts were more positive than in the private sector). In particular, there was consistent agreement that time for research is not built into teachers' workloads. Evidence from successful teacher projects (e.g. Westwell, 2006) suggests repeatedly that time is critical to efforts to promote research cultures; for example, one report concluded that 'the main resource required for research activity is staff time. Time is needed for planning the research, collecting data, analysis, reflection, and sharing results. Some release time may be necessary, especially when staff need to work together' (Sharp et al., 2006: 4).

While opinions about the lack of time teachers had for research were consistent in my programme of research, there were interesting differences among managers and teachers in relation to other factors that can contribute positively to a research culture. In particular, managers tended to see teachers' attitudes as being a significant factor in this respect, while downplaying the impact that their (i.e. managers') own attitudes to research had on teacher research engagement. Teachers, in contrast, felt that their attitudes to research were not as adverse as managers felt and that managers' support for research engagement was lacking. Given that a research culture implies a shared set of understandings and practices, this basic lack of consensus among teachers and managers has serious implications for the extent to which positive research cultures can be promoted in language teaching contexts.

Irrespective of these differences of opinion, there is no doubt that while time and funding do make a difference to the extent to which teachers and institutions can be research engaged, adverse teacher attitudes (to research and to professional development more generally) may outweigh such resource issues in determining the extent to which a productive research culture can develop. In addition to creating favourable external conditions for teacher research engagement, then, it is also important for organizations to address the attitudes which can hinder their attempts to develop a research culture. The view, for example, that research is academic and has no relevance to the classroom, or that effective teachers have nothing to gain by being research engaged, are clear examples of such adverse dispositions. Of course, in some cases similar views may be held by managers, and they too, therefore, may require awareness-raising development opportunities through which they can develop better understandings of how to create a research culture and of how this can strengthen the organization. Given a finding highlighted above, too, managers would also benefit from opportunities to better understand the impact that their own attitudes to teacher research engagement can have on the extent to which teachers are actually research engaged. There is clear evidence, particularly from projects in the state sector in the UK (Barker, 2005; Davies, Hamilton, & James, 2007; McLaughlin, Black-Hawkins, & McIntyre, 2004; Sharp, 2007; Sharp et al., 2005), of the central role that managers have in promoting teacher research engagement.

Managers were typically positively disposed to the idea of creating stronger research cultures in their institutions and suggested a number of strategies which would contribute to this goal. They were, however, acutely aware of constraints which extended beyond their own sphere of influence: for those working in language centres in university or further education contexts, the status of language teaching and of language teachers was seen to be low (and this minimized teachers' motivation to be research engaged); in the private EFL sector, managers felt constrained by commercial priorities, the inability to plan long-term, and the lack of commitment to the job manifested by many teachers. These are broader elements of the culture of private EFL schools which have undeniable implications for the feasibility of creating research cultures.

Overall, then, if we return to the stages of development in research cultures discussed at the start of this chapter (Ebbutt, 2002), I would have to conclude that there is little evidence here of research cultures in language teaching contexts. There are of course individuals, teachers, and managers, who do value research engagement, but there is no wider sense here in language teaching organizations of research engagement being 'at the heart of the school, its outlook, systems and activity' (Handscomb & Macbeath, 2003: 4) or of it being a central component in the way that such organizations strive for excellence. There is typically no expectation that teachers will be research engaged, or else teachers are encouraged to be so but not given any concrete support. There were also cases where teachers were seen to be research engaged, but their activities consisted mainly of reading practical teaching publications and developing and testing teaching materials and fell short of the kind of systematic empirical inquiry that research implies. The facilitative conditions for research engagement suggested by McLaughlin, Black-Hawkins, & McIntyre (2004) and Carter & Halsall (1998) at the start of this chapter simply do not exist. Culture is often defined simply as 'the way things are done'; research engagement, on the basis of the evidence generated by my programme of research, is not part of the way things are done in language teaching. In the final two chapters of this book I will respond to this conclusion by examining ways in which language teacher research engagement can be productively promoted. First I will discuss examples of actual teacher research projects, then, in Chapter 9, I will outline some principles for promoting teacher research engagement. These will be informed by the suggestions teachers and managers made in this chapter for creating stronger research cultures.

Notes

1   According to Bryman & Cramer (2005: 78), 0.8 is the alpha level which indicates a good level of conceptual relatedness among items.
2   I am aware that in the statistical methods literature debates exist about the use of Cronbach's alpha as a measure of internal reliability (e.g. Sijtsma, 2009); my use of this statistic for such a purpose, though, reflects widespread practice in social science research.

References

Bai, L., & Hudson, P. (2011). Understanding Chinese TEFL academics' capacity for research. *Journal of Further and Higher Education, 35*(3), 391–407.

Barker, P. (2005). *Research in schools and colleges*: National Educational Research Forum Working Paper 7.2. Retrieved 15 February, 2012, from www.eep.ac.uk/nerf/word/WP7.2withappendixe42d.doc?version=1

Borg, S. (2006). Conditions for teacher research. *English Teaching Forum, 44*(4), 22–27.

Bryman, A., & Cramer, D. (2005). *Quantitative data analysis with SPSS 12 and 13*. Routledge: London.

Carter, K., & Halsall, R. (1998). Teacher research for school improvement. In R. Halsall (Ed.), *Teacher research and school improvement: Opening doors from the inside* (pp. 71–90). Buckingham: Open University Press.

Davies, P., Hamilton, M., & James, K. (2007). *Maximising the impact of practitioner research: A handbook of practical advice*. London: NRDC.

Ebbutt, D. (2002). The development of a research culture in secondary schools. *Educational Action Research, 10*(1), 123–142.

Halsall, R. (1998). School improvement: An overview of key findings and messages. In R. Halsall (Ed.), *Teacher research and school improvement: Opening doors from the inside* (pp. 28–53). Buckingham: Open University Press.

Handscomb, G., & Macbeath, J. (2003). *The research-engaged school.* Chelmsford: Essex County Council.

McLaughlin, C., Black-Hawkins, K., & McIntyre, D. (2004). *Researching teachers, researching schools, researching networks: A review of the literature.* Cambridge and Cranfield: Faculty of Education, University of Cambridge and National College of School Leadership.

Schein, E. H. (1985). *Organizational culture and leadership.* San Francisco: Jossey-Bass Publishers.

Sharp, C. (2007). *Making research make a difference. Teacher research: A small-scale study to look at impact.* Chelmsford: Flare.

Sharp, C., Eames, A., Sanders, D., & Tomlinson, K. (2005). *Postcards from research-engaged schools.* Slough: NFER.

Sharp, C., Eames, A., Sanders, D., & Tomlinson, K. (2006). *Leading a research-engaged school.* Nottingham: National College for School Leadership.

Sijtsma, K. (2009). On the use, the misuse, and the very limited usefulness of Cronbach's alpha. *Psychometrika, 74*(1), 107–120.

Westwell, J. (2006). *Sustaining teacher researchers: What support really makes a difference?* Paper presented at the Teacher Research Conference 2006, Birmingham, UK. Retrieved 14 February, 2012, from http://media.education.gov.uk/assets/files/pdf/w/westwell.pdf

8 Facilitating teacher research projects

8.1 Introduction

In previous chapters I have provided an empirical analysis of various dimensions of teacher research engagement, drawing on the perspectives of language teachers and managers from around the world. My focus now turns to a discussion of initiatives through which teachers can be encouraged to do research. I will first comment briefly on existing literature which provides insight into such activity in the field of language teaching, before analyzing in detail two initiatives for supporting teacher research that I have been involved in. One of my purposes here is to highlight ways in which an awareness of many of the issues and constraints highlighted in previous chapters can inform efforts to support teacher research engagement. My analysis here is informed by personal experience and teacher feedback (via written evaluations) on the projects they took part in.

8.2 Promoting teacher research

Several published collections of research conducted by teachers generally (e.g. Meyers & Rust, 2003) and language teachers specifically are available. Burns (2010b), for example, reviews 12 volumes of language teacher research published since 2000, while Borg (2010) discusses additional earlier material as well as more recent publications. This literature provides positive evidence of engagement in research by language teachers in a range of global contexts. I have, however, been critical of such work on a number of grounds (Borg, 2010), in particular because much of it consists of dissertations produced in the context of higher education. For example, three of the volumes from Oman I have edited (Borg, 2006, 2008, 2009b) consist of BA dissertations, while the collection on teachers using tasks (Edwards & Willis, 2005) and that from Turkey (Phipps, 2006) are the result of MA dissertations. My experience over many years of supervising research projects on undergraduate and postgraduate degree programmes suggests that, in such circumstances, academic requirements can override teachers' concerns for conducting meaningful inquiry in their own contexts. In other words, teachers' priorities are typically to complete (within a restricted time) a project that allows them to obtain their qualification. I am not of course suggesting that research done in the context of formal study cannot inform teachers' understandings of their own practices (Wyatt, 2010 provides examples of cases where this does occur). Under such conditions, though, academic requirements can 'transform teacher research into an exercise driven by largely instrumental goals' (Borg, 2010: 406). Therefore, I would not view the context of formal study as a productive one in which to study the processes through which teachers learn to be research engaged. (Kiely et al., 2004, though, provide an interesting analysis of their attempts to promote such learning in the context of an MA TESOL programme.) Reis-Jorge's (2007: 415) experience of promoting teacher research in an academic context led him to conclude that if our goal is to promote teacher research, 'a formally designed research project produced to meet the criteria imposed by academic regulations may not be the most appropriate kind of project'. I do not think that the problem in such situations is the fact that the project is formally designed; rather, my concerns lie more with the impact that the academic requirements have on teachers' purposes in doing their research. An analysis of teacher research produced in the context of formal study, then, may not generate realistic understandings of teacher research engagement.

In this chapter, I would thus like to focus on the processes of supporting teacher research engagement outside the confines of formal study. This considerably narrows down the range of available material. The eight volumes in the *Teachers' Voices* series (e.g. Burns & de Silva Joyce, 2005; Burns & Hood, 1995) emerged from a series of action research projects run by the National Centre for English Language Teaching and Research (NCELTR) at Macquarie University, Sydney. Teachers in these projects worked on the Adult Migrant English Program (AMEP), a national programme funded by the Australian Government's Department of Immigration and Ethnic Affairs. These teachers worked collaboratively in studying specific themes (e.g. reading, course design, vocabulary teaching). Of particular interest here is the manner in which teacher research was supported on this project. A chapter in the publication that emerged from the first iteration of this project (Burns, 1995: 12–13) provides the summary of the processes involved, which is given in Figure 8.1.

Clearly, this programme of teacher research was well funded over a number of years and thus allowed for a substantial amount of structure and support to be built in. The project provided opportunities for dialogue among participants, an outlet for the dissemination of

1 Introductory workshop
- familiarisation with background and aims of project
- introduction to action research process, methods and procedures
- overview/discussion of shifts in AMEP curriculum approaches
- reflection and discussion of key concerns in competency-based approaches within teachers' own contexts
- development of proforma for systematic data collection
- clarification of agreed timeframes, additional sources of data, teacher-researcher teams

2 Collaborative teacher-researcher teams
- establishment of meeting times and action plans
- interviews/discussions between teachers and researchers
- classroom observations and joint teaching/participation in classroom
- recording of discussions/observations
- analysis of documentation collected – proformas, teaching plans, student writing, classroom materials, teaching centre plans / documents

3 Contact with other teacher participants
- telephone contact / discussion of progress
- collection of submitted data – proformas, teaching plans, materials etc
- ongoing liaison, monitoring and advice to participants

4 Meetings of project team
- collation of emerging data
- documentation of individual involvement
- comparison and analysis of emerging themes
- use of data on emerging issues to develop survey for program managers

5 Surveys and interviews with program managers
- investigation of managerial and administrative issues
- survey of program managers in all teaching centres
- face-to-face interviews with program managers in participating teachers' centres
- audio recording of interviews

6 Follow-up workshop
- dissemination of analysis of emerging issues to project teachers
- teachers' reflections and discussion of emerging issues
- problem posing and reflection on individual emerging issues
- establishment and refining of further specific research areas / issues for teacher investigation and documentation (e.g. developing units of work)

7 Writing up
- further analysis of specific areas through process of writing
- individual support to teachers' documentation of specific areas
- production of individual teachers' reports on specific areas

Figure 8.1   Summary of AMEP action research project (Burns, 1995: 14–15)

their work, and also worked closely with teachers' schools to maximize the internal support they received; external expertise was available to support teachers (including through the initial workshop) and participating teachers also received some financial compensation for the time they committed to the project. Such levels of resourcing for teacher research projects are unusual, but the *Teachers' Voices* series shows clearly that sustained and productive teacher participation in such projects is more likely when appropriate support structures are in place.

Further insights into the conduct of teacher research projects are provided by Nunan (1995), who considers three individual problematic cases. The first project took place in the 1980s, in the context of language curriculum reform in Australia, and involved secondary school teachers of a wide range of languages. Nunan describes two basic conditions he stipulated to the sponsors of the project at its outset: it needed to take place over time (i.e. 2–3 years) and teachers had to be given eight full days of paid release time. The first condition was agreed to; the second, through negotiation, was eventually revised so that teachers received eight half days of paid release time. After a promising start, Nunan reports on the critical challenges that the project faced. First, teachers were only allowed to research issues that the funders felt were relevant. This 'violates one of the fundamental principles of action research – the freedom of the individual concerned to determine what to investigate, how to investigate, and how to report' (p. 5–6). A second constraint was that official time for teachers to receive support outside the classroom from experts and peers was limited. Similar difficulties were reported in the two other teacher research projects Nunan describes in this paper and in his overall analysis of 'what went wrong' several adverse factors are highlighted, including a lack of time for teachers to do the research, interference by the administration, and a lack of skills and knowledge among teachers.

The Languages Inservice Program for Teachers (LIPT) was another large, funded programme in Australia that promoted action research. It ran from 1998 for four years and was, as with *Teachers' Voices*, characterized by the provision of various forms of support for teachers. In an evaluation of LIPT, Burton (1992: 3–4) describes the support received by facilitators and participants as follows:

- Systemic – teacher release time (TRT), eight days
- Peer group support: teachers joined a network group led by a facilitator
- Individual: teachers consulted their network group facilitator or a project officer on a one-to-one basis

- Organized input: conferences were held at strategic points during LIPT
- School involvement: LIPT projects officers invited contact with participants' school senior staff
- LIPT publications: after LIPT 1, all LIPT participants had access to the published reports from previous LIPTs.

This project thus, once again, benefited from various levels of support; according to Burton's evaluation, participants particularly acknowledged the importance of systemic support and input.

The papers in Tinker Sachs (2002b) emerged from a funded two-year action research project called *Fostering and furthering effective practices in the teaching of English*. This took place in Hong Kong in the context of education policy which encouraged (at least on paper) stronger collaborative links between universities and schools. This project thus took the form of a partnership in which university lecturers worked with classroom teachers in developing video cases of effective classroom practice. Tinker Sachs (2002a) provides particular insight into the challenges encountered on this project. One of these was recruiting teacher participants – from the original target of 25, only 8 sustained their participation for the whole project. Developing positive relationships between the lecturers and teachers was also difficult, given the varying roles these two groups customarily fulfilled and their different perspectives on effective practice in teaching English. The teachers also highlighted the time constraints they worked under (it was not clear whether the teachers received any reduction in teaching for the project) while there also seemed to be little support for or interest in the teachers' work within their schools (i.e. among colleagues and administrators). Overall, given these constraints, it was an achievement that eight teachers completed the project. In explaining why they did so, Tinker Sachs (2002a) suggests that above all it was their voluntary desire to improve their teaching which kept them going; the teachers also valued the support they received from the lecturers during the project.

One final initiative involving teacher research (again from Australia) is described in Burns (2011). This was a six-month programme through which six teachers in the Australian ELICOS (English Language Intensive Courses for Overseas Students) scheme were supported in conducting action research in their classrooms. This project was funded by Cambridge ESOL. In terms of its structure, the project consisted of three workshops (roughly two months apart and lasting a total of three and a half days) with email support provided to the teachers in between these workshops. Support was provided via an external facilitator and through the professional development officer of English Australia, the professional association for colleges involved in ELICOS. The outcomes of the six action research projects completed were presented through a colloquium at English Australia's 2010 annual conference and published in Issue 44 of *Research Notes* (www.cambridgeesol.org/rs_notes/rs_nts44.pdf). In reflecting on the project, Burns (2011) comments on the key conditions that facilitated it:

> … it was initiated and supported at the level of a whole educational system operating nationally. It was further supported by external sponsorship by a major international and high-profile organization … In addition, the colleges where the teachers worked gave their full support, both materially and professionally, to the additional work the teachers were doing. (pp. 3–4)

Additionally, teachers were volunteers and, within the priorities of ELICOS, free to decide on the focus of the action research studies. Challenges highlighted in this project related to sustaining virtual interaction among participants outside the group workshops, finding time to do research in addition to teaching and personal commitments, and selecting and implementing data collection methods.

A number of additional papers provide, on a much smaller scale to the initiatives described so far, insight into the processes through which language teachers engage in research. Denny (2005) discusses a collaborative action research project which involved teachers of English at a tertiary institution in New Zealand. The structure of this two-year project was described as follows:

> The group carrying out the classroom studies was set up at the end of 2002. There were eight members in 2003 and four in 2004. Each member carried out an investigation in his or her own classroom. The group met six times in 2003 and five times in 2004 to give mutual support, report on progress and discuss insights gained from their investigations. Between meetings they also talked informally and shared readings from the literature. At an initial meeting the principles of action research and data collection were briefly outlined and discussed. (p. 61)

The processes the teachers went through on this project were documented primarily through notes taken during teacher meetings. These showed that the predominant concerns of the teachers throughout the project were methodological ones (i.e. to do with designing instruments for data collection). Features of the project that facilitated teachers' sustained engagement in it were (a) some release from teaching; (b) voluntary participation; (c) an intellectual challenge; (d) an extended period of time to do research; and (e) teachers working in 'buddy' groups (i.e. pairs who met more frequently than the whole group did) – see also Atay, 2006, who paired up pre- and in-service teachers to do research. What was felt to be lacking, though, was input and support by an experienced action researcher; in particular, a workshop in which teachers new to research received guidance on research methodology would have improved teachers' ability to engage productively in the project.

Brindley (1991) examined the processes through which teachers become researchers in a small-scale study involving six respondents. His goal was to understand 'the perceptions of the research process of teachers who had newly become researchers' (p. 91). Through interviews with the teachers, the author elicited their views on the research process and on the kinds of support they appreciated. These included working collaboratively with colleagues or supervisors, hands on workshops and courses on research methods, institutional commitment, and access to literature. The conclusions to this analysis reiterate one of the key themes I want to stress in this chapter – the need for structure and support in initiatives which seek to promote teacher research:

> The accounts of the teachers in this study suggest that teacher educators who work in an institutional context can facilitate the research process in a number of ways. They can assist by providing teacher-researchers with initial support in framing research questions; by introducing them to research tools and methods which allow them to work through their own questions in a step by step fashion; by being available for consultation throughout the research process; by setting up research partnerships and/or networks as appropriate; by making sure that they are given due recognition for the time and effort expended; and by assisting with the publication and/or dissemination of the results of teacher-conducted research. (p. 104)

One final paper I would like to discuss here is Atay (2008). This study reports on a six-week teacher research programme run for 18 teachers of English at a university preparatory school in Turkey. The course took the form of four-hour sessions after classes each afternoon and was divided into three two-week blocks dealing with, respectively, theoretical knowledge of ELT, issues for investigation, and investigating the classroom and doing research. The second block covered the theory of doing research (e.g. ways of collecting data) and allowed the teachers to develop their research plans; in the final two-week block the teachers discussed their proposals and started their research projects. They were then expected to continue these projects independently (with email support from the tutor) and to submit a report. Six teachers did so by the end of the course.

Of the different teacher research initiatives described so far, this example seems to have taken place in particularly demanding circumstances; sessions were after school each day (i.e. no remission from teaching was made available to the participants) and the fieldwork was condensed into an (unrealistically) intensive period of two weeks. Some claims about the benefits of teacher research to the professional development of the participants on this course were made, but it is unlikely that significant impacts could have been achieved in the limited time available and in the circumstances that the teachers were expected to do their projects. It was not at all surprising that only a few teachers submitted a report of their work.

So far, then, I have reviewed a number of published reports of projects which encouraged teachers, outside the context of formal study, to engage in research or, in one case, which examined teachers' reactions to becoming researchers. These projects collectively highlight a number of features which influence the success of teacher research initiatives. One recurrent key feature is the availability of appropriate support, and, as noted above, this can take many forms: access to literature, on-going mentoring and feedback (including from external experts), theoretical input, opportunities for collaboration with peers, and institutional support, including time and physical resources. Clearly, where support is lacking, attempts to promote teacher research are less likely to succeed, even with motivated teachers.

Various models for promoting teacher research were also evident in the projects discussed above: large-scale, long-term and well-funded projects co-ordinated by expert researchers and supported at state or even national level; institutional or departmental projects initiated by teachers; and intensive short-term projects facilitated by a local or external advisor. Even where support is available, short programmes are less likely to be productive in achieving the kinds of benefits which teacher research has the potential to deliver; this is because the pressure to conceptualize, execute, and report a study in a limited time militates against the development of the understanding teachers need time to develop in order to conduct projects which are of value to their work.

At this stage I will proceed to discuss in detail two further initiatives for promoting teacher research that I have been involved in. In each case I will focus on the structures and processes involved rather than the actual outcomes, though, of course, in arguing for the success of these initiatives I will also point to some concrete outcomes that were achieved. At the outset it needs to be stated that I present these courses not as flawless prescriptions but as reflections on experiences that I and the participants have found of value in supporting teacher research engagement. There were naturally challenges in both courses and these too will be highlighted. Also, as noted earlier, the evidence I draw on here derives from my personal experience of these courses and from the written feedback about them provided by the participating teachers.

8.3 Researching ELT in Oman

I referred above to three collections of dissertations produced by teachers of English in Oman and which I edited. Additionally, though, and outside the formal academic parameters which governed the three earlier volumes, I also facilitated a separate research project for a group of teachers and supervisors working for the Ministry of Education in Oman. I will now discuss this project and reflect on some of the characteristics which, I believe, enhanced its effectiveness[1].

Background

From 1999, the University of Leeds and the Ministry of Education in Oman collaborated for a decade on the BA TESOL project, a large-scale teacher education initiative which enhanced the professional knowledge and skills of almost 900 Omani teachers of English. One spin-off from the larger initiative was a teacher research project for Ministry of Education staff, and it is this project that I discuss here. The rationale for this project was that

> ... teachers are more likely to become engaged in doing research if they are encouraged to do so within a structured and supportive framework in which they have opportunities to learn, experiment and to receive feedback from more experienced researchers. Teachers are not likely to engage in research in any sustained way if they are simply encouraged to do so. If the Ministry wishes research to become part of teachers' professional activities, a framework for enabling this needs to be put in place. (Course proposal, p. 1)

The course proposal also specified the following objectives:

1   to deepen participants' understandings of key issues in the conduct of ELT research
2   to develop participants' skills in designing, implementing, and reporting a piece of high quality ELT classroom research
3   to enable each participant to complete a piece of ELT classroom research
4   to create among participants a network of researchers who are able to continue promoting and supporting ELT research in Oman.

Participants on this project were 25 employees of the Ministry of Education in Oman. They came from all around the country and were volunteers. The project did not lead to any formal qualification.

Project design

The project lasted two years. As Figure 8.2 shows, it was divided into four phases of six months each. Each phase consisted of an initial intensive teaching block in Oman lasting one week followed by a longer period of independent study and research. For the input week, participants were released from work; during the independent study periods, they were at work but were granted a remission of one day a week to work on their research projects.

The intensive teaching blocks consisted of input and more practical hands-on and discussion activities in class, individual tutorials, and private library study. The focus of the input reflected the stage of the project we were at; for example, basic issues in doing research (e.g. writing research questions) were covered in Phase 1. During the independent study phases, participants were required to complete intermediate tasks, such as writing progress reports, submitting drafts of instruments, and, in the final phase, drafts of their report. They received written feedback on all the work they submitted. An online forum was also set up as an additional form of peer support, though, as I discuss later, this was not utilized.

For each phase there was one overall outcome. For Phase 1 this was a research proposal, for Phase 2 a pilot study report, for Phase 3 the completion of the fieldwork, and for Phase 4 the final report. The Ministry of Education were positively disposed to publishing the

Phase	Goal	Input	Output
Phase 1 Jan–Jun 2007	Write research proposal	Basics of educational research	Research proposal
Phase 2 Jul–Dec 2007	Complete pilot study	Collecting data	Pilot study report
Phase 3 Jan–Jun 2008	Complete fieldwork	Analyzing data	Fieldwork report
Phase 4 Jul–Dec 2008	Write up research	Analyzing and writing up data	Final report

Figure 8.2   Oman research project structure

final reports in a book if they were of suitable quality and participants were told this at the start of the course.

Project evaluation

Written feedback was collected from teachers at the end of each phase of the project; additionally, at the end of the project (and after they had submitted their final reports) teachers were asked to complete a written evaluation form (administered as an email attachment) which asked for their views on a range of issues such as the benefits and challenges they experienced, factors which motivated them to complete their research projects, and the kinds of support they found most valuable. The analysis below draws on these final written evaluations. Before discussing these, though, the success of the project can also be considered in terms of the number of participants who submitted a report and the quality of the work produced. Of the 25 participants who started the course, 19 submitted their final research report some two years later. Given the demands of the course, and the fact that it did not lead to any formal qualification, this must be considered an excellent completion rate. In terms of the quality of the work completed, this was generally admirable and all 19 completed projects were published in an edited collection (Borg, 2009a). Figure 8.3 lists the titles of these projects.

Turning now to an analysis of participants' written evaluations of the course, overall, these were very positive. As one teacher wrote, 'The course was of immense value to me professionally especially considering the fact that I did not have any pre-service or in-service training in this regard prior to the course ... It also deepened my understanding of the value of research for professional development and the exchange of knowledge during it was invaluable.' More specifically, they noted that through the project they had

- learned how to do good quality research
- learned how to evaluate research
- become equipped to help others do research
- been prepared to do further research
- become enthusiastic about doing research.

They also felt it had an impact on their theoretical knowledge and practical skills in relation to research as well as on their attitudes to research. As one teacher explained, 'First I felt that doing research is not interesting, but now I can say that doing research is very interesting.'

- EFL teachers' perceptions and practices regarding reflective writing
- Secondary school teachers' attitudes towards reflection
- The characteristics of post-lesson discussions
- Senior English teachers' views of the benefits of post-lesson discussions
- Peer observation: teachers' beliefs and practices
- High school English teachers' views about peer observation
- Teachers' beliefs about peer observation
- Supervisors' perceptions of the supervisory process
- English teachers' perceptions of professional development activities
- English teachers' perceptions of workload
- Using quality circles to solve work-related problems
- Students' beliefs about learning to speak English
- Using pictures in teaching vocabulary in elementary classrooms
- Teachers' beliefs about using group work in basic education
- Teachers' practices and beliefs about explicit grammar teaching
- Teachers' questions in the English language classroom
- Teachers' beliefs about learner autonomy
- Slow learners: how are they identified and supported?
- Teachers' beliefs about using Arabic in the English classroom.

Figure 8.3   Titles of Oman teacher research projects (Borg, 2009a)

In reflecting on the challenges they faced during the project, the two key issues highlighted by the teachers were access to resources and time. Regarding the first of these, a number of participants noted that finding suitable literature for their project locally in Oman was difficult. Participants were provided with reading packs and they were also supplied with electronic articles to support their work; however, they did not have direct access to electronic journals. In terms of time, the feelings of several participants were summed up in one comment which noted that 'time was a major challenge, because we had to teach and do our research at the same time'. Although a one-day release from work had been approved for all participants, the regional authorities around the country varied in the extent to which they provided this time consistently. In fact, only just over 26% of the participants said that day release was the time when they usually worked on their research, compared to 36% who said they did so mainly in the evenings.

The project did make considerable demands on the participants' time. In explaining what motivated them to persist for two years, participants said the most influential factors were their own interest in learning about and doing research, the knowledge that the project would prepare them for further studies, knowing that their final report would be published by the Ministry, and tutor feedback. Encouragement from colleagues, promotion, and being released from work were the three least motivating factors. Participants also felt the need to apply themselves as a way of showing their appreciation to their employer for providing the course; as one explained, 'I can say that you sometimes feel that the Ministry of Education provides us a good chance to improve ourselves and we should appreciate it. So we should do a good work in this course.'

As noted above, one form of support available to participants during the course was an electronic discussion forum. This gave participants the possibility to discuss their research with each other online. This facility was not used by participants, though, and they gave a range of reasons for this. Primary amongst their reasons was novelty – as one participant explained, 'I think this happened because we are not used to such method.' Concerns about the extent to which peer support and sharing would be valuable were also evident. One participant wrote that 'all of us don't know how to do research, so I was worried about asking anyone'; similar concerns about peers' abilities to help each other were reflected in the comment, 'The tutor was there to answer and he is more knowledgeable than others who might mislead us.'

Facilitative conditions

One aspect of the Oman course that was not ideal was that the teachers only saw myself and each other at the one-week meetings twice a year. They would have certainly benefited from ongoing local support and from opportunities to support one another in between these intensive blocks. Nonetheless, there were a number of features of the project which facilitated the positive outcomes it achieved:

1   Participants were motivated; the participants on this project were volunteers, genuinely interested in learning to do research, and persevered despite significant challenges.
2   The project focused not just on technical knowledge about doing research but, especially in Phase 1, on making explicit and reviewing participants' beliefs about the nature of research and of its role in the work of ELT professionals.
3   The project was sponsored by the Ministry of Education; participants appreciated this support and it also meant that it was possible for some release from normal duties to be provided.
4   It was extensive; the fact that it was spread over two years meant that the teachers' projects could unfold systematically and thoughtfully rather than being rushed; thus, for example, all participants did a pilot study and submitted a report on this

in the first six months of the course. These pilot studies made a significant contribution to the eventual quality of the projects.

5   It was structured; in between the intensive face-to-face meetings participants had a schedule of tasks to complete and were required to submit periodic progress reports. This gave them clear targets to aim for and enabled them to develop their projects systematically.

6   Participants received regular feedback on their work; although this did place considerable demands on me as the sole tutor, every piece of work that participants submitted received written feedback. This was important in enabling participants to identify and address significant potential problems with their research. Feedback also kept participants motivated.

7   The tutor was an experienced researcher familiar with the professional context in which the participants were planning and doing research. I had almost 10 years' experience of working with teachers of English in Oman and this background was invaluable; it allowed me to better understand the kinds of issues that were being researched and to support participants more effectively.

8   The project had a strong practical orientation; theoretical issues were discussed, but throughout, the focus was on how to plan, do, and report research, leading to a very concrete output at the end.

9   The research projects were conducted in participants' own working contexts, giving the work strong local relevance.

10 Opportunities for dissemination were provided. Participants were motivated by the prospect of their work being published.

11 The absence of the constraints associated with formal academic courses meant that on this course decisions about what content to cover and how to cover it could be made responsively, rather than being defined rigidly in advance. Through their regular input, participants were involved in on-going decisions about course content.

12 Participants decided what to focus their research projects on; there were no external pressures on the kinds of issues they could choose to examine. This element of choice ensured that their projects addressed issues they were interested in.

13 Although this remained an issue for some participants, access to literature was facilitated through reading packs, local academic libraries, and electronic resources made available by the tutor.

Procedurally, then, the project functioned well in sustaining the engagement in research of a group of language teaching professionals over a two-year period and allowing them to generate good quality studies. There were four outcomes I was less satisfied with, though.

One was the nature of a number of the projects participants undertook. In several cases, these were outward-looking (e.g. broader surveys of teachers) rather than an examination of some aspect of their own professional practices; in this sense, the project was not wholly successful in promoting teacher research as I defined it in Chapter 1. A second issue on this project was that there was little sense of collective enterprise or common sense of purpose; participants met twice a year for the input sessions but otherwise did not function as a research community – each individual focused on their own study. Third, although reports from the project were published, there were no attempts by the sponsor, as far as I am aware, to maximize the impact of this work and to consider what changes it might suggest to the ways the Ministry operates. For example, the project by A'Dhahab (2009) suggested that the requirement that they write regular written reflections on their lessons was perceived by teachers as an administrative task rather than a developmental one, and provided insights which policy makers could have acted on in very practical ways to review current practices. Finally (and this is a limitation common to the teacher research initiatives I discussed earlier in this chapter), evidence of any longer-term impacts of the research projects on the teachers' practices was not collected; I cannot claim, therefore, that as a result of taking part in the Oman project, participants were subsequently more effective (however 'effectiveness' is defined) in their work. Such a limitation has both conceptual and logistical dimensions; conceptually, establishing causal links between participation in a teacher research project and more effective practice is a complex undertaking; logistically, once projects end there is typically limited further formal contact between the facilitator and the participants, and thus no scope for the collection of evidence about longer-term impact of the project.

8.4 Researching 'Sense of Progress'

The second initiative for promoting teacher research engagement I will discuss here provides a contrast with the Oman project described above, yet, at a more fundamental level, it does highlight common facilitative conditions which can maximize the effectiveness of attempts to engage teachers in research.

Background

The project was entitled 'Sense of Progress' (SoP) and it was a project initiated by the British Council (the UK's international cultural relations body) in South-east Asia. Evaluations of the British Council's language teaching operations in the region had suggested that an important element of learner satisfaction was their sense of progress – the extent to which they felt they were learning. It was thus decided that developing a better understanding of 'sense of progress' (e.g. of what affects it and of how learners make judgements about it) would be of value to the organization. Teacher research was seen as an appropriate way of exploring these issues in language teaching centres around South-east Asia. It was at this point that I was invited to contribute to this project.

Following an initial discussion with the project manager responsible for this initiative, I produced a document in which I outlined some thoughts on how the teacher research projects might be set up. In particular, drawing on a recent review article on teacher research engagement (Borg, 2010), I suggested that attention to the following conditions would enhance the productivity of the initiative:

- appropriate understandings of what teacher research is, by both teachers and those supporting them
- support from mentors who have appropriate experience and/or understandings of teacher research
- incentives, to create and sustain teacher motivation to engage in teacher research
- feasibility, to ensure that the targets set are realistic
- relevance, to the teachers' working contexts and concerns
- structure, so that participants have a clear sense of direction and an understanding of what is required at each stage
- outcomes, so that at the end of the process there is a tangible product that can be shared.

One issue I particularly stressed at the planning stage was that the project would be more sustainable if the teachers were supported by senior teachers or middle managers who had been suitably prepared. The British Council were responsive to this and the other above suggestions.

Participants

Teachers working in ten language teaching centres in eight countries in South-east Asia participated in this course (the countries were Thailand, Vietnam, Korea, Japan, Malaysia, Singapore, Hong Kong, and Taiwan). They were all experienced and had a first degree and certificate- or diploma-level qualifications in TEFL. They were officially allocated three hours a week to participate in the project. Additionally, eight middle managers, from the same eight countries covered by the teachers, also participated in the project. Each manager was the mentor for the teacher (or teachers, in two cases) in their country.

Project design

The project lasted just over seven months. The first phase of this project consisted of two separate workshops for mentors and teachers. Each workshop lasted two full days and was held in Bangkok. In terms of content, the teachers' workshop covered standard issues relevant to the research process, e.g. understanding what research is, the research process, writing research questions, developing a proposal, collecting data. On both days, the afternoons were allocated to proposal writing (e.g. drafting research questions) as one of our goals was for the teachers to have an outline of their projects by the end of the second day. The managers' workshop also covered basic issues in the research process, though the emphasis was on their ability to support research rather than on actually doing it themselves.

Having the teacher and manager workshops consecutively allowed for interplay between the two. For example, teachers were asked in their workshop to draw up a list of the kinds of issues they would expect their mentors to help them with. Mentors were also asked to make a list of the kinds of support they felt they could realistically provide, then they were shown the teachers' suggestions. This was a useful way of minimizing significant differences in teacher and mentor expectations during the project. Teachers were also asked to identify the main challenges they felt they would experience during the project (see Figure 8.4); this list of challenges was also made available to the mentors as a way of sensitizing them to the kinds of support the teachers might need.

Within three weeks of completing the workshop, teachers were asked to submit a proposal and timetable for their projects to their mentors and to myself, and I provided individual written feedback

- In the later stages of analysis and writing up we may be pressed for time
- Time management
- Keeping volume of data manageable
- Deciding how to collect data
- Juggling the project and all my other responsibilities
- Designing a questionnaire
- Keeping to schedule
- Protecting hours down
- Finishing the project on time
- Refining the research questions
- Getting hold of relevant books

Figure 8.4   Main challenges anticipated by teachers on the 'Sense of Progress' project

on these. This was the only point at which I provided direct feedback to the teachers; for the remaining six months of the project, teachers sent queries and work for feedback to their mentors, and the mentors would consult me as required. This was one significant difference to the Oman project described above, where I was solely responsible for all the participants and for providing feedback on their work. During the fieldwork stage, teachers had access to a range of journals and, in some cases, to research methods texts which the teaching centres involved had been advised to purchase. A number of additional readings on doing research were made available electronically.

Project evaluation

Teachers were asked to submit final reports of up to 4,000 words by mid-June 2011. Seven teachers did so by this deadline (Figure 8.5 lists the titles of these projects). All teachers who submitted their reports, and the majority of their mentors, convened in Seoul in July 2011 for a review event. The purposes of this meeting were for the teachers to give oral presentations of their work, for us to review the project and to identify strategies for disseminating and maximizing the impact of the findings. The opportunity for teachers to present and discuss their findings was welcomed by all participants; it provided a concrete way of concluding the project and created much enthusiasm for seeking ways of using the results generated to inform the practice and policy within the British Council.

Participant evaluations of the project were elicited both individually and collectively. Individually, each participant completed a written feedback form in which they were asked to comment, in an open-ended manner on the positive aspects and key challenges of the project, and to assess the effectiveness of the various forms of support that were

---

- Learner expectations and sense of progress
- How Iranian students perceive and measure their current level of ability and sense of progress in regards to their writing skills at intermediate level
- Learners' response to the use of self-assessment as a tool to inform them of their progress
- Assessment, young learners and sense of progress
- Factors that intermediate level adult students feel have an effect on their sense of progress
- Factors that affect the sense of progress of pre-intermediate level learners
- Sense of progress: What are our primary parents thinking?

Figure 8.5   Titles of 'Sense of Progress' teacher research projects

provided. Collectively, at the final meeting in Seoul, participants worked in groups to generate lists of both the benefits they experienced through the project and the challenges. As Figure 8.6 shows, they identified a wide range of benefits, and these support and extend the discussion of the benefits of teacher research discussed in Chapter 1. Thus we see here references to 'a generative learning experience' which created enthusiasm and a broader view of research; it impacted on teachers' knowledge and on their understandings of their learners; and it was felt to be a catalyst for change, both in the teachers' own classrooms and also in their school, with potential for broader change within the organization too. Finally, participants noted the impact that doing and supporting a teacher research project had on their sense of unity and on their reputation and credibility. The comment that 'engaging seriously in research builds connections and lends kudos to both individual teachers and the organization as a whole' is, I think, a powerful testimony to the broader value of organizationally supported teacher research.

In terms of the challenges that participants experienced, these related to issues of time, support, resources, and communication. Both teachers and mentors faced many competing demands on their time during their project; the teachers would have appreciated more direct access to an outside expert for technical advice on aspects of their research. In some cases teachers did not have easy access to relevant literature; while more opportunities for peer interaction during the fieldwork stage (e.g. via an online forum or wiki) would, teachers felt, also have enhanced their experience.

Some six months after the end of the project, participants were contacted and asked to comment in writing on the extent to which their research projects had had a positive impact on their own work, that of their colleagues, and on their schools more generally. The responses were encouraging; for example, one teacher noted, 'It has definitely given me a better insight into how my students view assessment and how assessment systems can impact on my students', while another described the ongoing impact of her research into what 'progress' means to her learners as follows:

> As far as my own teaching goes, the project showed me that my instincts about my learners were right but that some of their difficulties in terms of their view of progress are far more deeply ingrained than I'd thought. I am now much more aware of just how important it is to address some of my findings, especially having high and unrealistic expectations. I have done a lot of work since in terms of highlighting to the learners the progress they make and they have been giving me positive feedback about how they feel in class. Also, myself and a colleague are still working towards helping them identify what progress is, and how to be able to recognise the progress they are making.

Research-related benefits

- The project provided 'space' and resources/support to carry out research and think about interesting issues.
- It was a real generative learning experience and provided an opportunity for CPD through reading and research that most of us haven't had the chance to do before.
- It gave a broader view of research.
- It fostered enthusiasm for action research and generated ideas for extended research.

Impact for learners

- The project led to a greater understanding of what learners are thinking, how they react to different activities and what they take from them.
- It showed the importance of enabling learners to make connections between activities and how raising awareness is important for learner autonomy.
- It reminded us how important it is to explain to learners what we are trying to do at every stage of our lessons.
- We gained insights into customers' needs/wants and their perception of the educational process.

Insights and information

- The project helped us gain knowledge. The research feeds into many aspects, e.g. course development, marketing, profiling of successful learners.
- It gave us an insight into the country we work in, the students, and parents.
- It helps us to be more 'customer driven', through identifying and closing gaps in perceptions.
- It challenges preconceptions for teachers, e.g. regarding what students think of self-assessment.

Teacher research as a catalyst for change

- Results of the project can be used for induction of new teachers.
- It provided a concrete way to inform our decisions and hence change the way courses are written and marketed, change assessment practices and meet customers' needs better.
- It has inspired colleagues to look at courses, do more research and change syllabuses.

Building connections

- It produced a unifying feeling across the region/network regarding involvement in research and not just the humdrum of everyday teaching.
- We enhance our reputation in the local community by sharing the results, leading to increased credibility amongst our own students and their parents.
- Showing that we are engaging seriously in research builds connections and lends kudos to both individual teachers and the organization as a whole.

Figure 8.6   Benefits of the 'Sense of Progress' project, according to participants

A third teacher explained his key finding – that 'sense of progress' is felt most keenly outside the classroom – informed a new advertising campaign showing learners using English outside a classroom setting; he also added that, 'Most importantly, the skills I learnt on the project enabled me to write and administer questionnaires and focus groups with more confidence and, I believe, validity. This has allowed me to investigate problems/opportunities with a renewed vigour.' Similarly positive reflections were provided by the teacher who wrote:

> The SoP project has indeed impacted positively on my own teaching. I have become more confident about setting self- and peer-assessed tasks for my students. I feel that I can justify why I am setting the tasks in such a way and that they should benefit my students in the long run, especially helping them to become more responsible and independent learners.

Overall, the feedback provided by the teachers six months after the SoP project emphasized its personal benefit to them and their teaching, although, as shown above, there was also some evidence that the findings from the project were being used more widely by the teachers' organization.

Facilitative conditions

The SoP project can be considered successful in a number of ways. Sustained participant engagement was achieved over several months and the overall completion rate (70%) was good; the quality of the research projects was (in my opinion) also sound and participants' evaluations of the project were, as we have seen, positive. The success of this project can be explained in relation to a number of facilitative conditions:

1 Organizational backing – the project was initiated, supported, and funded by the British Council
2 'Hours down' – the teachers were granted a reduction in their normal teaching duties to work on their projects
3 Opportunities for participants to enhance their technical knowledge of research, through the initial workshop
4 Mentoring throughout the project, via support from middle managers who had themselves been prepared for this role
5 A shared understanding by the teachers and their mentors about the purposes and parameters of the project
6 Access to resources, such as electronic journals and books on how to do research
7 Access to the expertise of an external advisor with experience of supporting teacher research

8 An emphasis on concrete outputs and dissemination, through a written report and an oral presentation
9 Motivated participants
10 Scope, within the established focus on 'sense of progress', for the teachers to identify issues for study that they were interested in and that were relevant to the work of their teaching centres.

Again, there is no suggestion here that the project was problem free; release from duties was, for example, implemented in variable ways across centres, while, as noted above, access to literature and to external advice was not always seen to be sufficient. It is hard to envisage any real-world teacher research project, however, that would be free of challenges, and overall there is ample evidence here that the SoP project was successful in enabling teachers to conduct projects which they found valuable to their practice. And in contrast to the Oman project described earlier, every project here focused on the teachers' own work and there was a sense of common purpose within the team. There was also a commitment to maximize the impact of the project more broadly within the organization, and above I quoted some evidence that suggests this did, at least at individual school level, take place.

8.5 Teaching research methods

A brief comment at this stage is merited in relation to the pedagogy of supporting teacher research. I have not included pedagogy in the lists of facilitative conditions outlined above, but it is clear that even where appropriate support structures, resources, and motivation exist, the absence of sound pedagogy in supporting teachers' understandings of and practices in research can limit what teachers achieve. However, while there is no shortage of books about doing teacher research in the field of language teaching (e.g. Burns, 2010a; Freeman, 1998), advice on the pedagogy of teaching research methods is scarce. In education generally, this is a topic that has been discussed periodically (e.g. Tashakkori & Teddle, 2003; Webb & Glesne, 1992), though typically in the context of research methods training for postgraduate research students. The few relevant sources that exist in language teaching (Diab, 2006; Kiely et al., 2004; Lorch, 2005) are also grounded in courses in undergraduate and postgraduate contexts. The teaching of action research has also been discussed in education (e.g. McKernan, 1996, Chapter 9) but, despite much attention to this specific form of teacher research in recent years, how it can be 'taught' to language teachers has not attracted much discussion, never mind empirical attention. This observation applies not just to teacher research but to the teaching of research methods more generally in language teaching and applied linguistics; we have no equivalent to, for example, *A Guide to Teaching Research Methods in Psychology* (Saville, 2008) or *Best Practices in Teaching Statistics and Research Methods in the Behavioral Sciences* (Dunn, Smith, & Beins, 2006). Clearly, an analysis of the characteristics of teacher research courses for language teachers is an area that merits research study in its own right, with particular attention to questions such as these:

1   What are the objectives of such courses for language teachers (e.g. propositional knowledge, technical competence, critical thinking – see Oliver & Williams, 2008)?

2   What content characterizes the curriculum of such courses (e.g. data collection strategies, statistics, mixed methods, foundational philosophical issues – see Page, 1997)?

3   How is the course structured (e.g. how long is it, how is material sequenced, what is the relationship between theoretical and practical components)?

4   What instructional practices are utilized (e.g. lectures, seminars, workshops, online materials – see Birbili, 2003 for several options)?

5   How is learning on such courses assessed (if it is)? (Several options are identified in the literature, such as oral presentations, article reviews, and reflective journals.)

6   What opportunities, if any, do teachers have for disseminating their research?

7   What facilitative conditions exist to enhance the effectiveness of teacher research courses (e.g. incentives for teachers, mentoring)?

8   What underlying principles and contextual factors, according to tutors, influence decisions regarding 1–5 above?

9   What are teachers' perceptions of the effectiveness and impact of the teacher research courses they attend?

10   What longer-term impact on teachers' work do teacher research courses have?

This chapter has provided insights into several of these issues for the two teacher research courses discussed here. What we need as a field, though, is a compilation and comparison of courses being taught in a range of language teaching contexts. I am sure that within our profession there exists much 'folk knowledge' (Glesne & Webb, 1993: 263) of what works in enabling teachers to become research engaged. At present, though, we lack both a research agenda for examining such issues (the list of questions above may provide some starting points) as well as the mechanisms through which those responsible for the design and delivery of language teacher research courses can interact and develop as a community of practice. I have for many years been passionate about enabling teachers to become teacher researchers; I have not been particularly successful, though, in identifying and developing sustained and productive networks with like-minded professionals in our field. I am sure many exist.

8.6 Conclusion

My focus in this chapter has been on the process of promoting teacher research engagement. Although much has been written about how to do teacher research and an increasing number of publications have reported the outcomes of such activity, there has to date been limited discussion of the processes through which teacher research engagement can be promoted. This is particularly true outside formal academic contexts. I have discussed in detail two initiatives I have been involved in, both set in motion by organizations for their staff as a form of professional development and which did not lead to any formal qualification. While contrasting in many ways, one unifying feature in both courses was the presence of a number of facilitative conditions which enhanced their effectiveness. Many attempts to promote research engagement among practising language teachers are unproductive because so many of the conditions I have highlighted here do not exist. I have also argued that more systematic study of courses of this kind from a range of contexts is required so that we can begin to develop a better understanding, grounded in evidence, of what works in relation to promoting language teacher research engagement.

At this point I move on to the final chapter in this book.

Notes

1   A video of a conference presentation I gave about this course is, at the time of writing, available at www.iatefl.britishcouncil.org/2010/sessions/2010-04-08/designing-effective-tesol-research-methods-courses-simon-borg (last accessed 21 August, 2012).

References

A'Dhahab, S. M. (2009). EFL teachers' perceptions and practices regarding reflective writing. In S. Borg (Ed.), *Researching English language teaching and teacher development in Oman* (pp. 1–15). Muscat: Ministry of Education, Oman.

Atay, D. (2006). Teachers' professional development: Partnerships in research. *TESL-EJ, 10*(2), 1–14.

Atay, D. (2008). Teacher research for professional development. *ELT Journal, 62*(2), 139–147.

Birbili, M. (2003). Teaching educational research methods. Retrieved 20 August, 2012, from www.escalate.ac.uk/resources/teachingresearchmethods/index.html

Borg, S. (Ed.). (2006). *Classroom research in ELT in Oman*. Muscat: Ministry of Education, Oman.

Borg, S. (Ed.). (2008). *Investigating English language teaching and learning in Oman*. Muscat: Ministry of Education, Oman.

Borg, S. (Ed.). (2009a). *Researching English language teaching and teacher development in Oman*. Muscat: Ministry of Education, Oman.

Borg, S. (Ed.). (2009b). *Understanding English language teaching and learning in Oman*. Muscat: Ministry of Education, Oman.

Borg, S. (2010). Language teacher research engagement. *Language Teaching, 43*(4), 391–429.

Brindley, G. (1991). Becoming a researcher: Teacher-conducted research and professional growth. In E. Sadtono (Ed.), *Issues in language teacher education* (pp. 89–105). Singapore: RELC.

Burns, A. (1995). Teacher researchers: Perspectives on teacher action research and curriculum renewal. In A. Burns & S. Hood (Eds.), *Teachers' voices: Exploring course design in a changing curriculum* (pp. 3–19). Sydney, Australia: NCELTR.

Burns, A. (2010a). *Doing action research in English language teaching. A guide for practitioners*. New York: Routledge.

Burns, A. (2010b). Teacher engagement in research: Published resources for teacher researchers. *Language Teaching, 43*(4), 527–536.

Burns, A. (2011). Embedding teacher research into a national language programme: Lessons from a pilot project. *Research Notes, 44*, 3–6.

Burns, A., & de Silva Joyce, H. (Eds.). (2005). *Teachers' voices 8: Explicitly supporting reading and writing in the classroom*. Sydney, Australia: NCELTR.

Burns, A., & Hood, S. (Eds.). (1995). *Teachers' voices: Exploring course design in a changing curriculum*. Sydney, Australia: NCELTR.

Burton, J. (1992). *The languages inservice program for teachers of languages other than English 1988–1991: An evaluation*. Adelaide: SA Education Department, Catholic Education Office & Independent Schools Board of South Australia.

Denny, H. (2005). Can busy classroom teachers really do action research? An action research study in an EAL tertiary setting. *New Zealand Studies in Applied Linguistics, 11*(2), 59–73.

Diab, R. L. (2006). Teaching practice and student learning in the introductory research methods class. *TESL-EJ, 10*(2). Retrieved 20 August, 2012, from www.tesl-ej.org/wordpress/issues/volume10/ej38/ej38a6

Dunn, D. S., Smith, R. A., & Beins, B. (2006). *Best practices in teaching statistics and research methods in the behavioral sciences*. Mahway: Lawrence Erlbaum Associates.

Edwards, C., & Willis, J. (Eds.). (2005). *Teachers exploring tasks in English language teaching*. Basingstoke: Palgrave Macmillan.

Freeman, D. (1998). *Doing teacher research*. Boston: Heinle and Heinle.

Glesne, C., & Webb, R. (1993). Teaching qualitative research: Who does what? *International Journal of Qualitative Studies in Education, 6*(3), 253–266.

Kiely, R., Clibbon, G., Rea-Dickins, P., Walter, C., & Woodfield, H. (2004). Teachers into researchers: A study of learning to research on a Masters in TESOL programme. Retrieved 12 February, 2012, from www.llas.ac.uk/projects/1454

Lorch, M. (2005). Turning students into researchers: Introduction to research methods in applied linguistics. Retrieved 20 August, 2012, from www.llas.ac.uk/resources/gpg/2273

McKernan, J. (1996). *Curriculum action research: A handbook of methods and resources for the reflective practitioner* 2nd ed. London: Kogan Page.

Meyers, E., & Rust, F. (Eds.). (2003). *Taking action with teacher research*. Portsmouth, NH: Heinemann.

Nunan, D. (1995). The more things change the more they stay the same: Or why action research doesn't work. In D. Nunan, R. Berry & V. Berry (Eds.), *Bringing about change in language education* (pp. 1–19). Hong Kong: The University of Hong Kong.

Oliver, M., & Williams, N. (2008). Engaging with the research methods curriculum. *Reflecting Education, 4*(1), 63–71. Retrieved 20 August, 2012, from http://reflectingeducation.net

Page, R. N. (1997). A thought about curriculum in qualitative research methods. *International Journal of Qualitative Studies in Education, 10*(2), 171–173.

Phipps, S. (Ed.). (2006). *Research news. IATEFL Research Newsletter, 17.*

Reis-Jorge, J. M. (2007). Teachers' conceptions of teacher-research and self-perceptions as enquiring practitioners – a longitudinal case study. *Teaching and Teacher Education, 23*(4), 402–417.

Saville, B. (2008). *A guide to teaching research methods in psychology*. Oxford: Blackwell.

Tashakkori, A., & Teddle, C. (2003). Issues and dilemmas in teaching research methods courses in social and behavioural sciences. *International Journal of Social Research Methodology, 6*(1), 61–77.

Tinker Sachs, G. (2002a). Fostering and furthering effective investigative practices. In G. Tinker Sachs (Ed.), *Action research in English language teaching* (pp. 23–65). Hong Kong: City University of Hong Kong.

Tinker Sachs, G. (Ed.). (2002b). *Action research in English language teaching*. Hong Kong: City University of Hong Kong.

Webb, R. B., & Glesne, C. (1992). Teaching qualitative research. In M. D. LeCompte, W. L. Millroy & J. Preissle (Eds.), *The handbook of qualitative research in education* (pp. 771–814). San Diego, CA: Academic Press.

Wyatt, M. (2010). Teachers researching their own practice. *ELT Journal, 65*(4), 417–425.

9 *Promoting language teacher research engagement*

9.1 Introduction

In this concluding chapter I will review the key findings to emerge from the book and consider, in response to these findings, concrete strategies for promoting language teacher research engagement. Such engagement is ultimately a practical activity and I thus feel it is important to outline what the programme of research I have discussed here suggests for how teacher research engagement can be made a more central activity in language teaching. As I suggested in the Introduction to the book, I would also like this chapter to provide the busy reader with a more direct way of discerning both the key research messages to emerge here and their implications. I will end the chapter with some methodological reflections on my programme of research and identify areas for continuing inquiry.

9.2 Rationale and sources of data

The rationale for this book was grounded in a tension I perceived between the potential value of teacher research engagement and its limited uptake in practice in language teaching. In other words, although much has been written about the many benefits to teachers, students, and schools or organizations that can result when teachers read and/or do research themselves, evidence of language teachers engaging in these practices remains limited. I have acknowledged the many publications which now exist and which provide examples of language teachers doing research; I am, however, also critical of these because they often emanate from academic contexts (e.g. BA or MA projects) which deflect attention away from the basic premise of teacher research (i.e. improving practice by understanding one's own working context) and report research conducted under conditions (e.g. full-time study) which are not representative of teachers' lives. Additionally, as I noted in Chapter 1, a significant volume of language teacher research is conducted by university language teachers, with much less evidence of engagement by teachers in primary, secondary, and high schools. Overall, too, the volume of teacher research that has been conducted represents only a small minority of the professionals involved in language teaching worldwide. The purpose of this book has thus been to critically examine the above assertions and to extend our understandings of the role of research engagement in teachers' lives. This is a worthy issue of study because of the clear potential that teacher research has to be a positive transformative influence on the work and development of language teachers. My aim, though, has not been normative; I have not argued that research engagement is an activity all teachers *should* do, but have focused on providing evidence which can assist in promoting teacher research engagement if it is considered to be a desirable activity. The latter is a decision which must always be made locally but the data I have presented in this book can allow such a decision to be made in a more informed manner.

In examining these issues, I have drawn on a programme of research and professional activity that took place between 2005 and 2011. The research component of this work involved 1,730 teachers and managers working in English language teaching institutions worldwide. Through four different studies, using questionnaires, interviews, and open-ended written responses (see the Appendices for the instruments), teachers' and managers' views about research and its role in the work of language teachers were elicited. Information was also generated about teachers' practices in reading and doing research and about the factors which support and hinder teachers' engagement in such activities. Additionally, I drew on my experience of two successful teacher research projects to provide further insights into the conditions which make teacher research more productive. Underpinning my analysis of all the above data was a conception of teacher research as systematic inquiry, conducted by teachers, into some aspect of their own context, with the aim of improving both understanding and practice. I have also stressed throughout that teacher research, like all research, needs to be made public – i.e. available for others to consider, respond to, learn from, and be inspired by – rather than kept private.

9.3 Key findings

Figure 9.1 summarizes 20 key findings to emerge from my research. I will now discuss these in relation to five key themes: (a) conceptions of research; (b) reading research; (c) doing research; (d) the benefits of research engagement; and (e) research cultures.

1   Teachers' and managers' beliefs about what 'research' is cohered around two extremes – formal academic activity and informal professional activity. Neither adequately represents the nature of teacher research.

2   In assessing the quality of research, an important criterion for teachers was the extent to which it gave them practical ideas for use in the classroom.

3   Almost 75% of teachers said they read research at least 'sometimes'. Due to variations in what both 'sometimes' and 'reading research' mean to teachers (see 5 below), this positive figure must be interpreted cautiously.

4   Almost 90% of teachers who said they read research said it had at least a moderate influence on their teaching.

5   There was little evidence that teachers engaged with research publications, as opposed to practical and professional publications. Teachers had negative attitudes towards research articles and saw them as irrelevant to the classroom.

6   Teachers' judgements about the relevance to practice of ideas encountered through reading were based on accumulated experience, common sense, and the congruence of the new ideas with teachers' existing practices and beliefs.

7   Three key factors limited teachers' engagement with research: a lack of time, the perceived limited practical value of published research, and a lack of access to such publications.

8   Almost 50% of the teachers said they did research at least 'sometimes'. Again, variations in interpretations of what 'sometimes' and 'research' mean (see 10 below) suggest caution in interpreting this finding.

9   Teachers' primary reasons for doing research were professional and pedagogical rather than instrumental (e.g. for promotion).

10 The predominant forms of 'research' which teachers said they do were individual and private reflections on teaching and evaluations of teaching and learning strategies and materials.

11 The primary reasons teachers gave for not doing research were a lack of time, a belief that doing research was not part of their job, and a lack of skills and knowledge.

12 Teacher identity was implicated in teachers' views about being research engaged. Becoming a teacher researcher implied developing a new identity that teachers did not want to, or felt unable to, assume.

13 The main benefits of research engagement, according to teachers and managers, were motivating teachers, keeping them fresh, encouraging reflection and developing their instructional repertoires.

14 Teachers who participated in actual teacher research projects reported benefits for their own teaching, knowledge, attitudes and understandings of learners, as well as benefits for their schools more generally. Teacher research was seen to enhance teachers' status as well as the credibility of their organization.

(Continued)

15 A concern for the quality of teacher research – in terms of research procedures and trustworthy findings – was not evident in teachers' and managers' commentaries on the value of such activity.

16 Negative views about the value of research engagement to teachers were based on a conception of research as theoretical knowledge external to teachers and having no relevance to classroom practice.

17 Teachers and managers who were less positive about the value of teacher research engagement associated research with theoretical knowledge which was not required for and could even be detrimental to effective teaching.

18 Teachers and managers did not assess highly the research cultures of the contexts they worked in. A lack of institutional support for research and negative teacher attitudes were seen, by teachers and managers respectively, as key reasons for the lack of positive research cultures.

19 Managers underestimated the impact that their own attitudes to research could have on the research culture in their schools.

20 The limited prevalence of research cultures in the private EFL sector was explained in terms of broader features of this sector such as transient teachers, unfavourable employment contracts, and commercial priorities.

Figure 9.1   Key findings

Conceptions of research

Teachers and managers hold a range of beliefs about what 'research' is that cohere around two extremes on a continuum of formality; at one extreme is the view, held by many (see especially Chapter 3) that research implies formal academic activity – associated with notions such as statistics, large samples, and objectivity – which has no relevance to the classroom. Teachers and managers with negative dispositions towards research typically held such a view. At the other extreme – and this was a view held particularly by those who were positively disposed to teacher research engagement – research was seen as various forms of professional activity which involved informal, individual, and very often private reflections on teaching materials and instructional strategies.

As I have argued, neither of these perspectives on teacher research is satisfactory. The more formal academic conceptions detach research from the practice of teaching and thus limit its perceived relevance to and feasibility for teachers. At the same time, definitions which see as research all forms of reflective practice, course design, and materials evaluation are too inclusive to capture the distinctiveness of teacher research as a professional development activity. A productive conception of teacher research lies in between these extremes – it is systematic, with the implications this has for the process of inquiry; at the same time it is motivated by, focuses on, and feeds back into, teachers' experiences in schools and classrooms. It thus has a strong personal and subjective dimension. I would like to repeat once more here that I am in no way criticizing the value of reflective practice and other less formal strategies for professional development – these are valuable processes for teachers to engage in. My goal here, though, has been to argue for the distinctive nature of teacher research and to show that much of the uncertainty that surrounds the status of this activity in our field stems from the definitional confusion that surrounds it.

Arguing for a more specific and consistently used definition of teacher research should not, also, be seen as an attempt to discourage teacher engagement in it; one overall goal of this book is in fact to facilitate such engagement. What I am arguing for here (see the definition of teacher research in Chapter 1), though, is a form of activity which is both feasible and rigorous; which allows teachers to explore in both a deeply personal and evidence-based manner their experiences as professionals, but which retains a concern for good quality inquiry, trustworthy discoveries, and scope for these to be communicated to others. Professional development work which does not share such concerns (and which thus does not meet the minimal requirements of research as I defined it in Chapter 1) need not appropriate the term 'research'. A lack of precision in the way this term is used, and which was illustrated in the data I have presented, also complicates, unnecessarily and unhelpfully, professional debate about teacher research (because it is not clear what the focus of this debate actually is).

Reading research

As shown in Chapter 4, the teachers in my programme of research reported encouraging levels of reading research, but these results must be interpreted cautiously. First, it was shown that when teachers quantify how often they read research they interpret the same frequency descriptors in various ways, often euphemistically (most typically, teachers said they read research 'sometimes' when 'rarely' would perhaps have been a more realistic estimate). Second, in explaining what kinds of research materials they read, teachers very often referred to practical teaching magazines and websites from which they obtained ideas which could be applied in the classroom. It is clear, then, that there is also much ambiguity among language teachers about what counts as a research publication. I must stress again that I am not suggesting that teachers should not read practical publications; these will always be of primary relevance to classroom practitioners. Teachers very often, though, either assume that practical materials which appear in journals are based on research or else that the act of looking through practical journals and identifying and reading articles in them constitutes engagement with research.

Overall, then, there was little evidence in the findings I have reported of teachers engaging with research publications. Some teachers referred to such publications in the context of their formal studies, but research findings reported in language teaching publications did not generally emerge here as an influence on teachers' thinking and teaching. Teachers commonly talked in negative terms about the theoretical and inaccessible nature of published research and of its limited relevance or applicability to the classroom. There were clearly strong adverse attitudinal forces at work here. In some cases these attitudes had been promoted by teachers' experiences of reading on formal courses – they did not feel the reading they were required to do had any bearing on the classroom. In other cases teachers held negative attitudes towards published research because it did not provide practical teaching advice (as we saw in Chapter 3, the presence of such advice was a criterion teachers often cited in making judgements about the quality of research). Such dispositions were often also held by managers. Two other factors which teachers cited as barriers to their engagement with research were a lack of time and a lack of access to research journals.

The majority of the teachers who said they engaged with research did say that it had some cognitive (e.g. on their knowledge) and/or practical (i.e. on their teaching) impact on their work. Of course, given the points made above, in many cases this meant that teachers read about practical teaching ideas which they then tried out in class. Insights also emerged here into the factors that mediated teachers' decisions to adopt in their teaching ideas encountered through reading. These factors were largely experiential – i.e. teachers drew on their accumulated experience and 'common sense' to make, often rapidly, judgements about the relevance and practicability of the ideas they read about. There was evidence here that teachers assessed as less feasible ideas they read about which were not congruent with their current beliefs and practices. Overall, the manner in which teachers mediated ideas they read about did not seem to be particularly critical.

Doing research

Teachers reported (see Chapter 5) modest levels of engagement in research. Again, given variations in how teachers interpreted frequency descriptors such as 'sometimes' and the term 'research', these findings must be interpreted cautiously. When teachers were asked to give examples of the research they do, the majority cited informal reflective evaluations of aspects of their teaching. And in explaining the impact of their research, teachers typically talked about the manner in which it allowed them to learn about new practical teaching strategies.

In line with such notions, teachers' motivations for doing research were largely personal, pedagogical, and professional rather than driven instrumentally by external targets such as promotion. Lack of time was (unsurprisingly) cited by teachers as the major obstacle to doing research; other factors, though, were also influential, such as the view held by teachers that doing research was not part of their job and that they lacked the skills and knowledge needed to engage in research. Lack of support for research (e.g. mentoring) was also often seen by teachers to be an obstacle to research engagement. Teacher identity was a concept that was implicated in teachers' accounts of why they struggled to be research engaged – i.e. being a teacher researcher calls for the development of a new identity which is at odds with conventional notions of teacher role. Teachers may reject such an identity, struggle to reconcile it with their perceptions of their role, or find that it is not supported by the contexts in which they work.

Benefits of teacher research engagement

Teachers and managers, to different degrees (teachers were more positive), recognized the potential benefits of research engagement for the quality of teaching. Collectively, respondents suggested a long list of specific ways in which they felt that reading and doing research could enhance teachers' work (see Chapter 6). These benefits focused largely on the role that research engagement could play in motivating teachers (individually and collectively), keeping them fresh, encouraging reflection, and developing their instructional repertoires. In respondents' comments on the benefits of research engagement, there was little direct reference to the concrete outcomes of such engagement; very often, in contrast, what was seen to be of value was the process itself. In other words, the process of engaging in classroom inquiry was seen to be motivating and to promote reflection and other benefits irrespective of whether such inquiry generated any 'findings' or outputs such as a report. Such a position once again highlights the more informal notion of research discussed above.

Much insight into the benefits of teacher research was also provided through the analysis of the two research projects I discussed in Chapter 8. Especially in the 'Sense of Progress' project, participants experienced a range of benefits, both conceptual and practical; in particular they felt that the systematic study of aspects of their work provided them with a deeper understanding of learners. They also felt that teacher research enhanced their status and the credibility and reputation of their organization.

Teachers and managers who were less positive about the value of research engagement for teaching cited three related arguments to support their position. The first was that being an effective teacher calls for much more than research knowledge; the second was that many examples exist of effective teachers who have no engagement with or in research; and third, that many teachers with superior 'research credentials' are ineffective practitioners. I do not dispute the substance of these arguments, though the thinking underpinning them is problematic. In the first argument, research knowledge is conceptualized as a theoretical entity that is generated outside the classroom and which has no implications for what teachers do; in the context of teacher research, though, research knowledge has a strong practical orientation and can contribute to the development of the wider range of knowledge, skills, and sensitivities which are needed for effective practice. For the second argument, it is of course possible to be an effective teacher (however that is defined) without research engagement; such claims, though, imply a resistance to professional development generally and a belief that improvement is required only where there are problems. Research engagement provides teachers with a means of ongoing professional growth; it is not simply a way of resolving deficiencies. In the third argument too, the research credentials being cited were typically academic ones; it was thus noted that holding, for example, an MA in Applied Linguistics does not necessarily make one effective in the classroom. This may be the case but academic qualifications are not my concern in promoting teacher research (in fact, in this book I have purposefully minimized attention to teacher research conducted for the purposes of a formal qualification). What I am arguing for here, rather, is teacher research as an eminently practical way of being a professional and one that bridges the gap between formal qualifications and effectiveness in the classroom.

Research cultures

The analysis of research cultures in language teaching presented here does not provide a positive picture of the extent to which teachers and managers feel that their working contexts are conducive to teacher research engagement. A lack of allocated time for such engagement was consistently seen to be a barrier, though there were sharp differences in the ways that managers and teachers assessed other aspects of their research cultures. Managers, for example, felt that adverse teacher attitudes (e.g. a lack of interest in professional development) constituted the most significant barrier to research cultures. Teachers in contrast, felt that limited support from their institutions was a key factor that hindered the development of such cultures. Clearly, both sets of factors – teacher attitudes and institutional support – have a significant influence on the extent to which teacher research engagement is a viable and productive activity that is embedded in schools. Additionally, though – and this is a factor whose influence seemed to be underestimated by the managers themselves – managers' attitudes to teacher research engagement also play a significant role in shaping research cultures. In fact, it is unlikely (as evidence from studies of research-engaged schools suggest – e.g. Barker, 2005; Davies, Hamilton, & James, 2007; McLaughlin, Black-Hawkins, & McIntyre, 2004; Sharp, 2007; Sharp et al., 2005) that a positive research culture can develop without leadership based on an understanding of the value of teacher research engagement and a commitment to making it work.

In explaining the lack of research cultures in language teaching contexts, teachers and managers, especially those working in the private EFL sector, referred to characteristics of the EFL industry generally. These included the transient nature of EFL teachers' careers and an associated lack of commitment to professional development, the complacency that characterizes many teachers who have been in the sector for a long time, the commercial priorities which govern how schools operate, and the restrictive nature, professionally speaking, of the teachers' contracts and job descriptions. Faced with these factors, it is difficult to make a case for teacher research engagement and, in the private EFL sector to which the above comments apply, significant changes are required in the mentality that underpins the industry before such engagement, and indeed professional development generally, can become more central issues. For example, there needs to be a recognition by those who run schools (and by those who accredit these schools) that investing in staff is ultimately beneficial for the organization. Collective action is needed to elevate TEFL from, by the admission of many of the teachers and managers who contributed to my work, its current status as a domain of activity that lacks a strong professional ethos.

9.4 Promoting teacher research engagement

I will now draw on the findings discussed above to outline a range of conditions and strategies through which language teacher research engagement can be promoted.

Basic principles

I would like to comment briefly on the epistemological stance (i.e. the view of what counts as knowledge, its origins and use) that underpins a belief in the value of teacher research engagement. This stance can be expressed as a series of basic principles and a commitment to them can be seen as a fundamental condition for promoting teachers' engagement with and in research. Here are a number of such principles (developed from those in Borg, 2010):

- classrooms and schools are a legitimate source of research knowledge about language teaching and learning
- academic research cannot provide incontrovertible evidence on which language teachers can reliably base their actions
- received knowledge (e.g. as acquired through reading) will always be mediated by teachers' cognitions and the socio-cultural contexts in which teaching and learning take place
- language teachers are uniquely positioned to conduct systematic inquiry that focuses on teaching and learning
- as professionals, language teachers must assume the role of generators of knowledge, not just consumers
- collaborations among language teachers, and among academics and language teachers, create productive mutually beneficial social spaces for knowledge creation
- systematic and publicly shared knowledge generation by language teachers, individually or collaboratively, has the potential to impact positively on learners, teachers, schools and policy-making more widely
- a concern for quality must be central if the findings of teacher research are to be a reliable basis for practical action.

An acceptance of these principles has implications for the manner in which the task of promoting teacher research engagement is approached. The relationship between academic research and teaching is not seen here to be a determinative one and this implies the need for teachers to develop the attitudes and skills which allow them to respond critically to the research they read and to view the ideas they encounter in their reading as options for them to explore in their classrooms (rather than prescriptions to be followed). Also embedded in the above principles is an enhanced notion of the language teacher as a professional who shapes their work through the knowledge that they generate systematically through classroom inquiry. The collaborative (or networked) and public dimensions of teacher research are also highlighted here; while the former is not a defining characteristic of teacher research, there is ample evidence of how teacher engagement in research is enhanced through the interactions of groups of teachers working together and with external collaborators. Bell et al. (2010: 52), for example, in their review of a range of teacher research projects, concluded that 'peer collaboration and critical friendship emerged overwhelmingly across all the study types as an essential support and motivator'. Finally, the above principles acknowledge the wide range of positive contributions to language teaching that teacher research can make. Efforts to promote teacher research engagement which, implicitly or explicitly, run counter to the above principles are less likely to be productive.

Teacher and manager suggestions

A more practical set of strategies for promoting research cultures in language teaching comes from the suggestions made in Chapter 7 by teachers and managers. Though managers felt such ideas were desirable, they were often uncertain about their feasibility, particularly because of some of the broader constraints which they felt regulated the work of language teachers. Nonetheless, collectively these proposals highlight a number of conditions which can support stronger research cultures in language teaching. A composite list of the strategies teachers and managers suggested is given in Figure 9.2; organizations that wish to promote a stronger research culture can first ask their staff to express their views on the current situation (using, for example, the item about research cultures in Section 3 of the questionnaire in Appendix 3). They can, depending on the results of the initial assessment, then consider which of the items in Figure 9.2 might be feasibly incorporated into the organization's work.

Facilitative conditions for teacher research projects

Further practical guidance for promoting teacher research engagement emerges from the analysis of the two research projects in

To promote stronger research cultures, schools can ...

- allocate official time for research on teachers' timetables
- balance business concerns (where applicable) with professional development concerns
- create a journal to allow teachers to get professional credit for their research
- create an awareness of the value of research to teachers
- create networks of teacher researchers within the school
- create opportunities for teachers to be part of a research team
- develop a shared understanding among teachers and managers of what teacher research is
- encourage staff to be proactive in being research engaged
- find out which teachers are interested in research and what support they need
- help teachers identify research that is relevant to the school's work
- include research in teachers' job descriptions
- make doing research relevant to teachers' professional goals
- make results of teachers' research projects available to other teachers
- provide teachers with access to research journals
- provide teachers with practical guidelines on how to do teacher research
- provide training/workshops on how to do research
- reward teachers' commitment to research through career opportunities
- use the results of teacher research to inform policy and practice in the school.

Figure 9.2   Teacher and manager suggestions for promoting stronger research cultures

Chapter 8. Figure 9.3 lists a number of conditions, drawn from these projects, which facilitate the success of such initiatives. The value of many of these conditions is confirmed by analyses of teacher research projects that have been conducted in education more generally (e.g. Bell et al., 2010; Davies, Hamilton, & James, 2007; Rickinson et al., 2004; Sharp et al., 2005). Thus, individuals responsible for initiating teacher research projects in language teaching contexts now have at their disposal a substantial volume of empirically based concrete guidance on the conditions which will maximize the success of such projects; in contrast, it is clear that where many of these conditions do not exist, initiatives will have little practical value. Figure 9.3 can be used as a checklist to assess, at the planning stage, the feasibility of attempts to set up teacher research projects, and to highlight any issues that need to be addressed before the project can be started. In some cases, a preponderance of negative responses might suggest that the project is not feasible and should be postponed until more facilitative conditions can be created.

If you are setting up a project to encourage teacher research, the following list of questions will allow you to consider whether the conditions are in place to make it successful. The more 'yes' answers you have, the more likely it is that the experience will be a productive one for everyone involved.

1 Are the teachers participating willingly in the project and are they motivated to engage in professional development generally and teacher research specifically?

2 Has the scope of the project and the nature of teachers' commitments (including any outputs that will be required) been clarified with teachers at the outset?

3 Have the benefits to teachers (and possibly to their schools) of the project been clearly defined?

4 Does the project provide teachers with opportunities to examine and review their beliefs about research and teacher research?

5 Does the project provide teachers with pedagogically sound and structured opportunities (e.g. through workshops) to develop their skills and knowledge in relation to doing teacher research?

6 Have some of the teachers' working hours been officially allocated to their participation in the project?

7 Will teachers have a say in the focus of the research they do?

8 Will teachers' research address issues that teachers feel are of professional relevance to them?

9 Are teachers' schools, colleagues and students aware and supportive of the project?

10 Does the project provide sufficient time (e.g. a number of months) for teachers to plan, conduct and report on (orally or in writing) their research?

11 Will teachers receive ongoing local mentoring for their research from individuals with appropriate experience, knowledge and skills?

(Continued)

12   Will teachers (and those who support them locally) have access to expertise and advice from an external collaborator with experience of teacher research?

13   Does the project have a clear structure, i.e. a starting point, intermediate targets along the way, and a completion date?

14   Will the project lead to a concrete product (e.g. an oral presentation or written report)?

15   Is the nature of the research teachers are planning feasible, given the time and resources available?

16   Will teachers have access to relevant journals and books, including books on how to do teacher research?

17   Does the project provide opportunities (physical and/or virtual) for teachers to collaborate, share ideas, and provide peer support?

18   Will teachers have opportunities during or after the project to share the findings of their research with others in and outside their school?

19   Will teachers' efforts and the outcomes of their research be acknowledged by their employers?

20   Will the management consider the implications of the research teachers do for policy and practice in their school more generally?

21   Will the project minimize additional work and disruptions to teachers' and their colleagues' routine professional activities?

22   Is the commitment teachers are expected to make to the project realistic given their working conditions (e.g. the nature of teachers' employment contracts and the number of jobs they have)?

Figure 9.3   A checklist of facilitative conditions for teacher research projects

Engaging with research

Much of the discussion above focuses on efforts to encourage teachers to do research. While this typically also involves teachers in reading research, I would like to comment here on ways in which teacher engagement with research can be promoted without teachers also actually doing research. In response to the findings presented in this book, here are five concrete strategies which can support teacher engagement with research:

1   Workshops for teachers through which they can become aware of a range of language teaching publications and discern the differences in orientation and purpose among them. Such an exercise

can support teachers in identifying research-based publications and distinguishing them from those with a stronger professional or pedagogical focus. The purpose of this exercise is not to promote the superior value of research publications but to enable teachers to understand the purposes and scope of the material they read (e.g. such work may reduce instances where teachers are critical of research articles because they lack practical advice for the classroom – teachers will better appreciate that this is typically not the function of research papers).

2 Workshops which broaden teachers' understandings of the ways in which reading research can support their professional development. For example, Rickinson et al. (2004) provides examples of teacher researchers talking about the benefits of reading research and these could provide the stimulus for a discussion among teachers. Extracts from Rankin & Becker (2006), an article which illustrates how a teacher used reading to deepen their understanding of their teaching, could also be used for a similar purpose. In Chapter 4, I also outlined five ways in which engagement with research can be of value to teachers – I called these new ways of seeing, doing, talking, knowing, and thinking respectively – and these ideas too might provide the framework for a workshop with teachers which encourages them to think about the contributions that reading research can make to their work.

3 Teacher study or support groups (Richards & Farrell, 2005) which meet periodically to discuss research articles (see Fenton-Smith & Stillwell, 2011 for a practical exploration of this issue). The selection of articles is determined by the members of the group and will normally relate to themes that are of relevance to their teaching context. Teachers read the articles prior to meeting, then during the meeting they contribute to a critical discussion of the key findings being proposed, the manner in which these findings were arrived at, and any implications that they might have for teachers' work. Brief summaries of these discussion points can be prepared after each meeting and made available to other teachers, via, for example, a school website, news bulletin, or noticeboard.

4 Workshops for teachers which make them aware of the sources of research available to them, in hard copy or online, and develop teachers' skills in searching for and locating such information. For example, there are a number of free journals for language teachers available online (e.g. *TESL-EJ*, *Asian EFL Journal*). I acknowledge that teachers will not have much time to spend

searching for articles, but one workshop which introduces them to the options available can contribute to the research culture of a school.

5 Investment by schools in relevant research publications. I recognize that journal subscriptions are expensive, and given the limited use that research journals typically have, schools will often not feel that the investment is justified. My modest suggestion here, though, would be that in addition to the practical and professional journals that schools do often purchase, one additional research journal be visible in the staffroom or library. Teachers may be consulted on the choice of the journal and also be asked to provide feedback on its value. Teacher study groups, as described above, could use articles from this journal as the basis of their discussions.

All of the above strategies involve teachers engaging with primary research publications. As I noted in Chapter 4, though, research in the UK has concluded that teachers are unlikely to sustain that form of direct engagement and what they require, therefore, are research digests or summaries, mediated by brokers, and which facilitate the teachers' task of extracting key findings from research papers and thinking about the implications of these findings for practice. Such resources in the field of language teaching are not available, and this therefore limits the extent to which teachers can feasibly be expected to engage with research in a regular manner.

9.5 Investigating language teacher research engagement

So far in this chapter I have reviewed the key findings from my programme of research and discussed practical responses to these. I will now provide some methodological reflections on my research and suggest areas where further research is needed.

My programme of research

Chapter 2 described the various studies which generated the data I have drawn on in this book. I also noted there the particular challenges that each study presented. Overall, I would assess the programme of research as being methodologically sound; instruments were systematically developed and refined over the lifespan of the programme and a consistent set of issues was addressed across different studies, thus allowing for the collective analyses I have been able to present here. The instruments utilized generated a substantial volume of quantitative and qualitative data which were both fully deployed in the previous chapters. The 1,730 participants worked in a range of global English language teaching contexts and included managers (367) as well as teachers (1,363).

As with any study, though, this body of work does have its limitations. The non-probability sample of teachers and managers in my work was self-selecting and will have represented individuals with some interest in teacher research engagement (this does not imply, though, as we have seen, that they were necessarily positively disposed to the idea). Over 80% of the sample worked in Europe, North America, and Asia, while the large majority of the managers worked in North America and the UK. Compared to the volume of questionnaires collected from teachers (which did, though, generate a good volume of open-ended data and were supplemented by further written follow-up comments from another 22 teachers), the number of interviews conducted (28, or 2.1%) was small. The wide geographical spread of the teachers was the main obstacle to the conduct of additional interviews with them. By comparison, the number of managers interviewed was high (59, or 16.1%), though 43 of these were conducted with individuals working for private language schools in the UK. Managers, or head teachers, working in the state sector, therefore, were not represented in my research, nor were any of the teacher interviews conducted with teachers working in this sector. Over 61% of the teachers completing questionnaires in my studies, though, did work in the state sector.

As noted above, the programme of research covered a consistent set of themes and these provided the focus for the chapters in this book: conceptions of research, engagement with research, engagement in research, research engagement and teaching quality, and research cultures. In exploring teachers' conceptions of research, the use of scenarios was an innovative strategy and the various questionnaire items I have developed in studying other aspects of teacher research engagement have generated credible data. My strategy in eliciting teachers' views about good quality research, though, is one I will continue to reflect on. For this issue (see Appendix 1, Section 3), respondents were asked to rate the importance they felt that eleven criteria had in determining research quality. The list did admittedly place too much emphasis on the technical dimension of research (i.e. related to its conduct) and did perhaps over-represent features of conventional scientific modes of inquiry (though as I noted in Chapter 3, respondents had the option of saying that criteria were not important and nominating others). In more recent work of this kind (e.g. two separate studies of the conceptions of research held by college English teachers in China – Borg & Liu, forthcoming – and by teacher educators at a university in Saudi Arabia – Borg & Alshumaimeri, 2012) I have extended the original list of 11 to 20 items which include more generic features of research (e.g. it is purposeful, it makes connections with existing literature) as well more reference to qualitative research. Results, though, remain unsatisfactory because the question seems to lack discriminatory power (i.e. very few of the 20 items in either of the above studies were rated as not being important in determining research quality). I will continue to explore alternative strategies for eliciting teachers' views of what good research is, including open-ended questionnaire items and interviews. There is a broader literature on academics' conceptions of research which can inform this process (e.g. Åkerlind, 2008; Kiley & Mullins, 2005; Meyer, Shanahan, & Laugksch, 2005; Prosser et al., 2008).

One other challenging area, methodologically, relates to the use of frequency descriptors in eliciting from teachers information about how often they read and do research. My work has shown that teachers will interpret descriptors such as 'sometimes' in different ways and this suggests the need for less ambiguous ways of capturing teachers' reported frequencies of research engagement. In more recent work, in asking about how often teachers read research I have experimented with response categories such as 'once a week' and 'once a month'; feedback from respondents, however, is that they find it difficult to quantify their reading in such terms. Thus I have yet to find a suitable alternative to the standard frequency descriptors used in the programme of research I have reported here, even though I am fully aware of their limitations. Suitable alternatives are even harder to find in asking about how often teachers do research; clearly, given the typically ongoing nature of the activity, answer categories such as 'once a month' would not be appropriate. These are issues I continue to explore.

Further research

There is welcome evidence in the literature of growing attention, motivated by my earlier publications in this area (e.g. Borg, 2009), to language teacher research engagement (Bai & Hudson, 2011; Bai & Millwater, 2011; Fenton-Smith & Stillwell, 2011; Gao, Barkhuizen, & Chow, 2011). As noted above, I have continued my programme of research and have recently completed studies of conceptions of research in China and Saudi Arabia. Beyond this stream of work, though, the research I have presented here suggests a number of both broader and more specific issues for further study. I articulate these issues below as questions.

1   What is the nature of language teachers' engagement with research? The manner in which language teachers engage with research (if, what, why, when, and how they read) and in particular the factors that mediate between the reading teachers do and their classroom practice are issues we know very little about, despite the preliminary findings I have presented here. There is clearly scope for more focused quantitative and qualitative research into this issue.

2   What are the characteristics of reports of research that language teachers respond positively to? Research in the UK (Cordingley & National Teacher Research Panel, 2000) has examined teachers' preferences for the format of research reports and a large-scale study of this kind is necessary in the context of language teaching. This could inform subsequent initiatives to start developing the kinds of mediated resources through which engagement with research can become a more feasible and regular part of teachers' professional activities.

3   How are teacher identities implicated in the practice of teacher research engagement? Some insights have emerged here of the ways that teacher research requires teachers to take on a new identity and of the positive and negative ways that teachers respond to this. This is a specific issue that has potential for very interesting indepth study, through interviewing or narrative writing. Longitudinal research tracking the emergence of teacher researcher identities and how they are integrated into or conflict with more conventional teacher identities also offers exciting possibilities.

4   In specific contexts, how do managers' (principals', head teachers', etc.) attitudes towards teacher research engagement influence the extent to which teachers can be research engaged and to which research cultures develop? My work here suggests that managers do not feel their attitudes towards research have a significant impact on teacher research engagement; I am sure they are mistaken, but we lack the empirical evidence to demonstrate this. Case studies of specific language teaching settings – particularly examples of effective practice in leading a research-engaged school – would provide an appropriate strategy for studying this issue.

5   What are the design features of courses which aim to develop teachers' attitudes, skills, and knowledge for teacher research

engagement? This question stems from my observations in Chapter 8 that we lack comparative documented evidence of the different ways that teacher research courses and projects are planned and delivered. An analysis of this issue can generate resources and guidelines to support individuals who run such courses and projects.

6   What are the benefits to teachers, learners, and schools of teacher research? In education, there is much literature on such benefits but contemporary evidence of this kind is lacking in language teaching. It is necessary, therefore, to identify contexts where teachers are engaged in teacher research projects, and to elicit from these teachers their stories of the highs and lows of the process. Evidence of success (as reported from the teacher research projects discussed in Chapter 8), especially, can play an important role in inspiring other teachers to become research engaged and in persuading authorities to support such engagement. Such evidence would help us to move beyond claims about the potential benefits of teacher research engagement to actual concrete evidence of such benefits in practice. Attention to ways of tracing connections between research engagement by teachers and benefits for learners would be a particularly important aspect of this strand of work.

7   What role does teacher research engagement play in the professional lives of language teachers working in primary, secondary, and high schools in the state sector? Although the perspectives of these individuals were represented in my research, greater qualitative insight is needed into the extent that reading and doing research are part of their work. Case studies of groups of language teachers in specific schools would be an appropriate way of investigating these issues, including broader analyses of the extent to which state schools in particular contexts constitute research cultures and the role that those leading the schools play in determining this.

8   What role does what I have called 'research education' (Borg, 2003) play in initial and in-service language teacher education programmes? One longer-term strategy for enhancing the status of language teaching as a research-engaged field is to integrate attention to research into teacher education programmes at all levels. This would need to extend beyond conventional models where teachers engage with research for the purposes of writing academic assignments without, though, connecting it to the actual practice of teaching. Rather, what is required is attention to research which is motivated by, informs understandings of,

and feeds back into, language teaching and learning. Crucially, I would argue, the message that research engagement is central to teaching is one that needs to be addressed as part of the early socialization processes of language teachers (even on entry-level certificate qualification programmes). The research question here, then, calls for investigations of current 'research education' practices, the documentation of the strategies through which teacher educators promote teacher research engagement (where they do), and analyses of the thinking and principles which inform the work of teacher educators in this respect.

9.6 Conclusion

Research engagement is not central to the 'way things are done' in language teaching. This is, in one short sentence, what the evidence presented in this book tells us. Constrained by definitional uncertainties about what research and teacher research entail, attitudes towards research engagement are polarized by an uninformed dichotomy between 'theory' and 'practice' in which research for teachers is conceptualized as either irrelevant academic activity or informal reflection on practice. Teacher research engagement – viewed as practice-driven, systematic, and shared active participation by teachers in reading and doing research – provides a productive interface between such divisive notions. It has undeniable transformative potential to enrich and improve the work of teachers, the experiences of learners, and the effectiveness and credibility of organizations (and is thus very relevant even in commercial contexts). Attempts to promote teacher research engagement, and research cultures more generally, can only flourish, though, when certain basic facilitative conditions exist. This book provides evidence of what those conditions are and of the limited extent to which they generally exist in language teaching contexts. A major challenge for us, then, is to consider, within individual schools and organizations as well as across the field more generally, how the key elements for productive research cultures can be created and sustained. It is unlikely that significant global progress on this front can be achieved without the support of major language teaching organizations and policy makers in education systems around the world; however, there is much that can be done at the level of individual schools, particularly where appropriate leadership is available. Similarly, teacher education institutions have an important role to play in creating in language teachers, from the outset, an understanding of the centrality of research engagement to professional practice. In many contexts where substantial investment is already made into the professional development of practising language teachers, the challenge is to consider how that existing investment might be redistributed to focus in part on facilitating teacher research engagement. Change of the kind I am advocating here is of course not going to be swift. It is my hope that the evidence I have presented here, though, can stimulate the kinds of informed decision-making in language teaching policy and practice that is required for our field to experience, in a more substantial and consistent manner, the undeniable benefits that teacher research engagement has to offer.

References

Åkerlind, G. S. (2008). An academic perspective on research and being a researcher: An integration of the literature. *Studies in Higher Education, 33*(1), 17–31.

Bai, L., & Hudson, P. (2011). Understanding Chinese TEFL academics' capacity for research. *Journal of Further and Higher Education, 35*(3), 391–407.

Bai, L., & Millwater, J. (2011). Chinese TEFL academics' perceptions about research: An institutional case study. *Higher Education Research and Development, 30*(2), 233–246.

Barker, P. (2005). *Research in schools and colleges*: National Educational Research Forum Working Paper 7.2. Retrieved 20 August, 2012, from www.eep.ac.uk/nerf/word/WP7.2withappendixe42d.doc?version=1

Bell, M., Cordingley, P., Isham., C., & Davis, R. (2010). Report of professional practitioner use of research review: Practitioner engagement in and/or with research. Retrieved 20 August, 2012, from www.curee-paccts.com/node/2303

Borg, S. (2003). 'Research education' as an objective for teacher learning. In B. Beaven & S. Borg (Eds.), *The role of research in teacher education* (pp. 41–48). Whitstable, Kent: IATEFL.

Borg, S. (2009). English language teachers' conceptions of research. *Applied Linguistics, 30*(3), 355–388.

Borg, S. (2010). Language teacher research engagement. *Language Teaching, 43*(4), 391–429.

Borg, S., & Alshumaimeri, Y. (2012). University teacher educators' research engagement: Perspectives from Saudi Arabia. *Teaching and Teacher Education, 28*(3), 347–356.

Borg, S., & Liu, Y. (forthcoming) Chinese College English teachers' research engagement. *TESOL Quarterly.*

Cordingley, P., & National Teacher Research Panel (2000). *Teacher perspectives on the accessibility and usability of research outputs.* Paper presented at the British Educational Research Association Conference, Cardiff University, 7–9 September 2000. Retrieved 15 July, 2011, from www.tda.gov.uk/upload/resources/doc/b/bera.doc

Davies, P., Hamilton, M., & James, K. (2007). *Practitioners leading research.* London: NRDC.

Fenton-Smith, B., & Stillwell, C. (2011). Reading discussion groups for teachers: Connecting theory to practice. *ELT Journal, 65*(3), 251–259.

Gao, X., Barkhuizen, G., & Chow, A. W. K. (2011). 'Nowadays teachers are relatively obedient': Understanding primary school English teachers' conceptions of and drives for research in China. *Language Teaching Research, 15*(1), 61–81.

Kiley, M., & Mullins, G. (2005). Supervisors' conceptions of research: What are they? *Scandinavian Journal of Educational Research, 49*(3), 245–262.

McLaughlin, C., Black-Hawkins, K., & McIntyre, D. (2004). *Researching teachers, researching schools, researching networks: A review of the literature.* Cambridge and Cranfield: Faculty of Education, University of Cambridge and National College of School Leadership.

Meyer, J. H. F., Shanahan, M. P., & Laugksch, R. C. (2005). Students' conceptions of research: I – a qualitative and quantitative analysis. *Scandinavian Journal of Educational Research, 49*(3), 225–244.

Prosser, M., Martin, E., Trigwell, K., Ramsden, P., & Middleton, H. (2008). University academics' experience of research and its relationship to their experience of teaching. *Instructional Science, 36*(1), 3–16.

Rankin, J., & Becker, F. (2006). Does reading the research make a difference? A case study of teacher growth in FL German. *Modern Language Journal, 90*(3), 353–372.

Richards, J. C., & Farrell, T. S. C. (2005). *Professional development for language teachers.* Cambridge: Cambridge University Press.

Rickinson, M., Clark, A., McLeod, S., Poulton, P., & Sargent, J. (2004). What on earth has research got to do with me? *Teacher Development, 8*(2/3), 201–220.

Sharp, C. (2007). *Making research make a difference. Teacher research: A small-scale study to look at impact.* Chelmsford: Flare.

Sharp, C., Eames, A., Sanders, D., & Tomlinson, K. (2005). *Postcards from research-engaged schools.* Slough: NFER.

Appendix 1 Teachers' questionnaire (Study 1)*

SECTION 1: ABOUT YOURSELF

1. Country where you work: _____

2. Town or city where you work: _____

3. Years of experience as an English language teacher (Tick ONE)

0–4 ☐	5–9 ☐	10–14 ☐	15–19 ☐	20–24 ☐	25+ ☐

4. Highest relevant qualification to ELT (Tick ONE)

Certificate ☐	Diploma ☐	Bachelor's ☐	Master's ☐

Doctorate ☐	Other ☐

5. Type of institution you teach English in most often (Tick ONE)

Private ☐	State ☐	Other ☐

6. Is your language school or centre part of a university? (Tick ONE)

Yes ☐   No ☐

7. The age of the learners you teach most often (Tick ONE)

12 or younger ☐	13–19 ☐	20–25 ☐	26+ ☐

8. How would you describe your work as an English language teacher? (Tick ONE)

I teach English full-time for one institution	☐
I teach English part-time for one institution	☐
I teach English part-time for different institutions	☐

*Please note that due to the book's format, the layout of the questionnaires has been modified from the original versions used during the study.

SECTION 2: SCENARIOS

This section presents 10 brief descriptions. Read each and choose **ONE** answer to say to what extent you feel the activity described is research.

1. A teacher noticed that an activity she used in class did not work well. She thought about this after the lesson and made some notes in her diary. She tried something different in her next lesson. This time the activity was more successful.

Definitely not research □	Probably not research □	Probably research □	Definitely research □

2. A teacher read about a new approach to teaching writing and decided to try it out in his class over a period of two weeks. He video recorded some of his lessons and collected samples of learners' written work. He analyzed this information then presented the results to his colleagues at a staff meeting.

Definitely not research □	Probably not research □	Probably research □	Definitely research □

3. A teacher was doing an MA course. She read several books and articles about grammar teaching then wrote an essay of 6,000 words in which she discussed the main points in those readings.

Definitely not research □	Probably not research □	Probably research □	Definitely research □

4. A university lecturer gave a questionnaire about the use of computers in language teaching to 500 teachers. Statistics were used to analyze the questionnaires. The lecturer wrote an article about the work in an academic journal.

Definitely not research □	Probably not research □	Probably research □	Definitely research □

5. Two teachers were both interested in discipline. They observed each other's lessons once a week for three months and made notes about how they controlled their classes. They discussed their notes and wrote a short article about what they learned for the newsletter of the national language teachers' association.

Definitely not research □	Probably not research □	Probably research □	Definitely research □

6. To find out which of two methods for teaching vocabulary was more effective, a teacher first tested two classes. Then for four weeks she taught vocabulary to each class using a different method. After that she tested both groups again and compared the results to the first test. She decided to use the method which worked best in her own teaching.

Definitely not research ☐	Probably not research ☐	Probably research ☐	Definitely research ☐

7. A headmaster met every teacher individually and asked them about their working conditions. The head made notes about the teachers' answers. He used his notes to write a report which he submitted to the Ministry of Education.

Definitely not research ☐	Probably not research ☐	Probably research ☐	Definitely research ☐

8. Mid-way through a course, a teacher gave a class of 30 students a feedback form. The next day, five students handed in their completed forms. The teacher read these and used the information to decide what to do in the second part of the course.

Definitely not research ☐	Probably not research ☐	Probably research ☐	Definitely research ☐

9. A teacher trainer asked his trainees to write an essay about ways of motivating teenage learners of English. After reading the assignments the trainer decided to write an article on the trainees' ideas about motivation. He submitted his article to a professional journal.

Definitely not research ☐	Probably not research ☐	Probably research ☐	Definitely research ☐

10. The Head of the English department wanted to know what teachers thought of the new coursebook. She gave all teachers a questionnaire to complete, studied their responses, then presented the results at a staff meeting.

Definitely not research ☐	Probably not research ☐	Probably research ☐	Definitely research ☐

SECTION 3: CHARACTERISTICS OF GOOD QUALITY RESEARCH

1. Here is a list of characteristics that research may have. Circle **ONE** number for each to give your opinion about how important it is in making a piece of research 'good'.

		Unimportant	Moderately important	Unsure	Important	Very important
a	a large number of people are studied	1	2	3	4	5
b	a large volume of information is collected	1	2	3	4	5
c	experiments are used	1	2	3	4	5
d	hypotheses are tested	1	2	3	4	5
e	information is analyzed statistically	1	2	3	4	5
f	questionnaires are used	1	2	3	4	5
g	the researcher is objective	1	2	3	4	5
h	the results apply to many ELT contexts	1	2	3	4	5
i	the results are made public	1	2	3	4	5
j	the results give teachers ideas they can use	1	2	3	4	5
k	variables are controlled	1	2	3	4	5

2. If there are any other characteristics which in your opinion a study must have for it to be called 'good' research, please list them here.

SECTION 4: RESEARCH CULTURE

1. Circle ONE number for each statement below to give your opinion about the general attitude to research in your institution.

	Disagree strongly	Disagree	Don't know	Agree	Agree strongly
Teachers do research themselves.	1	2	3	4	5
The management encourages teachers to do research.	1	2	3	4	5
Teachers feel that doing research is an important part of their job.	1	2	3	4	5
Teachers have access to research books and journals.	1	2	3	4	5
Teachers have opportunities to learn about current research.	1	2	3	4	5
Teachers talk about research.	1	2	3	4	5
Teachers are given support to attend ELT conferences.	1	2	3	4	5
Time for doing research is built into teachers' workloads.	1	2	3	4	5
Teachers read published research.	1	2	3	4	5

SECTION 5: READING RESEARCH

1. How frequently do you read published language teaching research? (Tick ONE)

Often ☐	Sometimes ☐	Rarely ☐	Never ☐

If you chose Rarely or Never go straight to Question 4 in this section.

2. You said that you read published language teaching research *often* or *sometimes*. Which of the following do you read? (Tick all that apply)

Books ☐
Academic journals (e.g. *TESOL Quarterly*) ☐
Professional Journals (e.g. *ELT Journal*) ☐
Professional Magazines (e.g. *ET Professional*) ☐

Newsletters (e.g. IATEFL SIG Newsletters)   □
Web-based sources of research   □
Other (please specify)   □

3. To what extent does the research you read influence your teaching? Choose **ONE**.

It has no influence on what I do in the classroom.   □
It has a slight influence on what I do in the classroom.   □
It has a moderate influence on what I do in the classroom.   □
It has a fairly strong influence on what I do in the classroom. □
It has a strong influence on what I do in the classroom.   □

Now go to Section 6

4. In Question 1 of this section you said that you read published research *rarely* or *never*. Here are some possible reasons for this. Tick those that are **true for you**.

I am not interested in research.   □
I do not have time.   □
I do not have access to books and journals.   □
I find published research hard to understand.   □
Published research does not give me practical advice for the   □
classroom.
Other reasons (please specify)   □

SECTION 6: DOING RESEARCH

1. How frequently do you do research yourself? (Tick ONE)

Often □	Sometimes □	Rarely □	Never □

If you chose Rarely or Never go straight to Question 3 in this section.

2. You said you do research **often** or **sometimes.** Below are a number of possible reasons for doing research. Tick those which are **true for you.**

'I do research ...

as part of a course I am studying on.	☐
because I enjoy it.	☐
because it is good for my professional development.	☐
because it will help me get a promotion.	☐
because my employer expects me to.	☐
because other teachers can learn from the findings of my work.	☐
to contribute to the improvement of the school generally.	☐
to find better ways of teaching.	☐
to solve problems in my teaching.	☐
other reasons (please specify)	☐

Now go to Section 7

3. You said that you do research **rarely** or **never.** Below are a number of possible reasons for not doing research. Tick those which are **true for you.**

'I don't do research because ...

I do not know enough about research methods.	☐
my job is to teach not to do research.	☐
I do not have time to do research.	☐
my employer discourages it.	☐
I am not interested in doing research.	☐
I need someone to advise me but no one is available.	☐
most of my colleagues do not do research.	☐
I do not have access to the books and journals I need.	☐
the learners would not co-operate if I did research in class.	☐
other teachers would not co-operate if I asked for their help.	☐
other reasons (please specify)	☐

SECTION 7: FURTHER PARTICIPATION

I would like to learn more about teachers' views of research and about the role it plays in their work. Would you be interested in discussing these issues further with me?

Yes ☐   No ☐

If YES, please write your name and email address here.

Name:
email:

This completes the questionnaire. Thank you for taking the time to respond.

Appendix 2 Written follow-up questions (Study 1)

Name:

Country:

Scenarios

> *In Section 1 of the survey you were asked to say to what extent you felt each activity described was research (on a scale of definitely not research, probably not research, probably research, and definitely research). Here I ask you to explain some of your answers.*

Q1.   You rated the scenario below as **definitely research:**

A teacher noticed that an activity she used in class did not work well. She thought about this after the lesson and made some notes in her diary. She tried something different in her next lesson. This time the activity was more successful.

Why did you feel this scenario was definitely research?

Q2.   You rated the scenario below as **definitely not research:**

A teacher read about a new approach to teaching writing and decided to try it out in his class over a period of two weeks. He video recorded some of his lessons and collected samples of learners' written work. He analyzed this information then presented the results to his colleagues at a staff meeting.

Why did you feel this scenario was definitely not research?

Characteristics of good research

> *In Section 2 of the survey you were asked to give your opinion about how important a list of characteristics were in making a piece of research 'good'. Here I ask you to explain some of your answers.*

Q3.   You said that 'the researcher is objective' was **very important.**

      (a) Please explain what 'objective' means for you in relation to research.

      (b) Why do you feel an objective researcher is a very important characteristic of good research?

Q4.   You said that 'the results apply to many ELT contexts' was **unimportant.**

      Please explain why you feel this is not an important characteristic for good research.

Reading research

> *In Section 4 of the survey you were asked how often you read research.*

Q5.   You said that the research you read has a fairly strong influence on what you do in the classroom.

      Could you explain what a 'fairly strong influence' means here?

Appendix 3 Directors' questionnaire (Study 2)

SECTION 1: YOU & YOUR CENTRE

1.1 Which of the following best describes the institution you work in? (Choose ONE by clicking on a shaded box)

Language School	University	Further/Higher Education College	International School/College	Other
☐	☐	☐	☐	☐

1.2 Maximum number of English language teachers (part & full-time) in your centre

1–10 ☐	11–20 ☐	21–30 ☐	31–40 ☐	41–50 ☐	50+ ☐

1.3 Total years of experience in ELT you have [teaching and management] (Choose ONE)

0–4 ☐	5–9 ☐	10–14 ☐	15–19 ☐	20–24 ☐	25+ ☐

1.4 How frequently do you read published research on English language teaching? (Choose ONE)

Never ☐	Rarely ☐	Sometimes ☐	Often ☐

1.5 How frequently do you do research yourself? (Choose ONE)

Never ☐	Rarely ☐	Sometimes ☐	Often ☐

SECTION 2: VALUE OF RESEARCH FOR ENGLISH LANGUAGE TEACHERS

2.1   How important do you feel it is for the English language teachers in your institution to read the following kinds of text? (Choose ONE answer in each case)

		Unimportant	Slightly important	No opinion	Important	Highly important
a	Academic journals (e.g. *TESOL Quarterly*)	☐	☐	☐	☐	☐
b	Books on how to do research	☐	☐	☐	☐	☐
c	Newsletters (e.g. *IATEFL Newsletters*)	☐	☐	☐	☐	☐
d	Practical 'how to teach' books	☐	☐	☐	☐	☐
e	Professional journals (e.g. *ELT Journal*)	☐	☐	☐	☐	☐
f	Professional magazines (e.g. *English Teaching Professional*)	☐	☐	☐	☐	☐
g	Research-based books about language teaching	☐	☐	☐	☐	☐

2.2   How important do you feel it is for English language teachers in your institution to do research themselves? (Choose ONE)

Unimportant	Slightly important	No opinion	Important	Highly important
☐	☐	☐	☐	☐

2.3   'Teachers who read and do research also teach more effectively in the classroom'. How do you feel about this? (Choose ONE)

Disagree Strongly	Disagree	Unsure	Agree	Agree Strongly
☐	☐	☐	☐	☐

2.4   Please explain your answer to question 2.3 here.

SECTION 3: RESEARCH CULTURE

Give your opinion about each statement below with reference to the EFL/ESOL teachers in your institution. Mark ONE answer for each statement.

		Disagree strongly	Disagree	Don't know	Agree	Agree strongly
a	Most teachers read published ELT research.					
b	Most teachers do research themselves.					
c	Most teachers like to talk about research.					
d	Teachers wanting to do research can get support from colleagues with research experience.					
e	Funding to attend ELT conferences is available to teachers.					
f	Teachers have opportunities to learn about doing research.					
g	Teachers feel that doing research is an important part of their job.					
h	Teachers have access to research books.					
i	Teachers have access to research journals.					
j	The management encourages teachers to do research.					
k	Time for doing research is built into (i.e. part of) teachers' workloads.					

SECTION 4: FURTHER PARTICIPATION

The next phase of this study will involve telephone interviews with a sample of academic managers in English language centres. Would you be willing to participate in an interview to discuss further the issues raised in this questionnaire? (Choose ONE)

Yes □   No □

If YES, please write your name and email address here so that I can contact you.

Name:
email:

Appendix 4 Director interview prompts (Study 2)

In Question 2.2, you say you felt it was [scale of importance] for teachers in your institution to do research. I'm interested in what 'research' means for you here. What kind of activity did you have in mind when you were saying that it is [scale of importance] for teachers to do?

Can you comment further on why you feel it is [scale of importance] for your teachers to do research?

In Section 3, you said that most teachers do not read and do research. Why do you feel that is the case?

OR

In Section 3, your responses indicate that a reasonably strong research culture does exist in your institution. What conditions or factors in your centre allow this to be the case?

Overall, are you satisfied with the current role that research plays in the teaching and professional development of your staff or is it an area of your centre's work that you would like to strengthen?

If YES, can you identify one key change which is required to allow this to happen?

Any other comments on this issue?

Appendix 5 Initial cover letter (Study 2)

Dear Academic Manager

You may have already read in an email or electronic newsletter from English UK or the British Council Accreditation Unit that I am conducting a study into academic managers' views about the role of research in the work of EFL and ESOL teachers in the UK. I am now writing to give you further information about this study and to invite you to participate.

English language teachers are often encouraged to read and do research in the belief that this enhances both their own professional development and the quality of their teaching.

In your position as academic manager (Director of Studies, Head of Department, Team Leader, Co-ordinator, Subject Leader) how do you feel about these issues? Do you feel that involvement in research by the teachers in your centre is desirable? What factors in your centre support or hinder such involvement? And in your experience does involvement by teachers in research improve the quality of their teaching?

I am very interested in your views on these issues and am inviting you to tell me what you think by completing a short questionnaire. I appreciate that you are busy and the questions will only take around **five minutes** to answer. You are not required to give your name or that of your institution.

There are three ways of completing the questionnaire. Please choose that which you prefer:

1   **Hard copy,** using the questionnaire enclosed with this letter. For your convenience, I have also enclosed a postage paid return envelope.
2   **Online,** at **http://www.surveymonkey.com/s.asp?u=582943258343**
    You will see a summary of all respondents' answers once you have submitted yours.
3   **On-screen,** using the Word version of the questionnaire which you can download from **http://www.personal.leeds.ac.uk/~edusbo/Survey.doc** and return by email.

Your responses will of course be treated confidentially and I will make a summary of the results available to you.

Thank you for your time. If you have any questions about this work please do contact me.

Yours faithfully

Simon

Index